The Chinese of Early Tucson
Historic Archaeology from the Tucson Urban Renewal Project

ANTHROPOLOGICAL PAPERS OF
THE UNIVERSITY OF ARIZONA
NUMBER 52

The Chinese of Early Tucson

Historic Archaeology from the Tucson Urban Renewal Project

Florence C. Lister and Robert H. Lister

THE UNIVERSITY OF ARIZONA PRESS
TUCSON
1989

About the authors

FLORENCE C. LISTER, formerly Research Associate of the Arizona State Museum and graduate in anthropology and education from the University of New Mexico, is a specialist in the history and technology of world ceramics. She has been senior author of more than a dozen articles and of a recent book on the subject published by the University of Arizona Press. She and Dr. Lister have made two trips to China, have studied museum collections of exported Chinese wares throughout the Far East and Europe, and are participants in the Overseas Chinese Group of the Society for Historical Archaeology.

ROBERT H. LISTER received a doctoral degree in anthropology from Harvard University and was formerly a Research Associate of the Arizona State Museum. He served as Professor and intermittently as Chairman of the Department of Anthropology at the University of Colorado from 1947 to 1971. He then joined the National Park Service where he was Chief Archeologist (1971–1972) and Head of the Chaco Center and the Southwestern Cultural Resources Center until retirement in 1978. Since then he and Mrs. Lister have coauthored six books dealing with various aspects of Southwestern archaeology.

Cover: Containers of Chinese medicinal preparations. See Figure 3.50 and Table 3.1 for contents, manufacturer, and provenience. (Photo by Helga Teiwes, Arizona State Museum, University of Arizona.)

THE UNIVERSITY OF ARIZONA PRESS

This book was set in Linotype CRTronic 10/12 Times Roman
∞ This book is printed on acid-free, archival-quality paper.
Manufactured in the United States of America.

93 92 91 90 89   5 4 3 2 1

Library of Congress Cataloguing-in-Publication Data

Lister, Florence Cline.
   The Chinese of early Tucson : historic archaeology from the Tucson Urban Renewal Project / Florence C. Lister and Robert H. Lister.
       p.   cm. — (Anthropological papers of the University of Arizona : no. 52)
     Bibliography: p.
     Includes index.
     ISBN 0-8165-1151-9 (alk. paper)
     1. Chinese Americans—Arizona—Tucson—Material culture.
2. Chinese Americans—Arizona—Tucson—Antiquities.   3. Tucson (Ariz.)—Antiquities.   4. Excavations (Archaeology)—Arizona—Tucson.   I. Lister, Robert Hill, 1915–   II. Title.
III. Series.
F819.T99C5L57   1989   89-5105
979.1′776004951—dc20   CIP

British Library Cataloguing in Publication data are available.

Contents

FIGURES

TABLES

Preface

From 1968 through 1973 the city of Tucson, Arizona, undertook a massive program of renovating eighty acres of its oldest downtown sector. The work was funded by the Department of Housing and Urban Development. Concurrent archaeological and ethnological investigations were conducted in the area by the Arizona State Museum, University of Arizona. The Department of Community Development of Tucson, which administered the HUD program, was especially supportive of the Museum's research needs and cooperated fully as the demolition schedule progressed.

The project was formally called the Pueblo Center Redevelopment Program. It became popularly referred to as the TUR (Tucson Urban Renewal) project, the acronym used throughout this volume. James E. Ayres, then on the archaeological staff of the Arizona State Museum, served as project director. He was aided in the field by volunteer students from the Department of Anthropology, University of Arizona, Tucson.

In concert with the municipal engineering schedule, the scientific work developed in two phases: (1) recording architectural data and collecting surface artifacts prior to demolition of buildings, and locating and excavating selected wells, latrines, and dumps in places where trash accumulation was likely; and (2) excavating sites from which buildings had been removed and salvaging cultural materials exposed prior to new construction (Ayres 1968c). Under a grant from the National Endowment for the Humanities, selected artifacts recovered were analyzed from 1975 to 1979 (Ayres 1980). The project area was inhabited at various times by Spaniards, Mexicans, Euro-Americans, Blacks, and Chinese during a span of years extending from 1776 to 1968. This report deals with the Chinese occupation.

Although the Chinese were, and have remained, a minority in Tucson's ethnic composition, much of their native material culture forms a cohesive, readily identifiable assemblage. This study focuses primarily on an ethnographic collection gathered from a complex of Chinese dwellings during phase one of the field program. Its importance lies not in its extrinsic value but in its size, diversity, generally good condition, and observable continuity of materials known from earlier periods of Chinese occupation in Tucson. These qualities are further enhanced by intimate observation of the surviving environment in which the objects were used.

The collection of Chinese goods recovered archaeologically receives less attention, inasmuch as we did not participate in the excavation or curatorial processes. Available field notes do not compensate for that lack of experience. There is no data base to support modern statistical analyses. These drawbacks were intensified when James Ayres, no longer with the Arizona State Museum, was unable to collaborate with us on this report. During the intervening years a number of coeval Chinese sites scattered about the West have been excavated using more refined techniques that have evolved as historical archaeology has matured. These sites have been reported on extensively and their artifacts typologically duplicate those retrieved in the TUR project. The data from Tucson substantiate the widespread homogeneity of overseas Chinese material culture and demonstrate the unbroken continuum from Tucson's archaeological to ethnographical contexts. Also of interest is some evidence for the increasing Chinese use of American goods. Hence, despite obvious limitations placed on interpretations, thorough consideration has been given to specimens recovered through excavation even though coverage of the archaeological evidence is uneven, depending on the nature of field records.

With full recognition of their inadequacies, the broad terms used in this report for the main ethnic components of Tucson society are Euro-American, Asian or Chinese, Hispanic, and Native American.

Acknowledgments

The Arizona State Museum and the National Endowment for the Humanities provided partial funding for this research. The Southwest Parks and Monuments Association supplied temporary quarters while data were being gathered. Without this help, our participation would not have been possible.

Sincere thanks go to the hard working staffs of the Arizona Historical Society; the Federal Archives, Los Angeles Branch; and the Arizona State Museum. From the Museum we are especially indebted to Raymond H. Thompson; R. Gwinn Vivian; Helga Teiwes; Kathy Hubenschmidt; G. Michael Jacobs; Diane Dittemore; Steven Rogers (now with the Wheelright Museum of the American Indian in Santa Fe, New Mexico); Sharon Urban; Jan Bell; Lee Fratt; and Jeanne Armstrong. Original line drawings by Robert H. Lister were drafted for final publication by Ron Beckwith

(Arizona State Museum). Photographs were taken by Robert H. Lister, Helga Teiwes, and James Ayres unless otherwise indicated. The Chinese characters in Appendix C were written by Hong Yu.

John W. Olsen, Department of Anthropology, University of Arizona, not only offered moral support as we probed unfamiliar ground but helped enormously in translating and interpreting scattered Chinese characters appearing on some artifacts. In addition, he contributed to this volume Appendixes B and C. A simple "thank you" is inadequate.

CHAPTER ONE

The Historical Record

Chinese immigrants lived in California for more than a quarter of a century before any of them appeared on the dusty streets of Tucson. During that time they had been welcomed, then rejected and persecuted. They had helped clean the Mother Lode of its riches, had led the way toward converting California's interior basin into a bread basket, had established a Chinese-style fishing industry along the coast, and had laid the nation's first railroad tracks across the Sierra Nevadas (R. H. Lee 1960; Lydon 1985; Lyman 1970, 1974). They also had created an inner-city ethnic community within the larger, heterogeneous agglomerate of San Francisco, where they perpetuated their life style within a foreign environment without appreciable integration into the host community.

TERRITORIAL PERIOD

No Chinese people can be documented as being in Tucson prior to the mid 1870s, despite loose claims for their presence ten years earlier. Such reports were based on unverified recollections of a 62-year-old Chinese grocer, Don Chun Wo, who had not come to Tucson himself until 1895 (Fong 1980: 23–24; Sonnichsen 1982: 111). Presumably, the Chinese were not attracted to the area because of its isolation in the midst of dry waste lands lacking placer fields or significant agricultural potential and because of the continuing threat of Apache raids. The federal census made in June of 1870 recorded no Asian names (U.S. Federal Census 1870).

Over the ensuing half dozen years, however, some Chinese are mentioned in newspaper accounts (*Arizona Citizen*, November 4, 1876; *Arizona Daily Star*, January 10, 1878 and September 3, 1879). Their arrival coincided with mounting Euro-American antagonism and with violent internal conflicts among the Chinese, both of which fostered movement away from the West Coast. The Asians may have come overland by wagon or stagecoach from the Colorado River terminal at Yuma, or, toward the end of the decade, they may have left the Southern Pacific Railroad construction crews as they worked their way eastward from California. By 1879 there were approximately thirty Chinese in town (*Arizona Daily Star*, September 3, 1879). They are believed to have been Sam Yap speakers from Guangdong Province of south China, who were responsive to social biases that had evolved and been nurtured in China over generations. Rather than submit to either confrontation or coexistence with ancient adversaries, the Sam Yaps soon moved out of

Tucson when a larger infiltration of Sze Yap speakers occurred after 1880 (*Arizona Daily Star*, Rodeo Edition, February 22, 1935).

The Southern Pacific Railroad reached the Tucson railhead in March 1880. Myrick (1975: 50) describes how 200 Chinese track workers marched to town with picks and shovels over their shoulders and set up a temporary camp at the local race track. A number of these Sze Yap speakers from the Toishan district of Guangdong Province soon decided to stay in Tucson. The federal census taken in June 1880 tabulated 160 Chinese, including 2 women, in Tucson (U.S. Federal Census 1880).

Other Chinese railroad hands preferred the security of $25 a month until they found a more inviting place farther along the tracks. The same census recorded 890 Asians in eastern Pima County, of which Tucson was the county seat. Of these individuals, 876 told tabulators their personal name was Ah, which actually is a term of endearment typical of Cantonese. Elsewhere in the county, 37 additional Chinese found in the mining and ranching hamlets of Patagonia, Santa Cruz, and Sonoita may have come into the territory either by way of the stage in the 1870s or the train in the 1880s.

Tucson's squat, contiguous, mud houses straggled along rutted dirt lanes must have seemed familiar to the men of south China because of the physical resemblance to some villages there. They first moved into what had been a historically important part of the settlement. It was a wedge-shaped tract lying immediately southwest of what had been a 10-acre walled presidio during the Spanish and Mexican occupations. That tract had emerged as the first central business district of the town, once the Americans began to assert their influence. Before the Civil War it was here, west of the trail grandly called the Royal Road, that Solomon Warner had opened a mercantile establishment, Mark Aldrich had run the first United States post office, and the Butterfield Overland Mail maintained a station for travelers and crews of the four weekly stages braving desert and warlike natives between the Rio Grande and the Colorado. The Tully and Ochoa Freight Company was once a primary link to the New Mexico portion of the original territory acquired from Mexico through the Treaty of Guadalupe Hidalgo. It had occupied the quarters later owned by furniture dealer Leo Goldschmidt. Most of the buildings used for these various purposes had been erected some years earlier, as Mexicans burst out of the confines of the original presidio. A three-sided deteriorating adobe compound located just to the north

Figure 1.1. Buildings along the west end of Pennington Street were among some of the earliest structures erected outside the Spanish presidio walls and already were dilapidated in 1881, when Chinese immigrants settled there. (Courtesy of the Arizona Historical Society, Tucson.)

had provided barracks outside the military enclosure for additional Mexican soldiers. American occupying forces later billeted there (Peterson 1966; Smith 1967: 215; Sonnichsen 1982: 43, 88, 102).

By the time the Chinese arrived, many of these structures already were in ruins because the central business district had shifted gradually a few blocks to the southeast (Fig. 1.1). Buildings were of the blocky, flat-roofed regional style, with thick mud brick walls, high ceilings of pine beams and saguaro crossribs, packed earthen floors, facades flush with the street, and privies out back. Apparently, one structure previously was sufficiently renovated to serve as a washhouse for a pre-1880s Chinese arrival, as noted by an advertisement in a local newspaper. "Tom, the Chinaman opposite the Cosmopolitan Hotel, is the first class washer and ironer of Tucson. Orders promptly attended to and clothes delivered and called for" (*Arizona Daily Star*, January 10, 1878).

Typically four or five structures sheltered a number of men. As was the case with the rest of Tucson in 1880, all the buildings into which these men moved lacked running water, gas lights, or electricity (Bret Harte 1980: 84; Sonnichsen 1982: 107–110). They also were devoid of furnishings. To subsist in these makeshift quarters and temporary shanties thrown up just to the west along an *acequia*, the men are assumed to have acquired a few basic household articles such as improvised burners or cook stoves (Fig. 3.8), utensils, kerosene lamps, and perhaps several of the earthenware water jars (*ollas*) that Tohono O'odham Indian women peddled on the streets for storage of drinking water (Fig. 1.2). Rudimentary tables, chairs, and bunks likely were made from scrap lumber.

Figure 1.2. Two Tohono O'odham women with large, wide-mouth, earthenware water jars resting on shoulder burden frames, photographed some time in the late nineteenth or early twentieth century. Water mains were installed in 1882, but the backyard *olla* remained a common feature in the Hispanic barrio and likely was used by the Chinese as well as other residents. (Courtesy of the Sharlot Hall Museum, Prescott.)

Figure 1.3. Chinese occupation in Tucson, 1883.

Table 1.1. Place of Chinese Residence in Tucson in 1880 (as indicated in U.S. Federal Census* and excluding private homes of Euro-Americans)

	1880
North of Congress Street:	
Main St. (or west side of Main St.)	51
Between Main St.—Levin's Gardens	5
Along ditch (acequia) west of town	4
Pennington St.	5
Dells between Main St.—Meyer St.	3
Court House Plaza	1
Cosmopolitan Hotel	1
Meyers St.**	12
Congress St.	18
South of Congress Street:	
Palace Hotel***	6
Out of town:	
Fort Lowell	11

*Incomplete residential information
**North assumed
***Residence at place of work assumed

Otherwise, it is thought that a whole gamut of small, portable Chinese goods soon was available for use by sojourners. According to the 1880 census, Wing Tai Sing had opened a store on the west side of north Main Street to serve the needs of his countrymen. His success depended on the shipping possibilities afforded by the new rails and the inherent conservatism of his clientele. The 1883 Sanborn fire insurance map shows that the potential sojourner market attracted at least three other Chinese merchants, who opened neighboring stores to sell customary comestibles, clothing, cooking gear and dishes, opium and tobacco, medicines, and toiletries.

Chinese Lodgings and Occupations

The earliest map of Tucson showing places of Chinese occupation was dated 1883 (Fig. 1.3). It confirms incomplete residential data in the 1880 census that this district west and south of the ancient presidio gate contained the heaviest concentration of Asian lodgings and businesses (Table 1.1). However, it was never an exclusively Chinese

domain; lower-class Hispanics shared tenements there and undoubtedly patronized Chinese-run stores. It is impossible to achieve an exact correlation between the map and the documents, but between them 60 Chinese individuals, 4 large dwellings communally occupied by them, 2 washhouses, 3 stores, and 2 opium dens, plus the outlying shanties, were explicitly indicated. No temple, or joss house, was identified. On Ott Street immediately to the east of this complex was another U-shaped unit containing a Chinese store, a saloon, and two wings utilized as rooming houses. Combined, all these buildings off both sides of Main Street and their tenants comprised the territorial Tucson Chinatown. Additionally, being under no locational restrictions, the Chinese dispersed to other sectors in order to be closer to potential customers, but seldom did they settle within the Anglicized central business district. In 1883 six laundries, three restaurants, one store, and a "keno den" were south of Congress Street, the artery through the center of town that served as a north-south dividing line. Other than those in Chinatown, three laundries and two stores were situated to the north.

In 1880, there was one secondary Chinese occupational area away from downtown Tucson and hence removed from the TUR district. That was at Fort Lowell, which in 1872 had been moved from its original location southeast of the center to a spot seven miles east on the Rillito Creek. Eleven Chinese worked there in 1880 and must have been provided housing.

The majority of the territorial Tucson Chinese population was prototypical sojourner: young single males, who probably were illiterate, unskilled, poor, highly ethnocentric, and with the single objective of economic betterment in order to return home as soon as possible to live the good life. Split among themselves by regional and clan rifts that had spanned generations, they were not a homogeneous block that would respond uniformly to exposure to the American way. Accommodation might result under those conditions, but assimilation requires a willingness to accept the educational, social, recreational, political, and economic aspects of a dominant society. According to the written record elsewhere, that willingness was lacking in a high percentage of Chinese arriving during the late nineteenth century (Ch'en 1979: 258–259; R. H. Lee 1960). Also curbing assimilation was the sexual imbalance, with Chinese women a prevailing rarity until well into the twentieth century. Thus, if aware of the opposing milieu into which they had entered, the earliest Chinese immigrants generally are viewed as remaining disaffected and self-focused. Add the Euro-American opposition that boiled up in nineteenth-century California and most western states (Hill 1973), and the overseas Chinese pattern of life became increasingly circumscribed and the possibilities for breaking out of it even more limited (Lyman 1974: 80).

In Tucson, Chinese cultural integrity can be assumed to have been reinforced daily by communal living for all those who were not employed by private Euro-American families as live-in domestics. Such a housing pattern may have been dictated by lack of available or affordable individual quarters, but more probably it was a preferred mode. Men's and juvenile boys' houses were customary in southern China (Prazniak 1984: 124). Additionally, the pattern provided defense against an outside, unfamiliar, and sometimes unfriendly world. The pressures attendant to the Chinese Exclusion Act passed in 1882, renewed in 1892, and extended indefinitely in 1902 quite surely drove this ethnic group deeper into its own system (for further examination of this phenomenon, see Spicer 1971: 795–800 and Sarna 1978). Other factors that might have forestalled significant cultural assimilation of these occupants of what had become a Tucson outskirts were the instability of this extremely mobile population, which was constantly on the move toward economic advancement, and the absence of the settling influence of families. In 1880 just a cook and a laundryman had wives living with them. Neither couple had children.

Still, in the late 1870s and early 1880s when the first Chinese came to town, there was some indication that the socioeconomic cleavages based on race, which were to plague other Arizona communities, might not evolve in Tucson. There was a widespread feeling among the town's residents of prosperity and well-being. A permanent military post promised hope for an end to the perennial Apache troubles, while putting money into local circulation. Regional mines and ranches were beginning to thrive, making Tucson their supply base. As a vital hub in the all-weather transportation routes leading off in cardinal directions, the village saw its size more than double in a 10-year period. Hotels, breweries, recreational parks, flour mills, grocery stores, livery stables, newspapers, schools, three dozen all-night saloons, and a well-patronized tenderloin district were attributes of a live-wire community on the move (Sonnichsen 1982: 88–91).

Furthermore, there were conditions peculiar to Tucson that had the potential for more rapid integration of the intrusive Chinese element. For three decades the majority Hispanics and minority Euro-Americans that comprised the local society had lived side by side harmoniously. Intermarriages, business partnerships, a sharing of life styles, and a common enemy in the Apache had produced a high level of cultural tolerance and reciprocity. As a reflection of this prevailing forbearance, the Chinese were not greeted with inflammatory newspaper editorials condemning their arrival or with cartoons ridiculing their physical appearance or mannerisms. There was no physical violence perpetrated against them. No Anti-Chinese League to force their ouster, such as leagues formed in most Arizona mining towns, ever was advocated. The prominent Fish and Stevens families, whose elegant homes were close to the Chinese quarters, are not known to have complained about their Asian neighbors. No residential or commercial segregation was imposed, after an appeal for confining Chinese businesses to a restricted zone was rejected by the city council as being unconstitutional (*Arizona Citizen*, March 7, 1893). Whether that desire to segregate the Chinese arose from racial bias or perceived threats to the Euro-American economy is unknown.

Nevertheless, if opportunities abounded for the old-timers, the newly arrived Asians found few economic doors open. Although the Euro-Americans likely regarded the Chinese as a cheap labor force worthy of exploitation and certainly little threat to their own positions of power, there was a basic problem with the Chinese themselves. Few had more to offer an employer than strong backs and an eagerness to work. Most were at a further disadvantage in not easily speaking or understanding English. Those factors qualified them only for unskilled or semiskilled jobs (Table 1.2). Half of them found work in some aspect of behind-the-scenes food services in the town's restaurants. Five cooks and a 15-year-old chamber servant were employed by the Palace Hotel situated on south Meyer Street, the only two-story building in Tucson. Six others tended garden plots at Fort Lowell. Presumably their expertise yielded more than enough produce for the needs of the soldiers' mess, inasmuch as five of them peddled vegetables and fruits to civilians around town. Four additional Chinese continued to toil in the local railroad yards, which earlier they had helped level (Myrick 1975: 56).

It is notable that two-thirds of the Chinese in Tucson in 1880 decided to be independently employed. They turned to washing and ironing clothes (Fig. 1.4). Laundrying was a viable occupation at the time because of a large, bachelor, Euro-American population and a growing number of monied families who could be expected to pay for such service. On the other hand, the dominant Hispanic community was not as promising a market because it was a long settled familial one wherein the women routinely carried out domestic tasks. More affluent Hispanic matrons hired poorer Hispanic household help. Even with this drawback, it is believed that

Table 1.2. Occupations of Chinese Residing in Territorial Tucson in 1880, 1890, and 1910

	1880	1900	1910
	Men: 158	Men: 211*	Men: 218**
	Women: 2	Women: 6	Women: 14
	Children: 0	Children: 5	Children: 25
Laundryman	98	31	23
Cook	26	34	36
Restaurant manager		5	12
Vegetable cleaner		1	
Waiter	2	12	1
Dishwasher	1	1	3
Farmer	6	36	30
Peddler	5		7
Railroad worker	4	13	5
Laborer	5	11	5
Servant	1	7	1
Butcher		1	
Barber			1
Hotel keeper	1		1
Interpreter			1
Merchant	1	40	63
Clerk		3	12
Doctor		3	
Druggist		3	
"Capitalist"		1	
Own income			8
No information	2	9	9

*related individuals, 2 Mexican females, 3 children of mixed parentage
**related individuals, 2 Mexican females, 1 French female, 11 children of mixed parentage

Figure 1.4. Kwong Hing, a 58-year-old laundryman, was included in the 1880 federal census, with no address indicated. In the 1901 Tucson city directory a laundry bearing his name is said to have been at 23 north Meyer Street, presumably shown in this photograph. However, the 1900 federal census lists five other men (three laundrymen and two cooks) residing there. The original proprietor may have died or returned to China prior to 1900 and his successors did not bother to change the sign out front. (Courtesy of the Arizona Historical Society, Tucson.)

sustained employment on railroad construction gangs may have allowed some Chinese to accumulate modest savings with which they set themselves up in the laundry business. This was a trade demanding little special skill and low capitalization. It would have been viewed as an advancement up the economic scale by those who came from a peasant background, even though such work was as scorned by men in China as by Euro-Americans on the western frontier (R. H. Lee 1960: 81).

The Chinese were undaunted by the fact that laundrying also was an occupation that demanded hard physical work and long hours for little remuneration. With a willingness to establish partnerships, three or four Chinese sometimes formed a joint business venture (Light 1972: 93; Ong 1983: 76). Partners were often clan or village related, who called each other "cousin." Pooled resources provided the necessary funds for rental of space, supplies of soap and firewood, and a few pieces of equipment. In addition to the satisfaction of proprietorship, this arrangement also allowed the option of the requisite trip back to China for family visits, while the endeavor continued to function in the hands of others. A division of labor existed, with some men washing, others ironing, and an occasional apprentice learning how to do both satisfactorily. They occupied shabby adobe rooms and assorted outbuildings humidified by wood stoves, boiling water, charcoal irons, and close quarters. Some, it is said, slept in shifts on floors beneath broad ironing tables. Outside, the wash-house yards were festooned with platforms and scaffolds of drying clothes and quagmires of stagnant sudsy water.

Two wash-houses in Chinatown must have served Asian customers, but the other nine dealt with Euro-Americans, Hispanics, and Blacks. Laundrymen, with a pair of delivery baskets balanced by a bamboo rod over the shoulders, became a typical sight on Tucson's streets. Siu (1964: 429–442) and Ong (1983) point out that the laundry installation was in itself a microcosm of China, isolated in effect from the impersonal Euro-American environment, and a means of rejecting assimilation into American patterns. It also provided valuable experience in private enterprise, which could be applied later to more profitable endeavors.

Meanwhile, another occupation for local Chinese had appeared at the inception of the colony that would lead to social stratification. Persons with sufficient initiative, education, and resources entered the ranks of mercantilism. At first their commercial contacts were strictly within the Chinese community, where they gradually accrued power because of sojourner dependence on them for goods and services and where they were agents in maintaining the ethnic boundary between the Chinese and other segments of the local society. Primarily because of a maturation of the assimilation process begun elsewhere, the merchants differed from the mass of sojourners in ways as diverse as place of birth, amount of education, finances, familial residence, and, in some instances, a forthright receptiveness of Americanization. It was this group who, having higher status, would emerge slowly into the societal mainstream.

One such shopkeeper of the first Tucson Chinatown was Jon Chin. He and his wife were second generation overseas Chinese born in California. Their three children were born in Tucson (U.S. Federal Census 1900). By reason of these births, all were American citizens. Quite possibly Jon Chin had received some formal schooling in California. A second merchant, Low Chon, and his wife were aliens, but their small son had been born in Oregon. Both men likely operated stores that primarily served Chinese customers, but they may have worn Western clothes and haircuts and been somewhat sophisticated in American-style business matters. The women can be expected to have been more sequestered and less quick to change their Eastern attire and manners. To what extent the furnishings of their rented homes on Ott and Pearl streets may have displayed a cultural blend is unknown.

Most notable of the emerging Chinese upper class was Chan Tin Wo. His prior background is uncertain, but early in the decade of the 1880s he arrived in Tucson with money to purchase a large Sonoran-style home that originally had been built in 1857 by Francisco G. Torano. It was at 88 Pearl Street in the heart of what later became Tucson's first Chinatown. Chan rented another structure on north Main Street to serve as a store. Within a few years he had a California-born wife and three children born in Tucson and a thriving business catering to Hispanic and Euro-American customers, as well as to Asians (*Arizona Daily Star*, May 2, 1890). By the end of the nineteenth century Chan had acquired four additional lots in a developing district east of the railroad tracks (Tucson Block Book, 1898, Arizona Historical Society). These purchases may have been real estate speculation because there apparently were no personal plans to exploit these properties, which were located in a Euro-American neighborhood. Chan also owned another lot in the Hispanic barrio at the corner of south Meyer and Kennedy streets, which he subsequently sold to countryman Don Yan. By 1900, census takers were so impressed with his holdings that they listed Chan as a "capitalist." More importantly, Chan had become Tucson's first naturalized Chinese American, despite a federal law prohibiting the granting of citizenship through that means to persons of his race, and he was active in civic affairs that included jury duty. Fluent in English, he was praised by the local Euro-American press as a respected intermediary between fellow Chinese and other Tucsonans (*Arizona Citizen*, November 4, 1904; *Arizona Daily Star*, November 9, 1884; June 19, 1889).

The tolerant atmosphere of the earliest era of Chinese presence in Tucson was to tighten during the 1890s, although the papers remained respectful, no formal sanctions were imposed, and the Euro-Americans likely regarded the Chinese as basically unassimilable because of racial distinctiveness. At that time there was a perceptible tipping of the balance of economic and social prestige, as well as approaching numerical superiority, toward the Euro-American societal component (Sheridan 1986: 15–96). As part of the Manifest Destiny philosophy, that prestige brought in its wake a rising prejudice on the part of Euro-Americans against the native Hispanics. These prejudicial feelings expanded to include the Chinese, most of whom were destined to enter the social hierarchy at the bottom level. That, in turn, pitted Hispanics against Chinese and lessened conflict between the Euro-Americans and the Asians.

Many Hispanics considered the Chinese to be inferior to themselves, according to Sheridan (1986: 84) even lower than the despised Native Americans. There were, however, many racial and ethnic parallels between the two groups that might have fostered bonds. The Mongoloid strain was so pronounced in some Hispanics that physical features such as physiognomy, stature, body build, hair type and color, and skin pigmentation were similar to those of the Asians. Cultural compatibility could be seen in spartan close-to-the-earth modes of life that were highly dependent on human muscle; strong family orientation; love of festivals, theatrics, music, and vibrant color; and unstructured cotton garb. Therefore, it is suggested that the hostility Hispanics felt for the Chinese centered on competition for employment and a working class nativism that spread like a cloud over the late nineteenth-century western frontier.

The labor caste system as it evolved in Tucson excluded Hispanics and Chinese from the same kinds of jobs and organized trade unions and restricted them to unskilled and semiskilled ranks, the Chinese proving most adept in the service sector. Whenever they decided to move within the employment structure, it had to be horizontally rather than vertically. Because of their greater power through numbers, the Hispanics gained the upper hand on some occasions but did not fare well on others. For example, after vitriolic protests by Spanish-language papers and incidents of violence, the railroads ceased hiring Chinese workers in areas away from Tucson but increased Asian employment in town, al-

though not significantly (Table 1.2; Sheridan 1986: 84). The Chinese were engaged in the local yards as engine wipers, water tank tenders, and depot janitors, with no possibility of gaining positions of greater responsibility.

One occupation that was to cause bitterness between Hispanics and Chinese was farming. Although this activity took place away from the TUR precinct, repercussions of it surely spread through the Hispanic neighborhoods. According to one informant, the first of Tucson's Chinese gardens was on a patch of ground east of the Santa Cruz River, worked in 1878 by Low Tai You (unidentified newspaper clipping, Arizona Historical Society). This early date is dubious, but by the middle of the next decade promising farm land on the opposite terrace of the river at the base of Sentinel Peak was being rented by countrymen from Euro-American owners (Fong 1980; Sheridan 1986: 65; Sonnichsen 1982: 112). Eventually more than 150 acres were under cultivation, watered by ditches off the river, and, in 1900, farmed by 34 Chinese. Typically, several relatives worked one farm. Such were the cases of three men named Wei, five named Wong, and three named Lim (U.S. Federal Census 1900). The desert had never been so bountiful, as these farmers intensely specialized in fruits and vegetables usually not grown by neighboring Hispanics or others tilling plots south of town. In the opinion of some, their lavish use of the Santa Cruz's limited surface waters hastened disastrous erosion of the floodplain, and it certainly brought them into direct confrontation with Hispanic farmers (Sheridan 1986: 65–67; Sonnichsen 1982: 112). The Chinese peddled their produce by wagon to restaurants and groceries run by fellow Chinese, as well as to Euro-American and possibly Hispanic homes (Fig. 1.5). A contemporary account provides an eyewitness view of this colorful part of the local Asian colony.

Figure 1.5. An unidentified Chinese gardener, with his nineteenth century horsedrawn delivery wagon, peddles his produce through town. (Courtesy of the Arizona Historical Society, Tucson.)

. . . adjoining their gardens are small huts built of adobes and ornamented by tin cans, barley sacks and bushes, in which two or three partners or 'cousins', as they call each other, live together. When working on their farms they present a very comical appearance with their blue trousers rolled up above their knees, barefooted and sometimes hatless . . . When in town the China farmer's appearance is more civilized. He wears dark blue overalls and a loose china jacket; his pig-tail is wound around his head in a queue under his large straw hat (unknown newspaper, 1897, Arizona Historical Society).

Occasionally the papers provided free, good-natured advertising for these men of the soil, who did much to make life more pleasant for persons who had chosen to live in such a sere land.

Mou Op, a Chinese vegetable gardener who lives in the valley just west of town, says he will have a box of ripe strawberries next week. He will very likely sell them at auction and with the proceeds go back to China on a special steamer and be a wealthy member of the emperor's court for the rest of his days (*Arizona Citizen*, March 15, 1893).

Chinese peddlers from the garden patches are bringing in cantaloupes and tomatoes to Tucson (*Arizona Republican*, July 15, 1898).

Two Chinese gardeners resided in town and probably cared for flower beds around Euro-American homes. One other rented land in the Tanque Verde area east of the settlement, where he raised potatoes, sweet potatoes, onions, and chili for buyers in Tombstone (*Arizona Daily Star*, May 11, 1889).

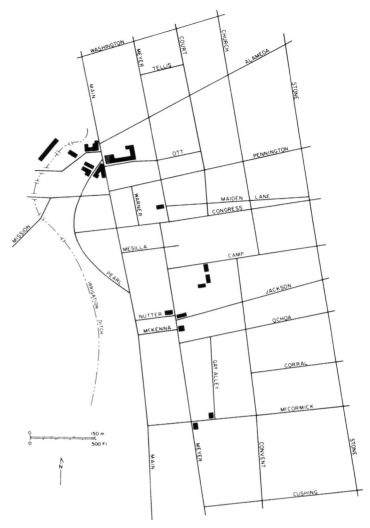

Figure 1.6. Chinese occupation in Tucson, 1896.

Chinese Solidarity and Associations

The overseas Chinese are known to have transferred their social organization to America. Clan and territorial associations to which all Chinese belonged quickly followed immigration to provide social assistance and cultural cohesion in an alien land. Whether such bodies were formally organized in territorial Tucson is not known, although census data confirm that relatives shared housing and often occupation. The most easily recognized local association was the Chee Kung Tong, present at least by the 1890s and probably earlier (Fig 1.6; *Arizona Citizen*, October 25, 1895). This secret fraternal society, originally with revolutionary aims and documented active involvement in the criminal arena of the United States, is fully described in Chapter 3. The Tucson chapter maintained a joss house in Chinatown that, together with opium dens and gambling parlors, was a focal point to which idle Chinese gravitated. Given the barren nature of their transitory residency, it was the sojourners who were most vulnerable to a panoply of vices that in the course of time and changing American standards transformed into illegalities. Sojourner participation in such activities as opium smuggling and use, prostitution, gambling, tong vio-

lence, and other circumventions of the laws of the land unfairly discolored Chinese reputations in the eyes of other Tucsonans. That view subsequently produced a ground swell of adversity on many levels, which drove this class of immigrant deeper into ethnicity and inner-community solidarity.

One expression of solidarity was the celebration of Chinese New Year. In China New Year's had not been a holiday with such elaborate observances as those staged in America by the overseas Chinese (Sarna 1978: 375). However, in Tucson, as elsewhere in the West, the day became a means by which sojourners could wrap themselves in the comfort of their cultural uniqueness and yet at the same time reach out for some degree of acceptance by the host society. Under the auspices of the Chee Kung Tong, itself a vehicle for perpetuation of Old World themes and attitudes, the Chinese community annually held a week-long open house to which all Tucsonans were invited. Barrages of firecrackers ricocheted along Pearl Street. Colorful paper lanterns and cloth banners bedecked the tong hall. Strange musical instruments caused an unfamiliar din. Tables loaded with exotic tidbits of food awaited guests. And local Chinese men donned their finest tunics, skull caps, and slippers (Fig 1.7).

Apparently a number of curious neighbors attended the festivities, viewing gawdy decorations and sampling party fare. Invariably journalists found good copy (*Arizona Citizen*, February 5, 1892 and February 12, 1907). But when the occasion had passed, no Euro-American or Hispanic groups are known to have responded in kind to these friendly overtures by the Chinese, with the exception of some church groups. Euro-American indifference, as much as enforced Chinese clannishness, must be held responsible for at least some of the introverted retreat by this body of immigrants.

A second territorial era fraternal organization, the Suey Ying Tong, is known to have existed in Tucson. Some Native American spectators are said to have attended its dedication, no doubt attracted by a firecracker barrage, free food, and unabashed curiosity (*Arizona Daily Star*, April 18, 1950).

Two developments occurred during the decade of the 1880s that affected the relationship between Hispanics and Chinese and that also determined the nature and permanence of the immigrant colony. One was the previously mentioned growing economic and social dominance of Euro-Americans. That dominance slowly forced lower-class Hispanics

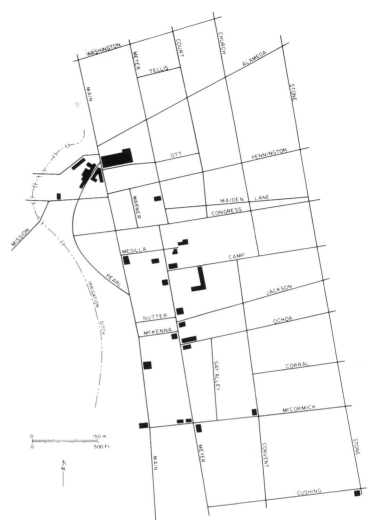

Figure 1.8. Chinese occupation in downtown Tucson, 1904.

Figure 1.7. A studio photograph taken 3 May 1894 shows an unidentified Tucson Chinese wearing his dress outfit of a heavy plush jacket characteristically fastened with ties on the right side and a stiff pillbox hat, under which his queue was tucked. (Courtesy of the Arizona Historical Society, Tucson.)

to relocate in a less developed, less Anglicized barrio south of the central business district, although since the Civil War there had been continuance of some American occupation there (Sheridan 1986: 79–82; Sonnichsen 1982: 107). The other development was the premium placed by the Exclusion Act on merchant status for Chinese, as opposed to that of unskilled labor. To become a shopkeeper not only meant independence but freedom from threat of deportation and opportunity to sponsor immigration of qualified relatives. Therefore, with the promising need for grocery and general dry goods stores to serve the expanding Hispanic neighborhood and the attraction of becoming self employed, some Chinese moved southward into a predominantly Hispanic quarter (Figs 1.6, 1.8, 1.9; Table 1.3). In partnerships of two or three persons, they set up shops and back-room lodging throughout the barrio in buildings identical to those occupied by Hispanics (Figs. 1.10, 1.11). They hoped through the Chinese network of trade connections to California to successfully compete with Hispanic shopkeepers, who often had to contend with sluggish north Mexican markets and high tariffs. The 1900 census tabulated 40 Chinese merchants in a total population of 224 Asians. The 1908 city

Figure 1.9. On unpaved south Meyer Street the Chinese opened small grocery and general merchandise stores (the buildings with awnings) interspersed among private dwellings. The horsedrawn wagon moving into the distance was similar to wagons used by Chinese gardeners to sell produce door to door. (Courtesy of the Arizona Historical Society, Tucson.)

Table 1.3. Place of Chinese Residence in Tucson in 1900 and 1910
(as indicated in U.S. Federal Census* and excluding private homes of Euro-Americans)

	1900	1910		1900	1910
North of Congress Street, core area:			Away from core area:		
Pearl St.	32	31	Southern Pacific Railroad dormitory	13	
Ott St.	10	7	San Xavier Hotel	8	
No. Meyer St.	11	15	Toole Ave.	1	3
E. Congress St.	2		1st St.	1	
W. Congress St.		16	5th St.		6
Franklin St.	1		6th St.	1	
No. Main St.	5	12	7th St.		1
W. Alameda St.	2	3	17th St.		2
Council St.	3		19th St.		1
Court St.	9		24th St.	2	
Court Plaza	3		4th Ave.		2
Pennington St.		2	5th Ave.		2
			6th Ave.		1
			8th Ave.		3
South of Congress Street, core area:			10th Ave.		2
So. Main St.	2	3	No. Zia St.	2	
So. Meyer St.	13	38	Colita St.	1	
Convent St.	8	18	Hoff St.		3
Mesilla St.	7		Anna St.		2
Church Plaza	4		Pima County Jail	2	
Ochoa St.	1	4	Indian Training School	1	
So. Stone St.	3	1			
Jackson St.		5	Out of town:		
Cushing St.		2	West of Santa Cruz River	43	
E. Broadway St.		5	West of Indian School Rd.		12
W. Broadway St.		13	Elysian Grove Rd.		13
Gay Alley		3	Old Yuma Rd.		2

*Incomplete residential information

Figure 1.10. A Chinese-run store in the early 1900s carries an American stock of groceries and dry goods for Hispanic and Euro-American customers. In addition, upturned Chinese rice-soup bowls are nested on the lower shelf, baskets on the upper shelf are probably Chinese, the dark hat hanging at the upper left is a style favored by many Asian immigrants, and the large rectangular cans on the shelves at right likely contained imported peanut oil or soy sauce. The proprietor has adopted Western clothes for his working day. His living quarters probably were several rooms through the door at the rear. (Courtesy of the Arizona Historical Society, Tucson.)

Figure 1.11. Charley Lee's grocery, as it appeared about 1899, was at 633 south Meyer Street in a flat-roofed adobe building typical of the Hispanic barrio. Serving a diverse clientele typical of territorial Tucson, Charley posted bunting-draped signs in Spanish and in English advertising non-Chinese foodstuffs. A man, perhaps the father, engages in some construction work, while two Hispanic boys lounge. The upturned pottery jar near the store entrance was Tohono O'odham Indian earthenware used by most residents to cool drinking water. (Courtesy of the Arizona Historical Society, Tucson.)

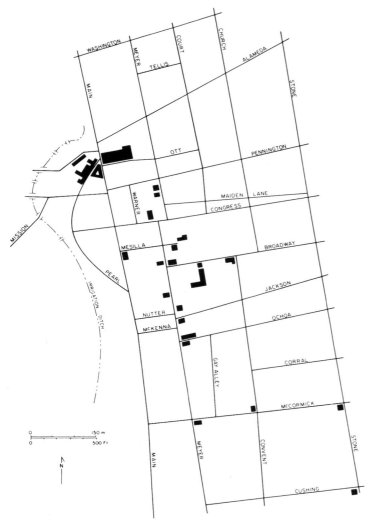

Figure 1.12. Chinese occupation in downtown Tucson, 1909.

sary to cultivate a consumer base there, and occasional inter-marriage with Hispanic women (*Arizona Republican*, August 7, 1898). An antimiscegenation law passed in Arizona in 1902 was not enforced in these cases; it was declared unconstitutional in 1967.

Illustrative of both racial intermarriage and a continued climate of tolerance on the part of some of the Euro-Americans was the following newspaper account of a 5-year-old orphan befriended by the Jon Chin merchant family.

Don Ah Look is a Chinese lad who was raised in Tucson. His father was a prosperous Chinese merchant and his mother was a Mexican woman.

The parents are both dead, and the little fellow has been brought up by friends of the family. He has relatives living in China who want to raise him and Don Ah Look will soon leave Tucson for the east.

Having been born in the United States, he is a lawful citizen of this country, and having lived in Tucson, he will some day want to return, for all who leave this ancient pueblo one day come back.

To be sure that the custom house officers will let him enter the country when he has grown to manhood, Sam Hughes and J. Knox Corbett [two of the most prominent Euro-American men of the community with homes on Main Street slightly north of Chinatown] lent their offices in his behalf and filed an affidavit with the picture of the Chinese boy accompanying it, to effect that the child was born in Tucson, and stating that he goes to China to acquire an education and will perhaps want to return to this country later on (*Arizona Citizen*, February 18, 1901).

Such Chinese-Hispanic interaction was a one-way route of cultural transmission, owing to Hispanic numerical superiority and ethnocentrism and to the critical scarcity of Chinese women and children, who perhaps would have helped soften some social barriers that were erected against an influx of foreign, unattached males. Further, in this Euro-American dominant town, it was an alliance that would continue to assign both groups to the lower societal stratum. The symbiotic dependence of Chinese merchants on Hispanic purchasers developed at this time would force them years later to move in tandem during the urban renewal upheaval.

Another small group of Chinese would-be retailers moved with Euro-Americans east of the Southern Pacific tracks, and still others opened businesses to serve Hispanics, establishing themselves north of town along the railroad. Several had short-order eateries near the railroad station.

Contemporaneous with the rise of the local merchant class, the Chinese laundry was disappearing. It was a victim, here as elsewhere, of mechanization. By 1900 there were two-thirds fewer laundrymen in town than there had been twenty years previously (Table 1.2). Some of the merchants, in fact, may have gained their business skill in that trade.

directory lists 37 Chinese businesses situated south of Congress Street, nearly half on south Meyer Street (Figs. 1.8, 1.12). Corner locations were preferred. There were as many as three or four similar stores, almost door by door, along some blocks. No supporting evidence for the conversion of Chinese gardeners into grocers such as these, as suggested by Schweitzer (1952), has been found during this study.

The assumption of roles as small tradesmen entailed some realignment of social concepts, because this occupation traditionally had been at the bottom of the Chinese social ladder. The bias against commerce and those engaged in it can be attributed to an ingrained defensive attitude of a basically agrarian society, such as China always had been. On a number of continents and oceanic islands, however, overseas Chinese considered commerce a way to success. In a perverse way the dependence for that success on an adversary ethnic group served to enhance their own position with fellow countrymen. Moreover, it was soon realized that in America financial success was linked to social acceptance.

With penetration of a Hispanicized territory came gradual acquisition of Spanish language, merchandising skills neces-

Social Stratification

Early in the twentieth century there was another change afoot within the Chinese colony. That was a steady, but limited, influx of American-born Chinese men and a few women. Caution must be taken with population figures because of statistical quicksands when dealing with the instability of Chinese occupation that intensified in Tucson. The town's location on transcontinental routes and its proximity to the permeable Mexican border fostered such an abnormally high mobility that absolute head counts were bound to be inaccurate. Notwithstanding, available records reveal that in the 1900 population, 11 Tucson Chinese men had been born in California, 1 in Nevada, and 1 (a 17-year-old youth) in Arizona; 4 Chinese women had been born in California. Ten years later the 1910 census for Tucson tabulated 51 men born in California, 1 in Nevada, and 1 in Arizona; 5 Chinese women had been born in California (U.S. Federal Census 1910).

Regardless of place of birth, Chinese allegiance to inherited roots typically was strong, but it was being tempered by a rising Americanization that included some command of English, education in public schools for their offspring, changes in costume and grooming, and a set of altered social values. Some 155 Chinese persons indicated literacy in English in 1910, but these figures are suspect because census takers, who are not likely to have been qualified judges, took Chinese claims at face value or did not ask relevant questions. However, English instruction had been available to the local Chinese for several decades (*Arizona Daily Citizen*, December 17, 1900).

If R. H. Lee's assessment (1960) of Chinese assimilation is correct, the most significant clue to their reorientation was religious conversion. The Congregational Church had been actively engaged in that program since the late 1800s, when it was reported, "The Chinese are apt scholars. They learn to read and sing with ease, and show a surprising amount of intelligence in their interpretation of passages of the scriptures" (*Arizona Daily Star*, April 24, 1889). In Tucson, the men in this category generally were restaurant operators, shopkeepers, clerks, or translators for the immigration service. In such positions they had almost daily association with Euro-Americans and improved economic opportunities (Table 1.2). Even so, there were subtle class boundaries between these two groupings that could be breeched only superficially. Most American-born Chinese moved into the Hispanic barrio, where the majority of their fellow alien Chinese also had moved (Figs. 1.8, 1.12; Table 1.3).

Inevitably, American-born Chinese were allied with occasional mainland Chinese who had decided to take up permanent residence in America, even though denied citizenship. This alliance sometimes was at considerable cost because any American citizen marrying a Chinese alien lost his or her citizenship (Lyman 1974: 106–107). The migrating Chinese elite were persons who had come with acceptable assets and occupation, frequently with a mate, and who preferred to socialize with the Chinese possessing more education and breeding than most sojourners.

Six such men with specialized occupations in 1900 were three doctors and three druggists, residing at 44 Mesilla Street and 187 east Congress Street. Inasmuch as those who would have sought their services were devoted to medicinal teas, herbs, and pills, their business must have been brisk. In the mainland Chinese social structure persons engaged in these occupations were of low esteem, but overseas they were ranked above the typical labor element (Davis 1971: 29). In any event, they likely had minimal contact with non-Asians.

A man who did cultivate the broader community was Lim Goon, listed in the 1908 city directory as having a grocery store on south Meyer Street and a restaurant on east Broadway. He probably came to Tucson by way of Sonora. In a description of an elaborate wedding ceremony at the Presbyterian Church, to which the most prominent Tucson Euro-Americans were invited, a newspaper reporter described fancy Oriental bric-a-brac and furniture in the Goon home on south Meyer Street. Also mentioned were silks, laces, crystal, and jewelry sent by the bride's relatives in China (*Arizona Daily Star*, March 28 and 29, 1908). It is possible that there were other Chinese domiciles in the barrio with comparable luxuries of which Euro-Americans were unaware.

Financial success is further suggested by the 1910 census tabulation of eight individuals having their "own income." Whether that meant that some men had come to Tucson after having accumulated savings elsewhere is unknown. They had been in the United States from 30 to 48 years and obviously had achieved the American dream of financial security. At least one of those with "own income," Heng Lee, variously had been a Tucson merchant and restaurant owner, was a naturalized citizen, and had married a Hispanic woman. The couple's three children were born in Tucson.

The number of Chinese residing in Tucson remained amazingly static for the first decade of the twentieth century, increasing by 7 males over 15 years of age. Such constancy of the colony was remarkable when considering population attrition through forced and voluntary return to China and the nation-wide Chinese trend toward withdrawal from outlying areas into large urban centers. At the same time, the overall size of Tucson had jumped to 13,000 persons. That growth stemmed from Tucson's role as a service center, with broad regional influence reaching many thousands more. As indicated above, some better jobs were available to upper level Chinese already present but were not sufficiently numerous to attract more Asian hopefuls. Lower level Chinese shopkeepers continued to be supported by Hispanic consumerism.

Fewer Chinese had to maintain themselves through domestic or manual labor, although 23 men continued to work in 7 hand laundries. There were 8 Chinese owned and operated restaurants, whose names in former times might have evoked Asian imagery. Instead, in the more prosaic

American cultural climate, they were called Arizona, California Short Order, Eagle, or Union. Even though their bills of fare included Chinese dishes, their managers featured Euro-American and Hispanic standbys. Kitchen work in the restaurants, as well as in private homes, occupied a total of 52 men. Farm plots south and west of town tended by 30 gardeners provided fresh produce that was marketed through the streets by 7 peddlers. The most notable occupational increase continued the trend toward merchandising. The 1910 census noted 63 Chinese men as proprietors of grocery or general stores, where 12 others waited on customers. The 1908 city directory contained names of 70 general stores owned by Chinese. In addition to those in usual districts north and south of Congress Street, there was a larger number in new Hispanic-occupied areas to the south of the original town (U.S. Federal Census 1910). The Chinese had indeed gained a measure of economic control over the Hispanics and likewise posed some important competition for the Euro-Americans. It was indicative of the rise in numbers of Chinese Americans that nearly one-third of those merchant-class men had been born in California. Almost as many had been admitted to the United States in the period from 1882 to 1909, when skilled labor rank was mandatory. Just 15 Chinese were known to have been resident prior to the first Exclusion Act.

There were 14 Chinese wives present in Tucson in 1910, 9 of them married to merchants. Lim Goon, an interpreter for the immigration service, and one store clerk also had Chinese wives. The mate of a native laborer had been born in China. According to her statement to the census taker, she had come to the United States at the age of three. Under what circumstance this occurred is unknown. Certainly, these women were an anchoring force.

At the same period when the elite of Chinese society was forming, there remained a hard-core group of lower-class men like the earlier sojourners. Unknown numbers of them had made their way illegally from Mexico into the United States, and they had spent years dodging the authorities (*Arizona Daily Star*, May 2, 1890). Mexico was a known port of entry. A Chinese association, called the Six Companies, boasted of Mexican leniency in allowing them to smuggle Chinese who docked south of the border into the United States (Perkins 1984: 221–222). This association provided many of the Asian transients with the proper papers, often removed from the dead or in other ways surreptitiously obtained. It then coached new recipients in proper answers to questions immigration officers were likely to ask about background, family, and kinds of employment. Nogales and stretches of deserted land on either side were well-used pathways of illegal entry from Sonora, occasionally with the aid of Mexican "pilots." From there, Chinese men straggled on to interior locations, planning to blend unnoticed into the Tucson Asian colony. Other hopeful sojourners slipped into the country at El Paso, where they hid aboard Southern Pacific trains, some jumping off in Tucson (Farrar 1972: 9–10).

Eight categories of federal officers were empowered to take action against a Chinese suspected of unlawful presence in the United States. These were a United States district attorney or his assistant, a collector or deputy collector of customs, an immigration inspector, a United States marshal or deputy marshal, and a Chinese Inspector. All became adept in spotting suspicious persons by their demeanor, by their appearance, by their lack of familiarity with surroundings, or by their possessing Certificate of Identification photographs or descriptions that did not match their personal characteristics. All those arrested had the right of appeal and could retain a lawyer, if so desired. Frequent repetition of names on voluminous legal documents suggests that some Tucson lawyers specialized in Chinese cases. In such proceedings, more often than not, the services of a Chinese translator were required, as well as those of a Spanish translator if Hispanic witnesses were called. Many appeal cases were successful in proving American birth, residency prior to 1882, or legitimate mercantile occupation.

Government court costs per deportation case were minimal by modern standards, ranging from ten cents for administering the oath to witnesses to five dollars for a hearing and judgment. Follow-up expense was more substantial. When deportation was ordered, the guilty usually were held in a local jail until there were a number of prisoners. Then, under guard, they were transported by train to San Francisco, where they were turned over to the purser of a vessel bound for China. The government paid for jail and transportation costs. Deportation to the nearby Mexican border was not allowed.

Most extant documentation concerning deportation matters in the First Judicial District, of which Tucson was the seat, and in the Second Judicial District, which encompasses Nogales, dates from the 1902 permanent Exclusion Act to the end of territorial status in 1912 (Register of Chinese Cases and Fee Book, First Judicial District; Book of Commissioners, Boxes 1–6, Second Judicial District, Arizona Territory, National Archives, Los Angeles Branch). During that time, 524 illegal Chinese were apprehended at Nogales. The number for Tucson was 95, although reports are not as complete. The years 1903 and 1909 appear to have yielded the greatest number of illegal aliens. A newsman of the time described a typical mass exodus and gave the hard-pressed inspectors a pat on the back.

> Deputy United States Marshal O'Neill of Tucson left Prescott yesterday having in charge two Chinamen who will be deported next Saturday from that city.
>
> A regular roundup has been made of the Chinamen in this territory in the past few months, and they are all herded in Tucson, forty-nine of them. They are all illegally residing in the territory and none of them can toe the mark when it comes to question of being personally identified with the photographs they carry.
>
> This is the greatest number of Chinamen to be deported from the territory in one shipment. An interesting story is given by the inspectors detailed for the

specific duty of hunting up those who are residing here illegally.

The common method of gaining entrance is through established channels on the border of smuggling them across the line. When once across they are equipped with spurious certificates taken from the effects of deceased Chinamen. Others enter on railroad trains from distant points and are open and defiant when accosted. They too are equipped with data and registration literature, furnished by a so-called Chinese importing society. Other ruses are in existence, also, but the bulk of offenders are confined to localities where the Chinese are numerous and not easily singled out.

The life of a Chinese Inspector is a vigilant one, and much effective work is done.

A few years ago one of these officials said that he had intercepted more Chinks through being conversant with the language than any other officer, and having a knowledge of their ways and haunts it was an easy matter to ferret out those violating the law (*Journal Miner*, August 8, 1909).

The illegal Chinese expectedly remained aloof from either Hispanic or Euro-American influences, intent instead on illusive economic goals that all too often drew them into unlawful activities. At best, they were manual laborers, dishwashers, or farmers. Ultimately those that were apprehended were deported no richer, and certainly no more Westernized, than when they arrived. Others voluntarily went home or drifted deeper into the secretive underground of more metropolitan ghettos.

By the early 1900s blocks north of Congress Street encompassing Chinatown were being deserted. Ramshackle buildings had become uninhabitable, and agitation for their removal was growing. Departing tenants undoubtedly carried away small possessions or threw them out with the trash. Looters likely made off with whatever was left behind. Surely the merchants moved out their commercial inventories and household wares lock, stock, and barrel. In 1910 the population of the blighted neighborhood had dwindled to a motley mix of 31 bachelor Chinese, 4 Hispanic families and 6 single Hispanic men, 1 Japanese male, and an itinerant Euro-American couple (U.S. Federal Census 1910). Two years later they, too, were gone (Fig. 1.13). The *Arizona Citizen*, January 5, 1911, reported, "To carry out a scheme for municipal improvement on the west side of the city along the same lines as the Paseo Redondo [approximately the area of the 1880s Chinese shanty town that had been removed earlier], the West Side Improvement Company has decided to demolish the entire block of buildings known as 'Chinatown.'" The relic landscape between Pennington and Alameda streets west of the northern extension of Main Street was leveled the next year to make way for a Womans Club; eventually low-cost housing filled in around it. In 1916 other blocks east of Main Street were cleared for city offices and a park. Some of the oldest extant structures in town, along with their associated privies, wells, and ref-

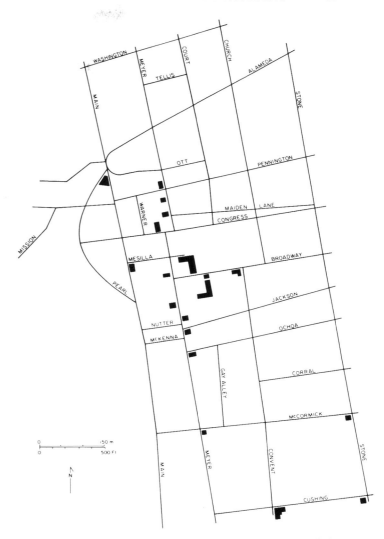

Figure 1.13. Chinese occupation in downtown Tucson, 1914.

use deposits were eradicated (Fig. 1.14). The territorial chapter in the history of the Tucson Chinese was closed.

As this era ended, much of an unassimilated, predominately male population continued to identify with China, even while making a living for many years on the Sonoran Desert. They represented the lower class of the local Chinese hierarchy. Whatever modest movement toward substantial acculturation had occurred came primarily from persons born in America. They comprised the core of an emerging upper class. However, for years even those individuals were to remain what Siu terms "marginal men," sharing two cultures but on the fringes of both (Siu 1952: 34).

STATEHOOD PERIOD

With the staged destruction of the first Chinatown, those occupants who did not take the occasion to return to either California or China moved south of Congress Street. That was where the bulk of their countrymen already were, where

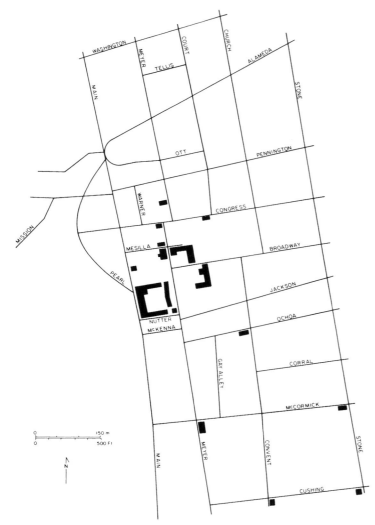

Figure 1.14. Chinese occupation in downtown Tucson, 1919.

Some Chinese opened a battery of "chop suey" restaurants and general stores with attached living quarters along the west side of Church Plaza, as it was called for many years even after St. Augustine and its adjoining convent were desanctified (Fig. 1.14). Gambling and opium retreats of bygone days were noticeably absent. The Chinese also took over a row of old dilapidated adobe houses in an alley off west Broadway, converting them into communal bedrooms. They found other places on south Meyer, Convent, Ochoa, and McCormick streets where groups of bachelors or the few individual families could dwell. A multi-roomed complex on south Main Street became a tenement for single men. One room soon was converted to a lodge for the Chee Kung Tong and another later housed the Tucson chapter of the political Guomindang. The tenement continued to be occupied until 1968.

Although census manuscript schedules are not available for this period, other sources indicate that the same dichotomy that had characterized the socioeconomic composition of the Chinese colony from its beginning continued. However, the upper class expanded slightly whereas the lower class diminished. A combination of law enforcement, World War I and constant fighting in China, and economic depression worldwide reduced illegal migration of laborers to a trickle. Many other drifters and unskilled workers already present in Tucson slowly were filtered out, presumably to return to their homeland or be absorbed into larger urban Chinatowns. A number of those who remained tended to congregate in the south Main Street tenement or sleeping rooms scattered about the surrounding district. There they existed through occasional employment in ethnically stereotyped tasks such as dishwashing, waiting on tables, or laboring on construction projects or, when there was no work available, through association relief. As a group they are the ones thought to have clung most tenaciously to their ethnicity, helped in part by the two traditional organizations in their midst that periodically drew them together and underscored their uniqueness from the town at large. Through time and uncontrollable political events, their ethnic staying power slowly became more sentiment than substance, as they were cut off from customary depots for Chinese material goods and sources of cultural rejuvenation. Home visits became both impossible and unnecessary, and burial among their ancestors lost its urgency.

Those Chinese of higher rank exhibited an increasing adjustment to, if not wholehearted adoption of, the American life style. Although for years the population figures for the Tucson Chinese colony remained about what they had been at the end of the territorial period, American-born females and children displaced departing alien males. Consequently, there were more traditional Chinese households living in private dwellings in the barrio, as well as family groups that consisted of a senior male member and one or more junior male relatives whose immigration he had been permitted to sponsor. These social entities created a moral bastion against

the cheapest housing was available, and where they were most culturally comfortable.

Again the Chinese moved almost as a collective body into a historic district. Previously in the early Euro-American days the district's center had been the open spot where mule-drawn freight wagons from southern New Mexico had thundered to a halt amid clouds of dust. Hence the square was named Plaza de la Mesilla, after the New Mexico settlement from which west-bound wagons departed. In the late 1860s, a massive Catholic church dedicated to St. Augustine graced the eastern flank of this plaza, calling the pressured Mexican-Americans to devotion and establishing a cultural epicenter around which they fruitlessly could rally against the growing Euro-American usurpation of what had been theirs. That grand old building had deteriorated ignominiously with the passage of time and purpose into a hotel and then a garage. The dirt plaza on which it fronted grew rank with weeds and drifted trash.

the discrimination that had been enacted during the statehood period, such as restriction from public swimming pools and movie houses (Tang 1977: 202–207). It was these individuals who continued to operate the small neighborhood grocery stores and "chop houses" typical of the southern sector of the TUR precinct. Conditions remained so quiescent for them that in 1935 there were almost the identical number of Chinese engaged in the same proportions in these and two related occupations as there had been in 1910 (Schweitzer 1952: 44). Although most of them then had the language and technical skills to qualify for more lucrative or prestigious employment, they were victims not only of lingering prejudice but of the severe depression that caused grief for all citizens. A Chinese Chamber of Commerce was established by the businessmen. They sought to protect their interests against occasional acts of violence perpetrated against them, but they seemed to be acts of criminality rather than racism. A Chinese Evangelical Church was positive indication of religious conversion. Chinese children attended public schools, going on to native instruction later in the day. Outwardly, these Chinese conformed to the local pattern in appearance, language, and most activities in which other ethnicities engaged. In numerous ways they began to participate in civic and cultural affairs of the community (Fong 1980: 27–28). Within their inner circles in varying degrees they perpetuated native language, food habits, ceremonies, costume, and pastimes, but, because of their legendary adaptability, they had avoided ethnic stratification (Noel 1968). Nevertheless, old bonds to the ancestral homeland, which many of them had never seen, were fraying for them as well as for the tenement dwellers.

The upheavals resulting from China's continual political travail, the worldwide economic depression of the early thirties, and two world wars halted or interrupted direct contact with the motherland. After China became an ally against Japan, in 1943 the United States rescinded the Exclusion Act. Some of its sociological damage was repaired when wives of men already resident were at last permitted to join their husbands, and naturalization proceedings for both sexes could be initiated (R. H. Lee 1960: 21).

Full assimilation and a greater spread in the social stratification that had been apparent from the initial settlement developed as economic and educational opportunities increased. Many upwardly mobile Chinese thus were prompted to move out of the old Hispanic barrio some years before the TUR project began. A few entered the professional world, but most remained in commerce. The 1950 city directory

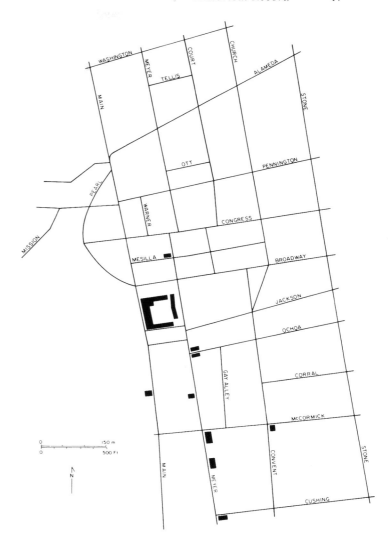

Figure 1.15. Chinese occupation in downtown Tucson, 1952.

listed 114 Chinese grocery stores, but also other Chinese-run enterprises such as a furniture store, a hardware store, two liquor stores, eight restaurants, and one drug store. Many of these were away from the urban renewal area. One by one the tiny, antiquated barrio shops left behind by former tenants were boarded up (Fig. 1.15). Those who stayed until the very end in the part of town where their forebears had settled were similarly being integrated into American society, albeit generally on a different stratum that continued their symbiotic relationship with local Hispanics.

CHAPTER TWO

The Tucson Urban Renewal Project

Nearly 80 acres of old downtown Tucson were renovated between 1968 and 1973. Preliminary work for this massive undertaking involved extensive excavations in areas known to have been occupied for a considerable time by the town's early Chinese population. The material items recovered reveal a history rich in ethnic tradition despite the rapidly evolving and changing western frontier.

Tucson Urban Renewal excavation proveniences were identified by a trinomial nomenclature. The first number refers to the administrative designation for the unit, usually a city block, assigned by the TUR authorities; the second number, separated from the first by a colon, designates individual lots within the unit; the third number, set apart from the second by a dash, identifies the type of feature. For example, 2 means latrine, 3 means well, and 5 means test trench. Letters attached to the third number as a suffix express the position of that feature in a sequence of such features. Thus, 2:1–2a is the first latrine excavated in lot 1 of unit 2; 3:4–5b is the second test trench dug in lot 4 of unit 3.

EXCAVATION OF FEATURES

Standard procedure for excavating most features, whether latrines, wells, or test trenches, was to remove deposits in arbitrary two-foot levels, measured and designated numerically from the surface. Test trenches and extensive features were gridded for horizontal control. Restricted units, such as wells and latrines, were excavated in their entirety by successive levels. Where possible, excavations were extended down to or into sterile earth. These deposits usually consisted of caliche, an easily recognizable crust infused with calcium carbonate that forms in the upper level of soil in semiarid regions such as southern Arizona. In a few instances stratified deposits of cultural materials were observable in trenches dug by work crews or in test pits. On such occasions further excavations proceeded to remove each identifiable stratum as a single level.

Picks, shovels, trowels, and brushes were routinely used for digging. A bucket attached to a windlass assisted in raising dirt from deep, confined units. Excavated deposits were sifted through quarter-inch or half-inch mesh screen when time permitted, and the quantity of items recovered justified this procedure. On other occasions, back dirt was troweled for specimens as it was removed from excavations. Objects were bagged and labeled by unit and level and also by sec-

tion if from test trenches. Test-trench sections varied from 3 feet to 4 feet wide and 6 feet to 10 feet long. The sides of trenches opened by demolition crews searching for buried sewers, water mains, or other features were sometimes smoothed to check stratigraphy. When warranted, some trenches were expanded to recover cultural remains and depositional data.

The excavation field crews, who recorded architectural details and collected specimens from abandoned structures, were under the general direction of James E. Ayres. The crews consisted mainly of volunteer and a few paid students enrolled primarily in classes of the Anthropology Department of the University of Arizona. Advanced students and occasionally faculty and staff members of the Anthropology Department and the Arizona State Museum assisted in directing specific investigations. Most field work was undertaken on weekends and over holidays, when students were free of classroom responsibilities. It was not always easy to recruit student assistance over sustained periods of time or to respond to work schedules or the findings of demolition crews that required immediate attention. Unfinished excavation units sometimes went untended for several days and on occasion artifacts were clandestinely removed, especially by bottle collectors.

Areas of Chinese occupation within the boundaries of the Tucson Urban Renewal project were pinpointed by maps, especially the Sanborn fire insurance maps. Municipal directories, block records, and newspaper accounts were also useful. In a few instances, recovery of complexes of specimens of Chinese derivation from areas not known to have been occupied by Chinese enriched the documentary evidence. The Sanborn maps for 1883, 1886, 1904, 1914, 1919, and 1952 were valuable in identifying Chinese dwellings, stores, restaurants, wash-houses, latrines, wells, a keno den, and opium dens. Sanborn maps and other kinds of written records distinguish at least 11 block locations of Chinese occupation of various sorts and 6 questionable block areas within the limits of the TUR project (Fig. 2.1). Each locality, its TUR identification, characteristics of the feature, and excavations undertaken there are enumerated below. Those proveniences not known to have been occupied by the Chinese but which yielded small quantities of Chinese artifacts are distinguished by numerical designations in brackets. Excavations known to have been near former Chinese installations, but which apparently produced no Chinese materials,

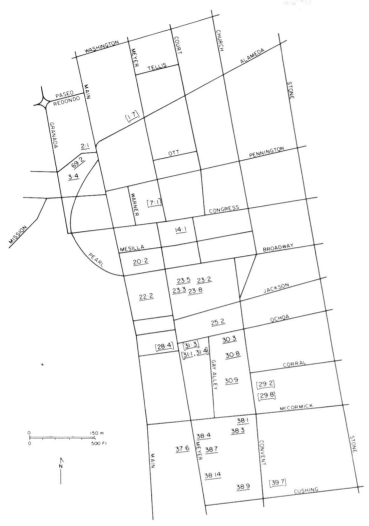

Figure 2.1. Excavations in areas of Chinese occupation in downtown Tucson. Numbers in brackets indicate proveniences not known to have been occupied by the Chinese but in which small quantities of Chinese artifacts were found.

are similarly identified in brackets. In those very few cases where only a random Chinese artifact was recovered, no site reference appears on the map.

[TUR 1:7]

Location. The southeast corner of the block bounded on the north, south, west, and east by Washington, Alameda, Main, and Meyer streets respectively.

References. No Chinese occupation is recorded in the area, which was part of the Spanish presidio during Tucson's earliest history.

Excavations. A Chinese ginger jar came from a series of east-west test trenches, [TUR 1:7–5a through 5d], located where a former non-Chinese building had existed (excavation map prepared by Pueblo Center Redevelopment Project, City of Tucson).

TUR 2:1

Location. North of Alameda Street between Granada and Main streets.

References. Sanborn maps of 1883, 1886, and 1896 indicate a concentration of Chinese occupation in the vicinity, including "shanties," dwellings, grocery store, laundry, and opium den.

Excavations. By November and December of 1967 the area, except for the Womans Club, had been cleared of structures and leveled. The Womans Club, built in 1913, was razed while archaeological testing was under way. A demolition crew trenching for old sewer lines north of the club building exposed a large ceramic vessel. Archaeologists expanded this trench by excavating a succession of culturally defined levels to a depth of about 3.5 feet, where sterile soil was reached. The small number of Chinese articles recovered included several kinds of ceramics, opium pipe bowl fragments, and a few coins. The tested deposits appeared to be scattered trash, the lower levels of which contained bottles and Mexican pottery dating between 1800 and 1860 (Renk 1968).

TUR 69:2

Location. Middle of Alameda Street 200 feet west of the intersection of Alameda and Main streets, 150 feet south of TUR 2:1.

References. Sanborn maps of 1883, 1886, 1896, 1904, and 1909 show a variety of Chinese structures in the area, including "shanties," dwellings, stores, laundries, and opium dens.

Excavations. Two adjoining test trenches, each about 20 feet long and slightly offset from one another, were dug through a trash deposit. They produced a quantity of Chinese artifacts. Other kinds of specimens from the trenches indicated that the trash dated between 1890 and 1900 (Goree 1971).

TUR 3:4

Location. South of Alameda Street between Granada and Pearl streets.

References. Sanborn maps of 1883, 1886, 1896, 1904, and 1909 pinpoint several buildings occupied by Chinese during the 26-year period represented by the maps. In the immediate vicinity of the excavations were dwellings, washhouse, opium den, store, and gambling place.

Excavations. Several features were excavated in the area that formerly had been to the rear of the group of Chinese buildings described above: four latrines (TUR 3:4–2a, 2b; 3:4–5b, a test trench in which two latrines were revealed), a well (TUR 3:4–3a), and two test trenches (TUR 3:4–5a, 5c). The lot had been cleared of structures and was being leveled and graded when the archaeological investigations took place in July 1968. Most of the subsurface features were located by an extensive series of auger borings and crowbar probes.

According to available field notes and collection records, at least two latrines and the well produced several types of Chinese ceramics. Latrines were 8 feet to 10 feet deep, and the well, which had notchlike hand and foot holes cut into its wall, reached a depth of almost 22 feet. Lower levels of debris from those features, all dug into hard caliche, were removed by windlass and bucket. Judging from a study of the non-Chinese buttons and coins recovered from those units (Goree 1971) and from a field evaluation of the age of the bottles retrieved, the well deposits date from about 1880 to 1900 and the latrine deposits from about 1860 to 1897.

[TUR 7:1]

Location. West of north Meyer Street, between Pennington and Congress streets.

References. Sanborn maps between 1883 and 1919 show two Chinese restaurants and two Chinese laundries in this block.

Excavations. Minimal testing in the center of the block, which would have been to the rear of the former Chinese structures, did not produce any identifiable Chinese materials.

TUR 14:1

Location. Small block limited by Congress Street on the north, Mesilla Street on the south, Meyer Street on the west, and Court Street on the east.

References. Chinese occupation in this area included a keno den, dwellings, grocery store, general store, and a restaurant, according to Sanborn maps for 1883, 1886, 1904, and 1909.

Excavations. In an attempt to locate a well and several latrines appearing on the 1883 Sanborn map, as well as possibly earlier features, approximately one-half of the block was tested by eight parallel east-west trenches spaced 3 feet to 5 feet apart. Each trench was 3 feet wide, extended from 50 feet to 80 feet in length, and was dug 5 feet to 6 feet deep. The area available for testing in July and August of 1969 was limited because of construction on Congress Street and heavy equipment operations to the south and east.

The trenches, designated TUR 14:1–5a through 5h, proved unproductive in locating trash deposits, but one latrine (TUR 14:1–2b) was revealed in Trench 5f. Another latrine (TUR 14:1–2a) was located to the east of Trench 5e.

The upper levels of both latrines were filled with sterile soil and with concrete blocks and other rubble resulting from the construction of buildings over them subsequent to their abandonment. One latrine was 18 feet deep, the other 22.5 feet deep. This depth necessitated the use of a windlass and bucket to remove the lower levels, which yielded a quantity of artifacts but only a few of Asian origin.

TUR 20:2

Location. Small block defined on the north by Mesilla Street, on the south by Broadway, on the west by Main Street, and on the east by Meyer Street. The Sanborn map

for 1904 identifies a Chinese grocery store on the northwest corner of the block. In 1919 a Chinese laundry faced Main Street and a Chinese store fronted on Meyer Street.

Excavations. A test trench (TUR 20:2–5a) dug between the two areas known to have been occupied by Chinese encountered two latrines (TUR 20:2–2a, 2b) which apparently were excavated. A few Chinese potsherds and several whole or restorable vessels came from this provenience.

TUR 22:2

Location. The block bounded on the north and south by Broadway and Jackson streets, and on the west and east by Main and Meyer streets.

References. The 1883 Sanborn map shows a Chinese restaurant on Jackson Street and a Chinese store and dwelling on Meyer Street. Subsequent maps reflect a comparable settlement pattern until 1919, when the Sanborn map shows the compound that covered three-fourths of the block contained approximately 35 single-room dwellings. All were occupied by Chinese. A joss house also was incorporated into the compound, and a Chinese store existed at the southeast corner of the block. Chinese continued to live in the compound structure until 1968. The evolution of the multi-roomed structure is described below.

Excavations. Seven latrines (TUR 22:2–2a through 2g) were excavated within the confines of TUR 22:2 (Fig. 2.2). All were found beneath the floors of rooms in units 2, 3, and 4 and were discovered by removing floor planking and joists

Figure 2.2. Excavation of TUR 22:2–2c. (Arizona State Museum photo by James E. Ayres.)

Figure 2.3. Trenching the courtyard of TUR 22:2. (Arizona State Museum photo by James E. Ayres.)

and probing beneath them with crowbars. Relatively soft, unconsolidated fill within four perpendicular walls cut into extremely hard caliche denoted their presence. They varied from 6 feet to 12 feet in depth. Two walls of TUR 22:2–2e were masonry lined. Latrines TUR 22:2–2c and 2g were connected by a subterranean horizontal tunnel. All yielded varying quantities of Euro-American artifactual materials. However, according to field notes (Ayres 1968a; Renk 1968), Chinese objects were limited. A few Asian potsherds and a jar came from the surface and upper level of feature TUR 22:2–2e, situated beneath the burned debris of Unit 2, Room 27, which also produced a single Chinese coin. Seven Chinese coins were recovered from the top level of latrine TUR 22:2–2c.

Two long, parallel test trenches (TUR 22:2–5a, 5b) were dug through the center of the compound courtyard in hope of finding additional latrines and trash deposits (Figs. 2.3, 2.4; Renk 1968). Spaced 11 feet apart, they were 3 feet wide and were divided into 10–foot-long control sections. Trench TUR 22:2–5a was 80 feet long and 2–5b was 100 feet long. Deposits above the sterile caliche proved to be shallow, ranging from 6 inches to 2 feet deep. In places the presence of horizontal lenses of adobe bricks led excavators to suggest that at some time parts of the courtyard had been paved. Findings from the test trenches proved disappointing. Neither concentrations of trash nor latrines were encountered. Other than two stray Chinese coins, field notes do not identify additional Chinese specimens from the sparse collections from the two probes.

Figure 2.4. Screening fill dirt removed from beneath Room 12 in Unit 4, TUR 22:2. (Arizona State Museum photo by James E. Ayres.)

TUR 23:2, TUR 23:3, TUR 23:5, and TUR 23:8

Location. Western one-half of the block bounded on the west and east by Meyer and Convent streets, and on the north and south by Broadway and Jackson streets.

References. The 1883 Sanborn map denotes a Chinese restaurant and laundry facing Camp (Broadway) Street. Maps for later years locate additional Chinese structures in this area, including a store and laundry on the southwest corner of the block and, beginning in 1896 and continuing until 1919, a group of as many as 10 contiguously arranged dwellings west of the old Belmont Hotel.

Excavations. Accessible field and catalog records reveal that six latrines and four test trenches were excavated in or adjacent to areas identified as having been occupied by Chinese. Three of the latrines (TUR 23:5–2a, 2b, and 2c) were situated behind former non-Asian dwellings or commercial buildings facing Meyer Street. One latrine (TUR 23:8–2a) was beneath a Chinese structure, and the others (TUR 23:2–2a and 3–2a) were near Chinese dwellings. A small assortment of opium pipe bowls and can fragments, potsherds, and whole or restorable ceramic vessels of Chinese origin were secured from the features excavated.

TUR 25:2

Location. The narrow west-east trending block between Jackson and Ochoa streets on the north and south, and Meyer and Convent streets on the west and east.

References. Sanborn maps from 1896 and 1914 show one or two Chinese stores on Meyer Street. The 1952 map places a single store on the southwest corner of the block.

Excavations. In Lot 2, in the unoccupied center of the block, four test trenches (TUR 25:2–5a through 5d) and a well (TUR 25:2–3a) were dug. Three Chinese ginger jars are reported to have been found in this provenience.

[TUR 28:4]

Location. Block 28 is a small entity defined by Ochoa Street on the north, an alley on the south, and Main and Meyer streets on the west and east.

References. Sanborn maps do not show any Chinese occupation of this block, although just across south Meyer Street there were Chinese stores from 1904 to 1952.

Excavations. It is recorded that a few Chinese potsherds were recovered from a latrine and test trenches [TUR 28:4–2a and 4–5a, 5b, and 5c] dug behind buildings on the southeast corner of the block.

[TUR 29:2, TUR 29:8]

Location. The block marked by Corral and McCormick streets on the north and south, and by Convent and Stone streets on the west and east.

References. Sanborn maps examined do not identify any Chinese occupation in this block.

Excavations. Several latrines and a well in [TUR 29:8] and a test trench in [TUR 29:2] were cleared in an area once surrounded by non-Chinese structures in the western half of this block. A small collection of Chinese and Japanese vessels and potsherds came from the several tests.

TUR 30:3, TUR 30:8, TUR 30:9

Location. The block delimited by Ochoa Street on the north, McCormick Street on the south, Gay Alley on the west, and Convent Street on the east.

References. In the period between 1889 and 1919, Sanborn maps show Chinese stores existed on the northeast and southeast corners of this block.

Excavations. Available field records do not indicate any excavations in this block. However, TUR collections include several fragmentary opium cans and some Asian potsherds from TUR 30:3, 30:8, and 30:9. Perhaps they represent surface finds.

[TUR 31:1, TUR 31:3, TUR 31:4]

Location. The northern part of the north-south elongated block marked by Ochoa Street on the north, McCormick Street on the south, Meyer Street on the west, and Gay Alley on the east.

References. Chinese holdings in TUR Block 31, as shown by Sanborn maps, depict a Chinese laundry on the northwest part of the block facing Meyer Street as early as 1883. From 1886 to 1952 a Chinese store was located on the northwest corner of the block.

Excavations. Two test trenches [TUR 31:1–5a, 5b], a well [TUR 31:3], and a latrine [TUR 31:4–2a] were dug in this block. Despite the former existence of two Chinese structures close to the excavations, there are no known records of Chinese materials being recovered from the diggings.

TUR 37:6

Location. Block 37 is a large unit, bounded on the north, south, west, and east by McCormick, Simpson, Main, and Meyer streets respectively.

References. The 1883 Sanborn map indicates a Chinese store on the west side of south Meyer Street a short distance from the northeast corner of the block.

Excavations. A well (TUR 37:6–3a), located behind non-Chinese buildings about 100 feet south of a former Chinese store, produced a Chinese vessel and a few potsherds.

TUR 38:1, TUR 38:3, TUR 38:4, TUR 38:7, TUR 38:9, and TUR 38:14

Location. McCormick Street on the north, Fourteenth (Cushing) Street on the south, Meyer Street on the west, and Convent Street on the east delimit this block.

References. A store on the northwest corner is shown on the 1896 Sanborn map as the earliest Chinese occupation of Block 38. Chinese continued to use that corner of Block 38 until demolition crews cleared the area in 1968. Then the property included a grocery store, storage facilities, dwelling, and rental units owned by Jeung Lee. The store was operated as the Suey Yuen Market, bearing the name of a former owner. It is more fully described below. In 1952 a second store, facing south Meyer Street midway on the block, is identified.

Excavations. An extensive series of excavations was conducted in this block, primarily in the central area behind the structures facing the four streets that surrounded the block. The digging of latrines, wells, and test trenches in TUR 38:1 and 38:3 in the northeast quadrant of the block, in TUR 38:4 and 38:7 on the west, in TUR 38:9 to the southeast, and in TUR 38:14 to the southeast produced a variety of Chinese earthenwares, one Chinese coin, several opium pipe bowl fragments, and a small number of Japanese potsherds.

[TUR 39:7]

Location. The southwest corner of the large block lying between McCormick and Fourteenth (Cushing) streets on the north and south and Convent and Stone streets on the west and east.

References. No Chinese installations were situated in the immediate vicinity of the archaeological explorations in this provenience. However, Chinese stores existed on either or both the northwest and northeast corners of the block between 1909 and 1952, according to Sanborn maps.

Excavations. Seven trenches [TUR 39:7A–5a, 5b, 5c, and TUR 39:7B–5a through 5d] tested the deposits behind the structures on the southwest corner of TUR Block 39. Several Chinese and Japanese vessels and a small quantity of potsherds were collected from them.

EXISTING STRUCTURES ASSOCIATED WITH CHINESE OCCUPATION

Suey Yuen Compound

One site that might have demonstrated occupation through a number of decades by a merchant-elite, acculturated group of Chinese was located at 253–265 south Meyer Street (TUR 38:4). The Suey Yuen grocery store-dwelling at the southeast corner of west McCormick and south Meyer streets housed three generations of a single family beginning at least by 1896. Prior to 1880, it had been the approximate location of the residence of territorial governor Safford (Smith 1967: 217). The owner in 1968, Jeung Lee, claimed that the store actually dated from the 1870s (*Arizona Daily Citizen*, August 8, 1968), but it does not appear on the earliest Sanborn fire insurance map of 1883.

Some thirty contiguous enclosed spaces arranged in a three-armed plan comprised the Suey Yuen compound (Figs. 2.5–2.10). Included were a salesroom, storerooms, living rooms, latrines, sheds, and a barn. Access to the central courtyard formed by the building wings was through a *zahuan*, or passageway, from the street. The exterior elevation of the building was the characteristic flat-roofed, cement-plastered, flush-facaded, blocky, regional style. The interior, with its maze of adjoining rooms of various sizes and shapes at different floor levels, exhibited a chaotic assortment of construction elements. Some materials were indigenous to the area, such as pine beams, saguaro secondary ribbing, and adobe bricks, and may have been in place when Chinese

Figure 2.5. North facade of the Suey Yuen store and dwelling at the southeast corner of south Meyer Street and west McCormick Street. At the center of the view were two apartment rentals. The section of wall with four high windows and a large display window under a metal awning was the store that fronted onto south Meyer Street. (Arizona State Museum photo by D. Hsu.)

Figure 2.6. West facade of the Suey Yuen building at 253–265 south Meyer Street, where the owner and his family lived. The store appears to the *far left*, the *zahuan* (entrance passageway) to the *far right*. (Arizona State Museum photo by James E. Ayres.)

Figure 2.7. *Zahuan* entrance of the Suey Yuen store-dwelling complex from south Meyer Street. (Arizona State Museum photo by James E. Ayres.)

Figure 2.8. Ceiling over the *zahuan* entrance. (Arizona State Museum photo by James E. Ayres.)

Figure 2.9. *Zahuan* ceiling construction of pine beams topped with saguaro crossribs and earth, characteristic of most barrio edifices. (Arizona State Museum photo by James E. Ayres.)

Figure 2.10. South face of an adobe hay barn and attached shed used as a garage located along the east side of the Suey Yuen store-dwelling complex. (Arizona State Museum photo by James E. Ayres.)

tenants moved in. Other materials were later replacements, such as plywood, linoleum, wallboard, and corrugated metal. Many structural changes had occurred over the years. Doorways and windows had been sealed, occasionally with shelving placed across the recesses. Fireplace chimneys had become stove flues. Electrical wiring in metal conduits had been added on wall surfaces. Tongue-and-groove wooden flooring had been laid. Flush plumbing had replaced earlier outhouses.

At the time of last occupancy of the structure, a series of five or six rooms next to the store served as lodging for the family. They had a generally neat, comfortable appearance. The remaining nine rooms along south Meyer Street and another six on the north wing were no longer in use. Two four-room apartments opening to west McCormick Street had been created in the northeast corner of the compound. Adjoining them to the south were three large structures. Two of these contained hay and grain in the pre-automobile era, and the third had been used as a modern garage (Fig. 2.10; Ayres 1968b).

Because the premises were occupied by a family that made plans for a new home and business in another part of Tucson, the rooms were cleaned of all furnishings and most accumulations of trash around the yard were disposed of before archaeological or wrecking crews arrived. The only remaining clue to former Chinese presence were two current Chinese calendars hanging on walls of the room thought to have been the parlor. The two rental units, however, were left littered with refuse, none of which was ethnic Chinese. The tenants are believed to have been of other cultural affiliation.

Limited testing failed to locate abandoned privies. Therefore, lacking a comparative Chinese ethnographic collection, no further study of this complex of rooms was undertaken.

Ying On Compound

The second Chinese-occupied building of significance to researchers was a tenement on south Main Street just three blocks from the original Chinatown (Figs. 2.11–2.14). It was expected to produce data about the lower-class Tucson Chinese. The architectural growth of this housing and the use of neighboring buildings on TUR Block 22 is of importance because of the ethnographic materials obtained and the archaeological investigations carried out there.

Surely all units of this block originally were built of local materials in the prevailing regional style of flat-roofed, cellular units flush with the street. A Chinese store and a Chinese restaurant had occupied such buildings on the east side of Block 22 as early as 1883 (Figs. 2.11, 2.15). Their rear porches and several privies were exposed to a row of dwelling rooms on the western side of the block facing south Main Street and to an alley along their southern flank, which apparently remained in either Hispanic or Euro-American hands throughout the territorial period. The Welish Brothers Importing Company used a series of the southern rooms until the 1880 completion of the railroad put it out of business, very likely loading and unloading wagon freight in the patio (Brandes 1962: 30). The Tucson 1898 Block Book indicates that at that time a member of the prominent Carrillo family had acquired title to the western two-thirds of the block, with M. Amado and C. T. Nutter owning the two

Figure 2.11. Chinese occupation of TUR Block 22, 1883.

Figure 2.13. Chinese occupation of TUR Block 22, 1948.

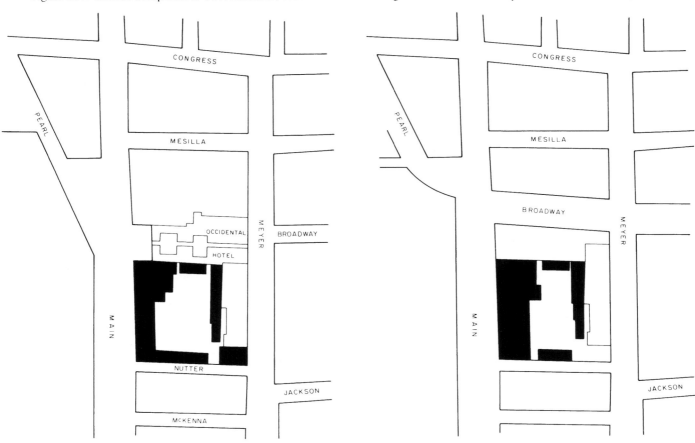

Figure 2.12. Chinese occupation of TUR Block 22, 1919.

Figure 2.14. Chinese occupation of TUR Block 22, 1952–1968.

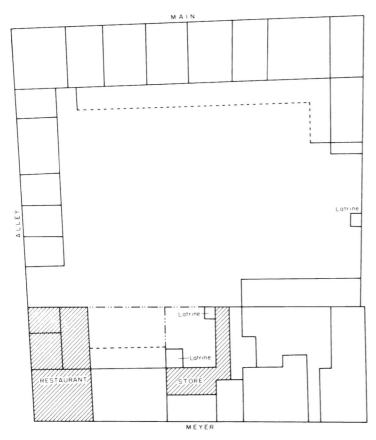

MAIN

ALLEY

Latrine

Latrine

Latrine

RESTAURANT

STORE

MEYER

Figure 2.15. Detail of Chinese occupation (hachured) of TUR Block 22, 1883.

parcels making up the eastern portion (Tucson Block Book, 1898, Arizona Historical Society).

The original U-shaped building that ultimately was to become the center of concentrated Chinese occupation in the southern barrio consisted of eight contiguous adobe-walled rooms fronting on south Main Street, with two rooms comprising a north arm and five rooms backing up to an alley on the south. A long portal off the major north-south unit connected the two wings. A single privy stood at the north property line adjacent to the two-story Palace Hotel, later renamed the Occidental (Figs. 2.11, 2.15).

Over the years the floor plan of the compound building continually was modified (Figs. 2.15–2.19). The original 15 rooms in linear arrangement expanded by 1904 to 28 rooms through enclosing the portal, building other rooms east into the courtyard, enlarging and increasing the number of rooms on the north wing, and partitioning one of the rooms on the south (Fig. 2.17). No latrine is shown on the map of the time, which suggests that one or more facilities must have been enclosed within the house block.

The mid-block Chinese store on the east side of Block 22 facing south Meyer Street had disappeared by 1889 (Fig. 2.16). By 1904 the Chinese-run four-roomed corner restaurant had become a large unpartitioned Chinese grocery (Fig. 2.17). There had been alterations in sizes and shapes of the adjacent south Meyer Street businesses, but the backs of the buildings still were accessible from the central patio of the western dwelling compound (Fig. 2.17).

The exact time when the Chinese moved into the complex of adobe row rooms facing south Main Street is uncertain. Some 1913 correspondence recovered from one room suggests that it may have been coincident with the leveling of the buildings north of Congress Street. At any rate, 1919 maps confirm that significant remodeling had been done in order to make the structure suitable for Chinese tenants (Figs. 2.12, 2.18). A line of 10 rooms built over filled-in privies, one of which was suggested as post-1897 in date (Goree 1971), and room foundations formed a new eastern wing that essentially enclosed an interior patio and cut off access to the east side of the block. Another line of four contiguous rooms, built over two latrines of the 1890s (Goree 1971), extended the north arm. The west unit was returned to more or less its original arrangement, from which it may be inferred that the 1904 additions had been frame rather than more substantial adobe. One room in the west wing was set aside as the new headquarters of the Chee Kung Tong, which had been displaced through the demolition of the original Chinatown. An additional room was created in the southern row of rooms by shifting partitions. If each tenant had a room to himself, the various sections of the building together could have housed 31 persons. A single latrine is shown on the contemporary map, although a second facility may have been under a shed roof off a room on the north property boundary. The patio latrine likely was the flush toilet still in use at time of abandonment. There was no running water in the rooms and no gas. Electricity had been crudely arranged in parts of the building.

In 1919 the Chinese-run grocery store still occupied the southeast corner of Block 22 facing south Meyer Street. In order to obtain routine supplies, a resident of the adjacent compound merely had to walk through the patio exit and turn left a few steps down the alley (Figs. 2.12, 2.18). In the event that he could not find something in particular, his countryman Don Kim ran Tucson's second largest store up the street at 30–42 south Meyer, where general merchandise, groceries, clothing, hardware, hay, and grain were offered for sale (Fig. 1.14; Tucson City Directory, 1918). Other comparable stores peppered the neighborhood.

For the next three decades the exterior elevation of the Chinese compound remained essentially unaltered, with the exception of a porch and small room added over part of the east wing (Fig. 2.19). There may have been interior changes, such as putting in or taking out partitions and sealing unwanted openings. A second latrine in the south part of the patio is indicated in 1948. A room in the west unit that opened to the street (indicated on Fig. 2.19 as Club) ceased to be used as a dwelling in order to serve as a meeting place for the Guomindang.

In 1948 no Chinese businesses remained on the Meyer side of the block. The landmark Occidental Hotel had been demolished so that Broadway could be extended west to Main Street. This left a strip of land vacant across the northern part of the block on which the Chinese tenement stood (Fig. 2.13).

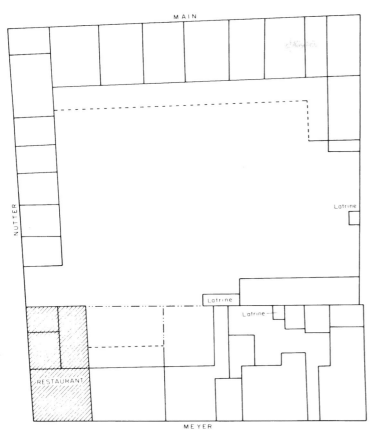

Figure 2.16. Detail of Chinese occupation (hachured) of TUR Block 22, 1889.

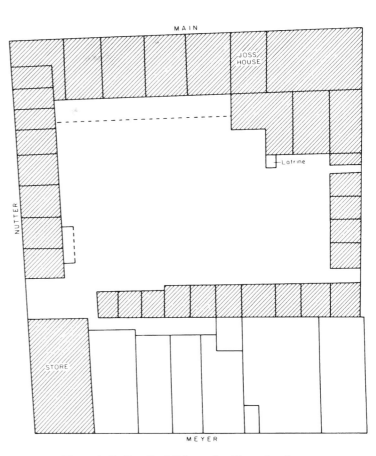

Figure 2.18. Detail of Chinese dwellings, joss house, and store (hachured) in TUR Block 22, 1919.

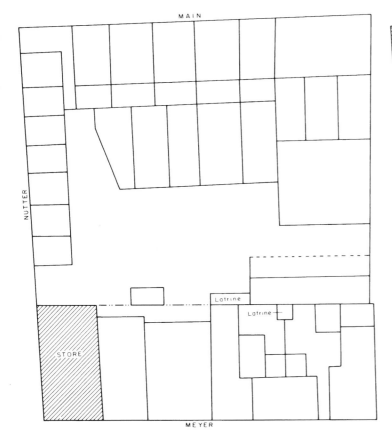

Figure 2.17. Detail of Chinese occupation (hachured) of TUR Block 22, 1904.

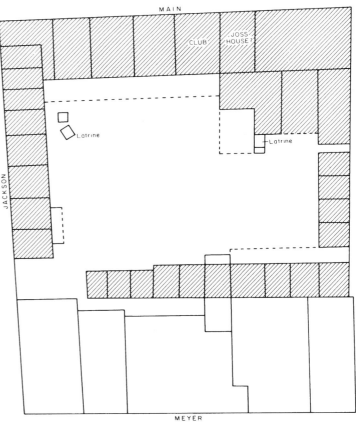

Figure 2.19. Detail of Chinese dwellings, joss house, and club (hachured) in TUR Block 22, 1948.

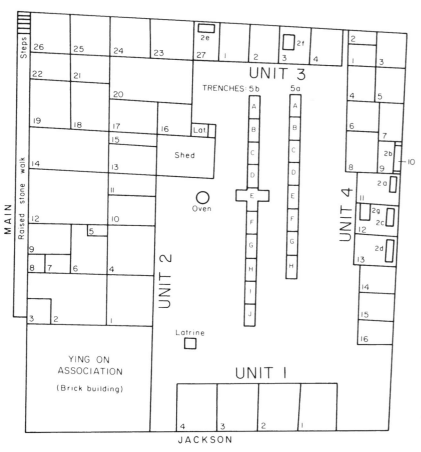

Figure 2.20. Chinese tenement on south Main Street and Jackson Street as it appeared in 1968, with excavated features indicated. The building had been remodeled in 1950.

Figure 2.21. The Ying On compound as it appeared in 1968 prior to demolition: *top*, the Ying On Merchants and Labor Benevolent Association building erected in 1950 at 103 south Main Street; *bottom*, the western facade (Unit 2). The two nearest flagpoles were over the doorways of the meeting rooms of the Chee Kung Tong (Chinese Masons) and the Guomindang (Nationalist Party).

Following World War II, the newly reorganized Ying On Merchants and Labor Benevolent Association, which had grown out of the earlier Suey Ying Tong, acquired the old compound buildings. In 1950 they undertook major changes that would remain unmodified until the final 1968 abandonment and demolishment. The Ying Ons tore down the southwest corner of the structure in order to erect a two-story brick meeting hall (Figs. 2.14, 2.20, 2.21).

At the same time a row of rooms was created from the interior porch off the west wing, bringing the number of rooms in that unit to 27, if a shed is included. All rooms were then dwellings, although flagpoles of former meeting halls remained on the exterior facade. An exception was a 1958 social hall known as the Chinese Club that used the room just to the north of the Ying On Association building. The north wing connected to the west unit by the shedlike feature (Room 27) still had 4 rooms, the east wing was expanded into 16 rooms, and the south unit was detached from the west wing so that 4 dwelling rooms remained. The total count reached 53 rooms. Access to interior chambers of the western and eastern units was through adjoining rooms because there were no central hallways. In the patio were a

shed, an oven, and two flush toilets, one of which shared a small attached building with a bath.

When researchers gained access to the compound buildings prior to their destruction in 1968, they encountered what appeared to be adobe homes nestled beside lush vegetation (Fig. 2.22). Once inside, there was a vivid record of the architectural changes and a huge accumulation of debris wrought by long human occupation (Fig. 2.23). Original construction had been revamped in a myriad of ways with generally inferior materials and slipshod workmanship (Ayres 1968a). Traditional rough-sawn roof beams topped with layers of saguaro ribs and earth were present, but at some time more efficient corrugated tin or wood shingles

Figure 2.22. An adobe room block (Unit 1) viewed from the central patio of the Ying On compound represented a peaceful haven amid bustling downtown Tucson. At the time of the TUR project, it was unoccupied. (Arizona State Museum photo by James E. Ayres.)

Figure 2.23. Room 11 of Unit 4 (TUR 22:2) was one of many habitations in the Ying On compound that housed a refuse midden of the discards of daily Chinese life. There are no articles visible that can be identified as ethnic Chinese. (Arizona State Museum photo by Helga Teiwes.)

Figure 2.24. Corner fireplaces, ubiquitous in regional Hispanic architecture, were converted by Chinese residents of the Ying On compound rooms into flues for cooking or heating stoves. Stove fittings appear midway in the illustrated chimney, but the stove itself had been moved elsewhere. Subsequently, a clothes rod was stretched diagonally across the room corner. (Arizona State Museum photo by James E. Ayres.)

had been applied over them. Occasional air vents and skylights had been cut through the roof to provide ventilation and light where needed. Some roofing had disappeared entirely or was in such bad condition that extensive leaking had occurred. Many ceilings still were of the customary cloth (*manta*), but cardboard or tongue-and-groove lumber had replaced others. Floors, often at different levels from room to room, were of concrete or wood, occasionally covered with worn linoleum. Walls were of adobe, brick, plywood, or plasterboard, not infrequently with several of these materials in a single room. Most electrical wiring was dangerously exposed, even in instances of rather recent replacement. Generally rooms contained a single, outmoded, surely inadequate, light fixture or a bare bulb on a cord. Over the years doorways, arches, and fireplaces had been blocked. Some chimneys had become vents for cooking or heating stoves (Fig. 2.24). Closets had been created in unused doorways or merely by a wire that stretched diagonally between

two walls. Clothes lines for laundry laced the ceilings. Such furniture as there was consisted of the simplest pine tables, chairs, and bed frames. Boxes served as cupboards. Cooking was done on wood or kerosene stoves.

Not all rooms of the compound had been occupied at any one time. It was obvious that as residents had died or moved on possessions left behind lay where last used in the emptied quarters. At the end, great drifts of trash, some of it undoubtedly many years old, were strewn over most of the crumbling structure.

Notes, drawings, and photographs of the building components were made. All items of identifiable Chinese derivation were collected, forming the bulk of the materials described in the following pages. Inventories and drawings of the total contents of one room occupied most recently were compiled (Figs. 2.25–2.31; Table 2.1).

Then the wreckers moved in, and this vestige of Tucson's second Chinatown vanished (Figs. 2.32, 2.33).

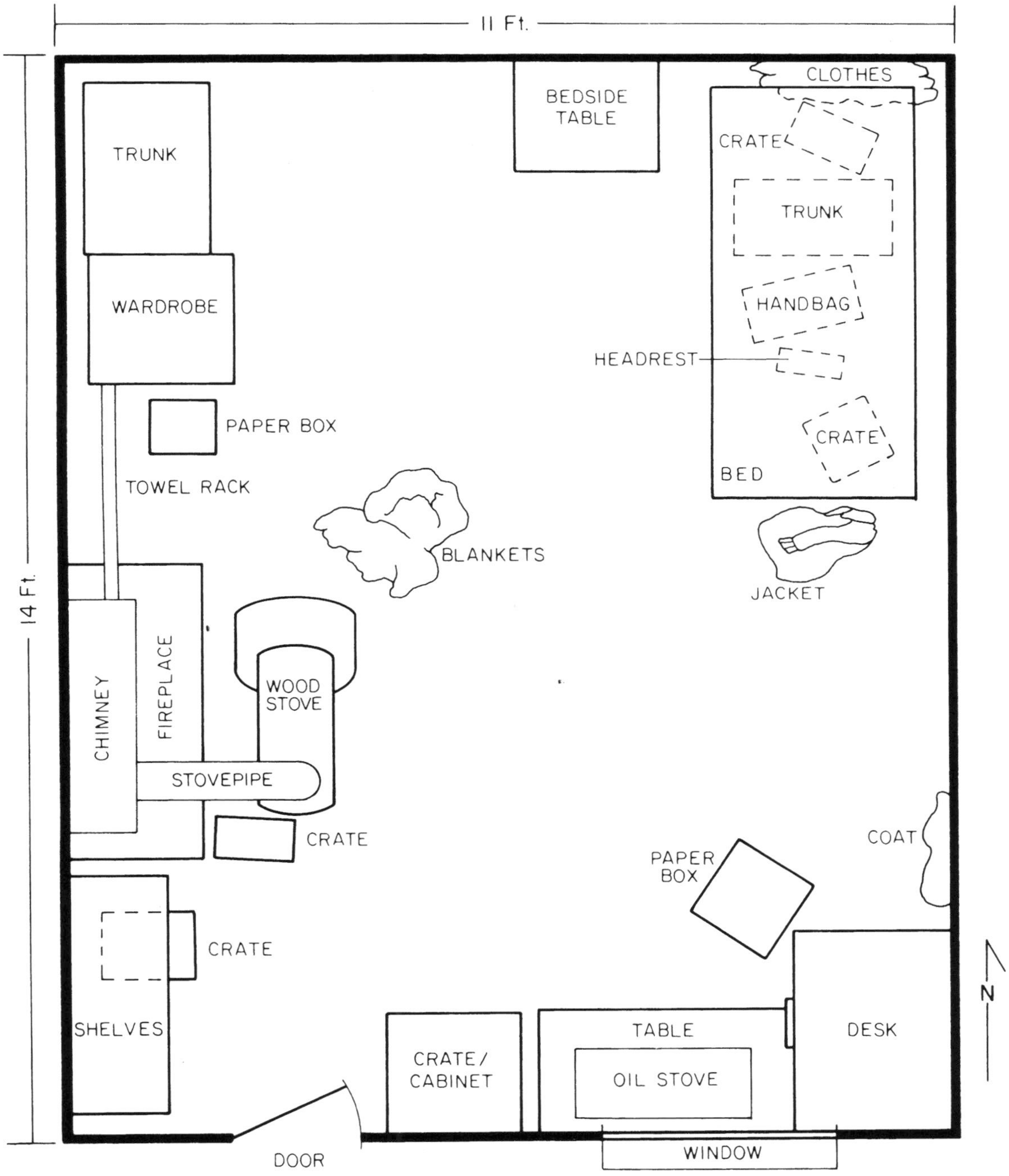

Figure 2.25. Room 2, Unit 3 (TUR 22:2), showing furniture and personal possessions of the former occupant as they were found just prior to demolition.

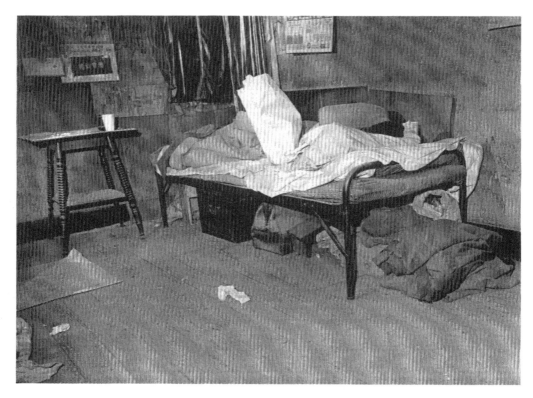

Figure 2.26. Northeast corner of Room 2, Unit 3 (TUR 22:2), after abandonment. Individual items are identified in Table 2.1. (Arizona State Museum photo by Helga Teiwes.)

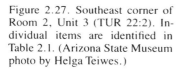

Figure 2.27. Southeast corner of Room 2, Unit 3 (TUR 22:2). Individual items are identified in Table 2.1. (Arizona State Museum photo by Helga Teiwes.)

Figure 2.28. Window ledge on south wall of Room 2, Unit 3 (TUR 22:2). Individual items are identified in Table 2.1. (Arizona State Museum photo by James E. Ayres.)

Figure 2.29. Southwest corner of Room 2, Unit 3 (TUR 22:2). Individual items are identified in Table 2.1. (Arizona State Museum photo by Helga Teiwes.)

Figure 2.30. Wood stove and fireplace in Room 2, Unit 3 (TUR 22:2). Individual items are identified in Table 2.1. (Arizona State Museum photo by Helga Teiwes.)

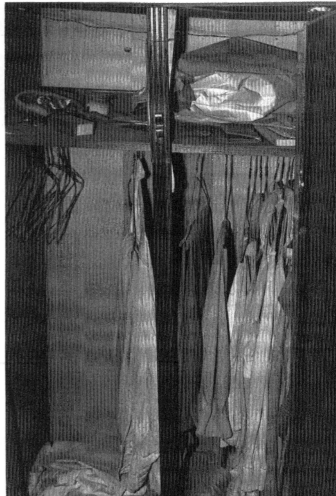

Figure 2.31. Wardrobe against west wall of Room 2, Unit 3 (TUR 22:2). Individual items are identified in Table 2.1. (Arizona State Museum photo by James E. Ayres.)

Figure 2.32. A 1968 view north across the Ying On compound patio shows demolition under way: *left*, the remains of the west wing (Unit 2), with the attached shingle-roofed latrine that once had been the hiding place for emptied containers of illegal opium; *center*, the four-room north wing (Unit 3); *right*, one of the last utilized Chinese dwelling rooms; and *center right*, a corner of the east wing (Unit 4). The low buildings in the background also were removed to make way for a new civic center. (Arizona State Museum photo by James E. Ayres.)

Figure 2.33. Dismantling of Unit 2 of the Ying On compound, 1968. (Arizona State Museum photo by James E. Ayres.)

Table 2.1. Inventory of Items Recovered from Room 2, Unit 3 of TUR 22:2, in 1968

CHINESE ARTIFACTS	ceramic soup spoons	2 medicine boxes
		skull cap
	ceramic spirit bottle sherd	Chinese newspaper
		calendars with Chinese writing
	brass ladle	opium pipe stem
	chopsticks	opium scale
	rice-soup bowl	opium pipe bowl
	headrests	opium pipe bowl made from Mexican jar
	Chinese checks	
	gambling booklets	
	Chinese bag	
EURO-AMERICAN ARTIFACTS	trunk with clothing	shoe laces
Clothes	suit coat	plastic clothes bag
	belt	suit coat
	shirt	hat
	jacket	apron
	pants and other clothes in paper bags	socks
		underwear
		1 glove
	ties	vest
	shirts and pants in wardrobe	sweater
		handkerchiefs
Linens	dish towel	sheets
	blankets	bath and hand towels
	pillow	
	quilt	
Toiletries and Notions	razor strap, case, blade	shaving brush
		umbrella
	keys	3 pairs of reading glasses
	sun glasses	
	billfold	Mexican coin purse
	clothes hangers	mirror
	needle	facial tissue
	scissors	cuticle scissors
	manicure kit	comb
	hair brush	2 finger rings
Medicines	BC tablets	Hospitality Kit, Johnson & Johnson
	Geritol	
	pill bottles	
	Bufferin	Primatene box
	Alka Seltzer	jar of salve
	rubbing alcohol bottle	prescription tablets
		Anacin
		vitamins
		antiseptic container
Recreational Items	2 cigar boxes	Raleigh cigarettes
	ashtray	tobacco can
Papers	Physical examination card, U.S. Selective Service	cardboard and wrapping paper
		English phrase book
	paper towels	shopping bag, paper bags
	comic book	
	envelopes and writing paper	personal letters

Table 2.1.
(continued)

Cooking and Eating Tools	strainers	2 styrofoam cups
	can openers	frying pan
	saucepans and lids	whetstone
	saucer with nails	toothpicks
	Hills Brothers coffee can with knives and spoons	glass cup with nails
		cooking spoons
		wire trivet
	thermos	coffee pot
	ceramic cup, dish, bowls	cups with knives and spoons
	enamel bowl	glass bowl
	drinking glass	funnel
	tin mug	knives
	chopping block	pie tin
Groceries	1 lb. Hills Brothers coffee	Hills Brothers coffee cans with flour, beans, 4 eggs
	Instant Postum	
	Wesson Oil bottles	box of oatmeal
	bread wrapper	Calumet Baking Powder
	can of corn	Pream
	pail with Ideal Mincemeat label	soap
		3-in-1 oil
	Black Flag insect spray	monosodium glutamate box (used for stove ashes)
	coupon from Suey Yuen store	
Hardware and Housewares	padlock	whisk broom, scrub brush
	mop, broom	
	metal pipe	saws, saw blade
	dog collar chain	gallon pails
	ash scoop	hinges, nails, screws, spring
	poker	
	tire iron	sandpaper
	hatchet	hammer
	electric fan	top of oil lamp (for opium use?)
	fly swatter	
	mousetraps	book of matches
	ball of string	tin box
	bamboo pole	glue
	metal files	kerosene can
	flashlight	empty jars and bottles
	electric cord, light bulbs, light socket	
		liquid solder
Furniture	folding cot	bedside table
	desk table	stove table
	wooden crates	portable wardrobe
	wood stove	kerosene stove
Miscellaneous	Indian basket with odds and ends	1864 Guatemalan coin
	trunks	handbag
	U.S. penny	

CHAPTER THREE

Chinese Material Culture

The material objects used by the Chinese community generally are sufficiently distinct to permit their separation from the mass of goods discarded by Tucson's larger Hispanic and Euro-American populations. Such items provide evidence for an ethnic identity that persisted throughout the diverse and rapidly changing cultural environment of early Tucson (see Spicer 1971 and McGuire 1982 for discussions of this phenomenon).

One collection of Chinese artifacts came from excavations in city blocks, adjacent to areas of Chinese occupation, where surface structures had been destroyed either years prior to or at the time of the 1968–1973 urban renewal, or both. These complete or fragmentary items of ceramic, glass, or metal endured the conditions of deposition, although in the case of metal, with considerable corrosion. Objects of a more fragile nature had suffered not only from decay or from demolition, but also from a traditional funerary practice of burning a deceased person's belongings (Burkhardt 1953: 97). A description of a typical Arizona sojourner funeral and ceremonial burning of his possessions appeared in Prescott's *Journal Miner*, August 25, 1908. In Tucson, as in all other Chinese sites probed in the West, the archaeological record is skewed accordingly. However, what has been recovered through excavation of overseas Chinese sites is so remarkably homogeneous and unchanging through time that Tucson's sample serves to further substantiate the pattern.

A meager collection of sherds from the late eighteenth- to early nineteenth-century Spanish presidio area is not included in this study. The sherds are representative of a trade in Chinese porcelains from Manila to New Spain and onward to border installations. The fragments are too small in size and too few in number to offer much more than a hint of a widespread trade pattern shared with other northern Spanish borderlands (Barnes 1983).

The second collection of Chinese articles to be considered is composed of examples of the imperishables recovered during excavation and, more importantly, a rich inventory of fiber, cloth, leather, and paper artifacts not generally available archaeologically. These objects were taken from a block of tenements and an adjoining association building scheduled for destruction (Figs. 1.15, 2.20). Various parts of the four units of the structure had been lived in by Chinese from about 1919, or perhaps a few years earlier, until 1968, although there had been Asian use of some buildings outside the east arm of the compound as early as 1883. The most intense occupation of the block structure apparently occurred about 1935, when a newspaper account described it as home to thirty or forty Chinese men (*Arizona Daily Star*, February 22, 1935). During the later years of this long occupational period there was a relaxation of customary funeral rites, and personal possessions were not destroyed but simply left scattered in vacated rooms formerly housing the deceased. In other cases, tenants apparently left behind unwanted articles when they moved to new quarters. For unknown reasons, the Ying On Merchants and Labor Benevolent Association officials also did not bother to carry many records, photographs, and furnishings to their new hall erected in another location away from the zone marked for leveling.

Both the archaeological and ethnological collections reflect a steadfast affiliation by the Chinese to their ethnic base and the physical goods pertaining to it. The generally low quality of these objects confirms the poor economic standing of sojourners and of most inhabitants at the Chinese sources of supply in the homeland and abroad. By contrast, analyses of ships' manifests indicate a flourishing traffic in Oriental luxuries brought from China to San Francisco after 1850, luxuries intended for an affluent non-Chinese market (Giles and Layton 1986). Such items, however, are not present in most archaeological sites in the western United States.

CULINARY ARTIFACTS

Large tracts of China are not arable, yet for millennia the country's population rose dramatically. These two conflicting conditions forced the Chinese to constantly and fully exploit the local flora and fauna and to attempt to utilize introduced elements of other environments in order to survive. These factors led to such an unparalleled focus on food and its preparation that eating and drinking of prescribed foods and beverages became a language of all social behavior from birth to death (Hahn 1968). Virtually every able-bodied adult acquired familiarity with rudimentary cooking procedures, a skill that supported the migratory overseas bachelors in caring for personal needs and in gaining employment. Although centuries of confrontation with threat of famine taught the Chinese the value of innovating palatable dishes out of what Westerners tend to consider inedible plants or animal parts, food prejudices do flourish. Buddhism demands vegetarianism, but generally biases are predicated on environmental shortcomings or social viewpoints.

In south China beef and dairy products, for example, either are unknown or are disdained, in part because lack of sufficient range land severely limits any cattle industry and in part because in earlier days the hated nomads of the Asian interior so largely depended on them (Anderson and Anderson 1977: 326). Nevertheless, through trial and error, the Chinese learned how to dry, to pickle, to salt, and to preserve an incredible assemblage of foods and how best to package them for storage or for cartage. Internal distribution within China of provisions peculiar to certain districts became a major business. Once containers of ceramic, metal, fiber, cloth, or wood were engineered to meet specific physical conditions of their intended contents (candied or raw, liquid or powdered, dried or viscous, bulky or small), they remained unmodified for generations.

Starting in the late Ming Dynasty, south China periodically disgorged its restless hungry peasantry to southeast Asia, to the south Pacific, and, in the mid-nineteenth century, to the Americas, and it was inevitable that familiar foodstuffs, in characteristic packaging, went along. Dietary habits are among the most resistant to change, a phenomenon appreciated by entrepreneurs of all nationalities. The large-volume, trans-Pacific traffic that evolved after 1850 brought impressive inventories of Chinese commodities to immigrants settling in the western United States. Evans (1980: 89) cites an 1850s checklist of seven major categories of commodities, including foodstuffs; Spier (1958: 80) notes 131 different items on invoices of food shipments between 1850 and 1854. For a century, both the foods and the varied containers in which they were packed are presumed to have originated in provinces nearest to the principal ports of south China active in the trade.

Some archaeological substantiation in Tucson for this international commerce in Chinese foods intended for migrant or expatriated Chinese consumers comes from one source: the ceramic containers in which they had been exported. Although certainly important, other kinds of packaging did not survive subsurface deposition.

Ceramic Shipping Containers for Foodstuffs

It is probable that as early as 1880, when the Southern Pacific Railroad tracks had been laid from the West Coast to Tucson, mass-produced stoneware receptacles of comestibles, known as *Min Gei* (Whitlow 1981: 38), reached Chinese-run grocery stores being opened to serve the expanding Asian market in urban and in adjacent desert areas. Evidence of them has been noted in all three excavation areas in the part of town where the Chinese are believed to have settled first. Commodities in these ceramics continued to be purchased by the Chinese during the first two decades of the twentieth century, as they gradually dispersed into the Hispanic barrio. They still were being used at the terminal date of this study (1968), when abandonment of the Ying On compound became necessary. Their sources after 1949, perhaps even as early as 1937 and the Second Sino-Japanese War, would have been Hong Kong or Taiwan. All these containers, as well as recovered tablewares, have been described previously (Olsen 1978), so this presentation is primarily photographic, with some tentative temporal interpretations.

The stoneware shipping containers recovered from archaeological excavations may be classified into five general groupings. Squat, wide-mouthed jars were designed to hold one or two pounds of dry or nonviscous foodstuffs such as salted vegetables, dried fruits, dried mushrooms, shrimp paste, or bean curd (Fig. 3.1). In the haste of large-scale manufacture of these containers, journeymen potters obviously worked without benefit of templates. Their jars likely were symmetrical when taken from the wheel but tended to slump or warp during uncontrolled drying or firing conditions. Glaze defects, such as pinholes, crawling, or fingerprints left where the jar was held during dipping further emphasize lack of care in processing, glaze application, and firing. Some of the jars had been sealed with lids. These thin disks of grainy clay had slightly upturned rims for a nested fit with vessel mouths, and they probably were sealed into place with white clay, a substance found around the perimeters of four nearly complete examples. Perhaps they had been covered with a paper label. The friability of such delicate lids indicates they were intended solely for one-time use in transit. When used for storage purposes, the jars may have had cloth bean-bag or flat wooden covers, as are common in modern China (Fig. 3.2). Ceramic lids were fired off the jars and probably tucked into unfilled corners of the same kilns.

Similar squat, wide-mouthed jars have been recovered from most Chinese sites in western America, including Ventura, Sacramento, Donner Pass, San Francisco, Woodland, and Lovelock (Chace 1976: 517, 519; Praetzellis and Praetzellis 1978, Fig. 101d and 1979, Fig. 1b–d; Felton and others 1984, Fig. 11c; and Pastron, Gross, and Garaventa 1981: 410–413).

Very small jars probably were used to ship candy, medicinal preparations, or dried seasoning such as cilantro, fennel, aniseed, star anise, or Sichuan peppercorns (Fig. 3.3c–e). A complete specimen similar to that in Figure 3.3e is illustrated by Pastron, Prichett, and Ziebarth (1981, Appendix C, Fig. C.03, *left*).

Another group of stoneware food containers are round-bodied, flat-based, and narrow-mouthed receptacles. They have a downward-tilted and irregular hand-modeled pouring spout welded to the vessel by a coil of clay that was not totally smoothed away on the upper shoulder. Five complete jars of this type and sherds from at least five others were recovered in the TUR project. The spouts were closed during shipment by a wad of plastic clay that hardened when exposed to air. The small collared openings were closed with a cork or wooden stopper. The jars probably were glazed by a dipping technique, and some sherds reveal incomplete covering of interior surfaces. Typically, bases and an inch (2.54 cm) of the lower exterior body remain unglazed. It has been suggested that in addition to soy sauce, jars of this sort may have contained black vinegar or molasses (Olsen 1978: 36).

Figure 3.1. Stoneware food containers. *a*, A modern, squat, wide-mouthed globular jar intended to reach an English-speaking market has a paper label and oiled paper seal. Identical jars in contemporary Chinese stores in the United States, Tahiti, and Australia suggest a ceramic form made specifically for the twentieth century Chinese export trade. (Height, 9.0 cm; orifice diameter, 5.5 cm.) *b*, *c*, Small, wide-mouthed, shouldered jars for one pound of nonviscous foodstuffs. Although these two specimens came from contexts that possibly were separated by three-fourths of a century, the only stylistic difference between them was accidental. (Average heights, 10.0 cm; average orifice diameters, 6.3 cm.) *d*, *e*, Medium size, wide-mouthed, shouldered jars for foodstuffs. (Average height, 13.7 cm; average orifice diameter, 8.0 cm; average lid diameter, 8.2 cm; average lid thickness, 0.03 cm.) Provenience: TUR 22:2, Unit 2, Room 20 (*a*), Room 19 (*c*); TUR 3:4–3aL10 (*b*), 3:4–2aL2/3 (*d*), 3:4 (*e*); TUR 14:1–2aL8 (lid).

Figure 3.2. Storage jars in a street stall in modern southern China, with improvised covers of flat pieces of wood or a filled pouch with handle. The dippers were used for removal of jar contents.

Figure 3.3. Stoneware food containers. *a*, *b*, Lids. *c*, *d*, Small cylindrical jars, with interiors and exteriors covered with thin honey-colored glaze (*c*) or with thick glossy, brown glaze (*d*). Flat-topped, knobless lids rested on shoulder flanges and perhaps had been sealed in place with a paper label. Lids are glazed on exterior only (*a*, *b*, *d*) or remain unglazed (*c*). Two fragments of similar jars had molded illegible characters on their bases. (Jar heights range from 6.0 cm to 7.0 cm, orifice diameters are 6.5 cm.) *e*, Small, narrow-mouthed, cylindrical jar, wheel-thrown and covered with a thick, pin-holed, brown glaze, has a restricted orifice and horizontally flared rim. It probably was stoppered with a cork and wooden plug. (Height, 8.5 cm; maximum diameter, 7.5 cm.) *f*, *g*, Spouted jars. (Average height, 12.7 cm; maximum diameter, 14.2 cm.) Provenience: TUR 22:2, Unit 2, roof (*a*, *d*); TUR 29:2–L5 (*b*), 29:2–L1 (*f*); TUR 2:1–L5b (*c*, *e*); TUR 69:2, surface (*g*).

Figure 3.4. Large globular jar found 1.1 m below the floor of a burned room in the Ying On compound in the upper level of an abandoned latrine. Throwing rings on body walls and basal marks from being cut from a wheel head are evident. The narrow mouth had been sealed with a lid secured in place by straps through small shoulder lugs. The pot had been used secondarily for storage and remains of an improvised coffee-can lid were associated with it (*right*). (Height, 23.0 cm; maximum diameter, 23.0 cm; TUR 22:2–2eL1, beneath floor of Unit 2, Room 27.)

Other possibilities are Hoisin sauce, oyster sauce, rapeseed oil, or sesame seed oil. The uniformity in size of these jars is twice that of comparable jars reported by Brott (1982: 49). They conform to the largest of three gradations of the form recorded in the San Francisco waterfront collection (Pastron, Gross, and Garaventa 1981: 404, Fig. 9.15).

Commodious, heavily potted jars transported cooking supplies such as soy sauce, vinegar, or peanut oil (Figs. 3.4, 3.5). Intact examples are not common in archaeological contexts because their size made them vulnerable to breakage. A single vessel (Fig. 3.4) came from the TUR work. Elsewhere these jars, in various states of preservation, have been reported from Donner Pass and Ventura (Chace 1976: 521–522), Woodland (Felton and others 1984, Fig. 10d), Sacramento (Praetzellis and Praetzellis 1979, Figs. 21b and 25b), and San Francisco (Pastron, Gross, and Garaventa 1981: 407–410). The jar from Tucson may be as much as forty to fifty years more recent than the others, but how long it might have been in service prior to its final deposition is unknown.

A high-shouldered jar made of a distinctive light-firing clay containing iron particles that caused speckling commonly is termed a ginger jar. Seven whole or restorable vessels of this type are in the TUR collection (Fig. 3.6). The jars were molded in two parts and luted together at the leather-hard stage. However, a slight size variation among the collection specimens indicates a number of comparable, but not identical, molds were used at the workshop. A white engobe in a wide band on the exterior jar body carries simple encircling linear patterns executed in a blue pigment. The pigment typically was so unstable under stoneware temperatures and a clear glaze that it flowed excessively. The same glaze covers the interior and exterior basal area within the ring foot. The flat-topped, knobless lid fit over a short straight neck to rest on the upper jar shoulder and probably was fired in place, since there were no touching glazed surfaces. Often, but not invariably, lid tops are covered with the same colorless glaze as on jar bodies. Likely the output of a particular but unidentified factory, these jars were made to hold some special product like ginger root in syrup or

Figure 3.5. Two kinds of large unglazed ceramic jars commonly seen in southern China. For long distance transport the jars are fitted with unelaborated, knobless ceramic lids sealed into place with a malleable substance that air hardens. In the absence of handles, bamboo covers facilitate handling.

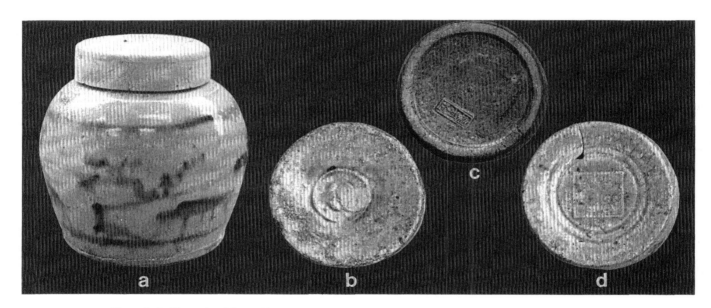

Figure 3.6. Ginger jar, lids, and base. Lids have impressed patterns on upper surfaces under a transparent glaze (*b*, *c*), and all jars recovered carry an impressed seal on their bases (*d*). (Jar height, 12.5 cm; maximum diameter, 14.7 cm; orifice diameter, 6.0 cm; average lid height, 2.5 cm; TUR 25:2–5cL6.)

crystallized ginger. Other suggested commodities are preserved onions, green plums, seaweed, gerkins, preserved fish, or chopped garlic.

In addition to the illustrated food containers, many of which surely were put to secondary uses, it is probable that some recovered fragments may have come from huge glazed jars or tubs. No vessels of this type were retrieved intact from TUR activities, but sherds of such a container were recovered in Levels 4 and 5 of a trench at TUR 2:1, in the earliest Chinatown. Although the original intent of the makers of large glazed stoneware containers may have been to create the kinds of receptacles essential for large-scale storage of farm products such as rice, wheat, or even water, it is probable that for export the practical Chinese filled them

with more valuable items (for example, pickled duck eggs, water chestnuts, or lotus root) that would have brought sufficient returns to compensate for handling otherwise unprofitable, cumbersome, and breakable cargo. Brott (1982: 24) suggests that a hole was punched into the bases of those vessels containing products packed in liquid so that they could be emptied more readily, a process that surely would have ended in breakage.

Hundreds of Chinese provincial kilns still produce such large vessels (Fig. 3.5), but more commonly they are unglazed earthenwares. If unglazed jars of this sort reached Tucson, perhaps their fragments were included in the original sorting with Tohono O'odham Indian earthenwares. Although made by different methods, the pottery nevertheless

Figure 3.7. Cooking or kitchen ceramics: *left*, small, tapered, ring-footed bowl; *right*, thin ceramic pans with exterior body ridge. (Height of bowl, 3.1 cm; diameter, 10.0 cm; average height of pans, 4.5 cm; average orifice diameter, 12.6 cm.) Provenience: TUR 3:4–5bL2 (bowl); TUR 22:2, Unit 2, Room 11 (top pan); TUR 29:2–5 (bottom pan).

could be confused in casual observation.

The various kinds of shipping containers were turned on potters' wheels, were poured into molds, or were formed in sections through a combination of both techniques, then luted together. The vessels were covered with a basic, low-cost iron oxide glaze identified as *jian you* (Olsen 1978: 36). Hurried production of expendable ceramics crafted for immediate, rough usage is evident in slight variations in size within categories and casual attention to finishing details. Forms and vessel sizes were dictated by intended purposes. These had been so solidly established in marketing practices that for the more than eight decades represented by TUR materials there was no appreciable modification within each category. That kind of stylistic continuity makes impossible the dating of specimens through physical attributes, with the exception of minor glaze differences and the presence of English labels on what must be regarded as modern examples.

Nonceramic Shipping Containers

Abandoned quarters in the Ying On compound yielded some paper cartons that had held imported rice or tea and some cooking oil tins. One small rectangular can that had been opened with a manual can opener bears a partial impressed English label and sun-face trademark, but the words "Made in Hong Kong" suggest the possibility that it contained something other than food.

Ceramic Cookpots

Earthenware and stoneware cooking vessels are not well represented among the Tucson finds, nor are they numerous in China. Other than thick-walled, sandy-textured pots in which soups and stews are simmered, the basic utensils customarily are of metal that can withstand the intense heat of

charcoal braziers. Ceramic vessels, however, are used in preliminary food preparation, to store cooked dishes, or possibly to steam foods (although most typically steamers are of bamboo). These are small bowls such as illustrated in Figure 3.7 and thin ceramic pans with exterior body ridge and lower wall that have been tapered with a swipe of a trimming tool to facilitate nesting of like vessels (Fig. 3.7 *right*).

Kitchen, Cooking, and Eating Tools

In China, most cooking is accomplished over single or double charcoal braziers or portable clay stoves with few utensils or hand tools (Fig. 3.8).

Figure 3.8. Cooking facilities in a village in southern China may be similar to those used by late nineteenth century sojourners squatting in abandoned buildings on Tucson's west side. The basket to the left of the stove is similar to baskets recovered from Ying On rooms once used by Chinese (Fig. 3.10). The bags contain cubes of charcoal, a typical cooking and heating fuel in China that may have been replaced in the Arizona desert by mesquite.

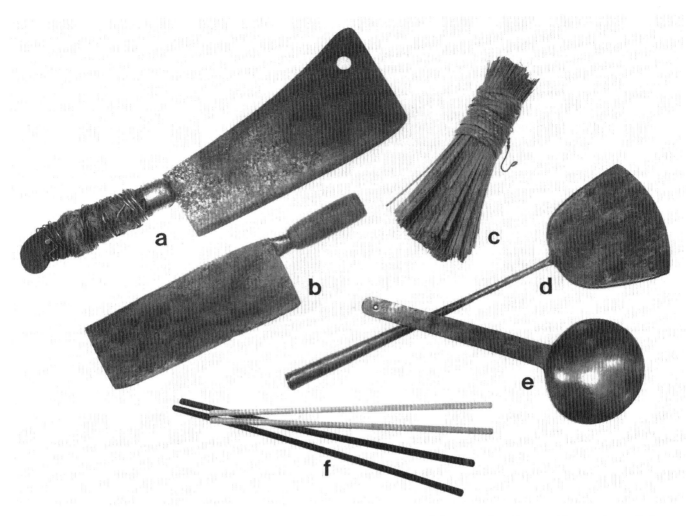

Figure 3.9. Cooking and eating tools from TUR 22:2. *a*, Metal cleaver, an American-made implement, bears a stamp *Foster Bros. Trade 9* on one face. Its original wooden handle had broken and been crudely replaced by fiber rope and wire. A hole for suspension is in the upper corner of the blade. *b*, The blade of a smaller cleaver is more rectangular and shows signs of heavy use in chopping through hard substances, such as bone. It is an imported product with Chinese characters stamped on the blade. *c*, Brush made of fine strips of stiff bamboo bound around a wooden core, customarily used to scour woks. An attached bent wire permitted suspension. A second brush was recovered from the Chee Kung Tong room, suggesting that at times food preparation may have taken place there. *d*, Iron spatula with curved lower edge to fit the contour of a round-bottomed wok. The face of the spatulate end is stamped *HCKL*; the handle is rolled metal. *e*, Brass ladle that appears to have been hand formed over a mold. Shaping and hammering scars are visible on the round bowl. *f*, Two pairs of chopsticks. (Lengths and widths in cm: *a*, 38.2, 11.5; *b*, 29.2, 7.3; *c*, 18.0, diameter 4.8; *d*, 37.9, spatulate end 11.3; *e*, 27.0, bowl diameter 10.5; *f*, 26.6 top pair, 30.2 bottom pair.) Provenience: Unit 4, Room 12 (*a*), Room 11 (*f*, one pair); Unit 2, Room 25 (*b*), Room 19 (*c*), Room 1 (*d*); Unit 3, window ledge (*e*), Unit 1, Room 4 (*f*, one pair). (Arizona State Museum photo by Helga Teiwes.)

By necessity, the Chinese sojourners or settlers coming to America eventually would have learned to cope with wood or kerosene stoves, but it can be assumed that customary small objects would have been imported, along with groceries, from the motherland. No such equipment from the TUR excavations can be identified as uniquely Chinese, but some was found in the quarters of the Ying On compound (Figs. 3.9–3.12). Among kitchen implements recovered was a bamboo brush, metal spatulas and ladles, and 39 chopsticks of ivory, bamboo, other woods, and plastic (Fig. 3.9*c–f*). Also included in culinary gear were six cleavers, the ubiquitous Chinese chopping-cutting tool. Of several sizes present, two have rectangular blades and two have blades whose lower edge is more rounded (Fig. 3.9*a, b*).

During the infamous tong wars of the late nineteenth century, hired killers, who were members of fighting secret societies, customarily used a cleaverlike weapon (see Chesneaux 1971, Fig. 4, where they are called Triad fighting swords). From that vicious practice, the killers were identified in the Euro-American press as hatchetmen. Their weapons differed from kitchen cleavers in having a blade whose lower edge was longer than the upper edge, a weapon that undoubtedly could slice expeditiously through human bones.

All the cooking and eating objects are of types still in use every day in Chinese kitchens, and all certainly have a lengthy previous history. For unknown reasons, typical woks and wire mesh spoons are absent from the collection.

Figure 3.10. Chinese-made kitchen storage baskets from TUR 22:2. *Left*, large over-two, under-two, twilled ring basket with slightly rounded base and direct rim. Natural and pale purple weaving materials form a diamond-patterned centerpiece. (Diameter, 39.5 cm; height, 10.0 cm; Unit 4, Room 11.) *Center*, deep, square-based, flared, cylindrical wicker basket, with rim reinforced on the exterior by four twisted coils below the wrapped rim coil. Weaving elements of the base form the warps of the sides; wefts are narrow strips of vegetal material. Formerly a fine piece of cordage had been woven into the basket just below the strengthening coils. (Diameter, 25.3 cm; height, 22.0 cm.) *Right front*, small, flat-based and square-based wicker basket made of flat strips of bamboo lashed vertically over narrow vegetal weft. A partial paper label with illegible Chinese characters is glued to the back side. Figure 3.11 shows this basket in situ. (Diameter, 16.8 cm to 17.3 cm; height, 11.7 cm; Unit 4, Room 12, on table.) (Arizona State Museum photo by Helga Teiwes.)

Figure 3.11. Debris in Room 12, Unit 4 (TUR 22:2), including the basket in Figure 3.10 *right* shown as it was found (*upper left*). The thermos behind it is a typical modern fixture in Chinese lodgings for keeping hot water ready for tea. (Arizona State Museum photo by James E. Ayres.)

Figure 3.12. An insect-eaten, large steamer tray with outer frame made of six concentric layers of bamboo strips held together with wooden pegs and a rack of lashed bamboo strips on supporting slats. The *Made in China* marking on the rim, accompanied by some Chinese characters, identifies the tray as a modern export item, probably from Hong Kong or Taiwan. (Diameter, 45.0 cm; height, 8.2 cm; TUR 22:2, Unit 2, Room 22; Arizona State Museum photo by Helga Teiwes.)

Three Chinese baskets of the types commonly used to store or to sift dry products are in the collection (Figs. 3.10, 3.11). Two are wicker; one is of twilled construction. A large bamboo steamer tray was probably used over a basal wok of boiling water to steam foods (Fig. 3.12). Three small Indian-made baskets supplement those from China (Fig. 3.13).

Late Qing Tableware

Nearly all the recovered tablewares are known, from research accomplished elsewhere, to have come into general use by Chinese commoners during the late half of the lengthy Qing Dynasty (1644–1911). The tablewares are divided into six groupings, and all but one continued being used in Tucson for perhaps three decades into the Republican era, even though production in China of these particular styles may have ceased. The categories include three patterns of eating and drinking vessels for individual service, which, to some undetermined degree, may have been successive. Also present are a special service plate that may or may not have been part of a set, two kinds of spouted, handled receptacles, and a series of unmatched serving bowls or sauce dishes.

Typically in a home setting laboring-class Chinese relied for personal use on four small, individual ceramic forms: a teacup, a rice-soup bowl, a soup spoon, and a saucer. However, early overseas Chinese, particularly single men living in work camps or rooming houses, managed with only an all-purpose rice-soup bowl and perhaps a ceramic spoon. One of the styles of such bowls, widely distributed abroad wherever Chinese migrants found work up to about 1880, was characterized by an underglaze blue pattern known to archaeologists as Double Happiness (Brott 1982: 53–54; Pastron, Gross, and Garaventa 1981, Fig. 9.25). Expectedly, inasmuch as the major movement of Chinese into the city did not occur until after 1880, this style was absent in Tucson.

The Tucson tableware inventory began with a low caliber style that now is called Three Circles and Dragonfly. Olsen (1978: 15–16), in his preliminary report on TUR Chinese ceramics, termed it Swatow or Blue Flower Ware; more re-

Figure 3.13. Tohono O'odham Indian baskets from TUR 22:2, used by Chinese tenants of the Ying On compound. The coiled baskets have a bear grass foundation and willow and martynia sewing elements. (Diameters and heights in cm: *left*, 22.5, 8.0; *center*, 16.0, 5.0; *right*, 18.5, 7.5, from Unit 3, Room 2; Arizona State Museum photo by Helga Teiwes.)

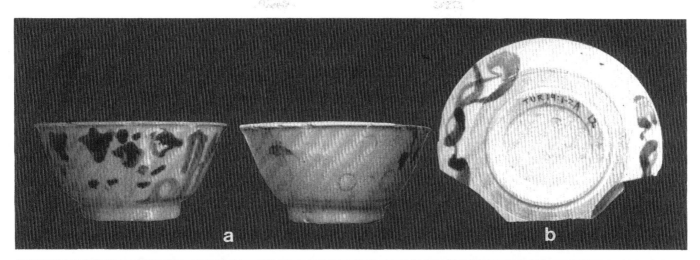

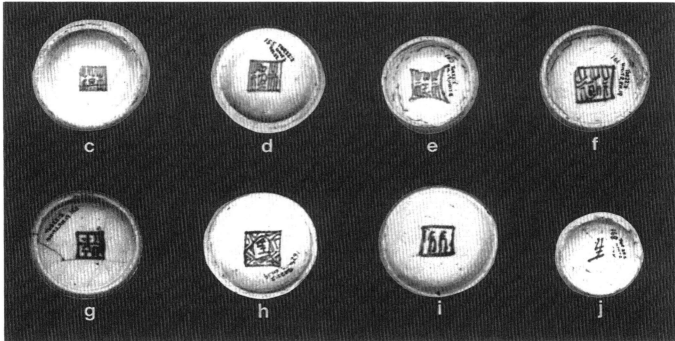

Figure 3.14. Three Circles and Dragonfly rice-soup bowl (opposite sides, *a*) and saucer base (*b*), and bases of Celadon rice bowls with various marks painted in blue prior to firing (*c–j*). Diameters and heights in cm: (*a*) 13.9, 6.8; (*b*) 8.2, 1.4. Provenience: TUR 3:4–5bL2/3 (*a*); TUR 14:1–2aL2 (*b*); TUR: 22:2 (*c*), 22:2, Unit 2, Room 22 (*d*), Room 19 (*e, f, h*), Room 21 (*g, j*); unavailable (*i*).

cently Felton and his coauthors (1984: 40) call it Bamboo. It is a grayish, coarse stoneware confined almost entirely to rice-soup bowls with many surface flaws and casually brushed underglaze slate blue decoration. Its forms were restricted to those suitable for individual use. Not as plentiful as the two styles that gradually replaced it, Three Circles and Dragonfly was dispersed throughout the TUR district wherever there had been former Chinese occupation. Twelve complete, or fragmentary but identifiable, such bowls and one less common saucer (Brott 1982: 53; Pastron, Prichett,

and Ziebarth 1981, Vol. 3, Fig. C.05) were recovered from six different locations (Fig. 3.14*a*, *b*). Three of these proveniences (TUR 2:1, 3:4, and 69:2) were in the clustering of dwellings that comprised the original Chinatown (Fig. 1.3). It is probable that eight bowls, as well as an assortment of related sherds, resulted from that 1880 to 1910 occupation. One bowl was retrieved from a well situated in a block (TUR 37:6) within the Hispanic barrio, where a Chinese store appears on an 1883 map (Fig. 1.3). That bowl may have been acquired by a Hispanic customer of the store, later to be discarded with non-Chinese trash. Two partial bowls were left in the Ying On compound (TUR 22:2, Figs. 2.14, 2.20). Either they were objects that somehow had survived for a very long time, or, less likely, the ware continued to be made later than generally believed. A saucer came from a latrine in an area near a keno den (TUR 14:1, Fig. 2.1). Inasmuch as keno was based on a Chinese-introduced game (Culin 1891: 15), the gambling parlor likely was run by Asians from at least 1883 until some time prior to 1896 (Fig. 1.3). More positive evidence for a Chinese presence were dwellings and a grocery store in the block that mappers indicated as existing from 1904 to 1909 (Figs. 1.8, 1.12). A Three Circles and Dragonfly sherd lot was taken from a latrine and trenches in City Block 38, where from 1896 to 1914 there were variously two to five Chinese stores open for business (Figs. 1.6, 1.8, 1.12, 1.13). Proprietors of such stores lived in the rear of their places of business and likely were responsible for the use and breakage of these ceramics.

The comparative scarcity of the Three Circles and Dragonfly type and its technical characteristics (stoneware rather than porcelain and of limited form variation) suggest either that it was early in the local sequence or the product of a provincial factory lacking the higher standards to be observed in the other coeval tablewares. Felton and others (1984: 96–97) consider it a cheaper product more apt to have been used by lower-class workers.

The second category of Qing tableware is known as Celadon, an unfortunate choice of nomenclature because, except for color, it bears little resemblance to the icy, jadelike celadons of the Song Dynasty (A.D. 960–1279). Winter Green, a name drawn from overseas Chinese business records, is more suitable (Felton and others 1984: 40). Vessel exteriors of the late nineteenth- to early twentieth-century style are a light greenish blue, interiors a creamy white, and bases of cups and bowls often are enriched with blue seals said to have a variety of meanings (Pastron, Prichett, and Ziebarth 1981, Appendix C, Table 9.07). The ware is moderately thin, but is not transparent porcelain. It was mold made, serviceable but unadorned, and obviously mass-produced for a large commoner market. It appeared in a greater variety of forms than the presumed predecessor type. Included in the style were rice-soup bowls, teacups, wine cups, tapered and hemispherical small bowls of several capacities, and spoons. The uniformity of sizes within these subdivisions and the vessel finish parallel those of contemporary Western industrial ceramics and likely the pieces were turned out by the same assembly-line methods. The variety of form implies an elaboration of peasant-level life style, which history seems to deny.

Celadon ceramics were comparatively common in Tucson, with an estimated fifty specimens represented in complete or fragmentary condition (Fig. 3.14*c–j*). They were recovered in four localities identified with territorial occupation (TUR 2:1, 69:2, 3:4, 14:1; Figs. 1.3, 1.6, 1.8, 1.12, 2.1), as well as in the later Ying On compound (TUR 22:2; Figs. 1.14, 1.15), indicating a use-life of fifty or sixty years.

Celadon pottery also was found in excavations in four non-Chinese contexts (TUR 28:4, 29:8, 34:1, 34:7), the first two of which were situated near former Chinese stores.

Celadon is a type commonly encountered in other late nineteenth-century Chinese sites in the West (Chace 1976: 15; Felton and others 1984: 40; Pastron, Gross, and Garaventa 1981: 432–436; Praetzellis and Praetzellis 1979, Fig. 4; Whitlow 1981: 35).

A chronologically late version of the style was exemplified by five bowls with an exterior glaze of a much lighter green color over more heavily potted vessels found in abandoned Ying On rooms.

Another individual tableware style recovered in the TUR project was represented by 39 complete or nearly complete vessels and 32 lots of sherds from an estimated 54 additional vessels of a ware now called Four Seasons (Enamelled Flower Ware in Olsen 1978: 20–21; Four Flowers in Felton and others 1984: 40). It is a mold-made style also widely found in Chinese contexts elsewhere (Brott 1982: 56–57; Chace 1976: 525; Praetzellis and Praetzellis 1979, Fig. 5; Whitlow 1981: 30–34). The name comes from engraved, overglaze floral patterns on a white ground symbolizing the seasons of the year and possibly having other meanings as well. It is a type that illustrates the Chinese desire for objects that were functional but also beautiful and emblematic of religious beliefs. The range in form and size of Four Seasons ceramics is greater than that of the other two categories of individual eating dishes, but whether such variation reflects a still more complex social atmosphere is dubious. These objects were meant to appeal to the river boatmen who plied the canals, peasants who worked the fields, tradesmen who sat behind counters of road-side stalls, and those who courageously ventured thousands of miles overseas seeking financial improvement.

The Tucson sample contains bowls with four size variations, flatware that includes saucers and plates, wine cups, scallop-edged oval sauce dishes, and spoons with slightly faceted bowls (Figs. 3.15–3.20). Even with this elaboration and the decorative mode that required more time in execution, the ware was a relatively coarse product made to sell for modest cost and representative of a period in Chinese ceramics Willetts and Poh (1981) call "devolution."

Four Seasons ware was recovered in five locations occupied from about 1880 to 1910 (TUR 2:1, 69:2, 3:4, 14:1, 23:8; Figs. 1.3, 1.6, 1.8, 1.12, 2.1) and in the Ying On quarters (TUR 22:2; Figs. 1.14, 1.15, 2.20) that were not vacated until 1968. Comparable Four Seasons vessels purchased from several antique dealers in China were dated by them to the brief Tong Zhi reign of the Qing Dynasty (1862–1874). Olsen (1978: 21) has identified seal marks on some of the Tucson pieces as of this period. However, when considering proveniences of recovered examples, the ware must have continued in use, and probably in production, for more than an additional half century. The word *China* painted in red on the bottom of one derivative sauce dish (Fig. 3.19) substantiates this later continuation, although several basal red

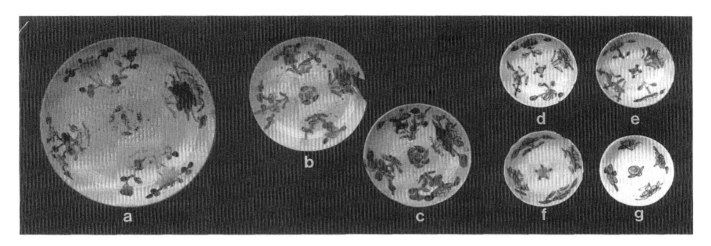

Figure 3.15. Four Seasons porcelain tableware: *a*, plate; *b*, *c*, saucers; *d–g*, sauce dishes. (Diameters and heights in cm: *a*, 21.7, 3.6; *b*, 13.3, 2.5; *c*, 12.0, 2.5; *d–g*, 7.7, 2.5.) Provenience: TUR 22:2 (*a*), 22:2, Unit 2, Room 11 (*c*), Unit 3, Room 2 (*d–g*); TUR 3:4–2a (*b*).

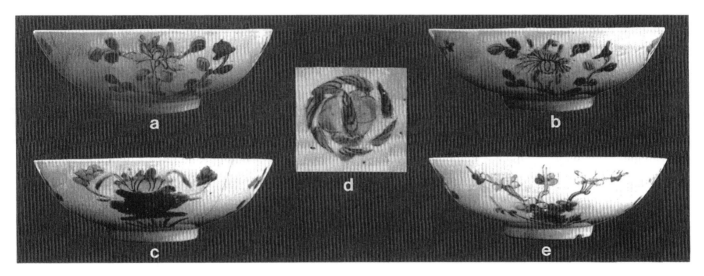

Figure 3.16. Four Seasons serving bowl showing floral motifs representing the seasons of the year and symbolizing other Taoist concepts (Brott 1982: 56–57; Praetzellis and Praetzellis 1979: 147): *a*, peony, spring, good fortune; *b*, chrysanthemum, fall, pleasure; *c*, lotus, summer, purity; *d*, centerpiece, flower medallion or peach; *e*, plum, winter, courage. (Diameter, 21.0 cm; height, 7.3 cm; TUR 22:2.)

Figure 3.17. Four Seasons wine cups, with basal view. (Diameters, 4.5 cm; heights, 2.4 cm.) Provenience: TUR 22:2, Unit 2, Room 13 (*left*, *right*), Room 1 (*center*).

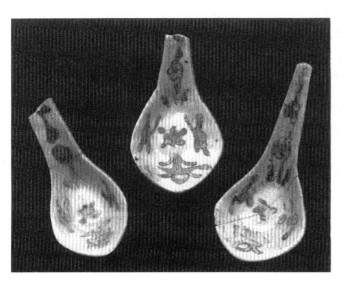

Figure 3.18. Four Seasons soup spoons, with flared bowls and low ring feet, recovered from the area of earliest Chinese occupation. These spoons are identical to others retrieved from the abandoned rooms in the Ying On compound occupied into the 1950s and 1960s. (Lengths, 11.2 cm; bowl widths, 4.7 cm; TUR 2:1–L5b.)

Figure 3.19. Mold-made sauce dish, with word *CHINA* fired within the ring foot, probably is a late export version of the Four Seasons style in vogue for many decades. The decorative method and palette are comparable to, and the floral elements are reminiscent of but not identical to, earlier prototypes. (Length, 13.3 cm; width, 8.7 cm; height, 2.5 cm; TUR 22:2, Unit 4, Room 11.)

Figure 3.20. Four Seasons and Nonya Ware bowls, Fragrant Flowers and Calling Birds sauce dish, and polychrome bulb planter. Tableware from TUR 3:4, 22:2; food containers from TUR 1:7, 3:4, 14:1.

Figure 3.21. Three Circles and Dragonfly, Celadon, and Rice-grain porcelain rice-soup bowls, carp plate, and blue on white teapot lid. Tableware from TUR 3:4, 22:2; food containers from TUR 1:7, 3:4, 14:1.

arabesques, perhaps a reference to the Buddhist eternal knot, may be earlier.

The three Qing tablewares for individual use (Three Circles and Dragonfly, Celadon, and Four Seasons) comprise a ceramic triad characteristic of virtually all excavated sites in the West occupied from about 1860 to 1900. Three Circles and Dragonfly generally is more abundant in sites dating early within this time span; the other two styles appear most commonly in the later decades and in almost the same proportions to each other (Brott 1982: 56–57; Evans 1980, Table 2). As yet more discrete dating is not available, nor is it likely to be, inasmuch as Chinese ceramic styles are notably long-lived. The Tucson ceramic data fit this nineteenth-century pattern but indicate an extension of the use of Celadon and Four Seasons into the middle of the twentieth century.

Turning to objects designed for communal use, a white porcelain plate with a motif depicting a carp surrounded by eelgrass probably was a special piece reserved for festive occasions (Fig. 3.21). Willetts and Poh (1981, Figs. 28, 29, 34) report that this style was exported in quantity to Indonesia in the late nineteenth- to early twentieth-century eras. A comparable plate purchased in an antique shop aboard a Yangtze River boat was said to represent an 1821 to 1850 manufacturing date (Fig. 3.22 left); if correct, that date makes it at least seventy or more years older than the example recovered in Unit 2, Room 22, of the Ying On house. This Chinese style today is perpetuated in ubiquitous Japanese copies.

Another vessel style for group service is a later nineteenth-century Shanghai or Canton ware. Although it is known in jar, basin, box, vase, and bowl forms, the Tucson specimen (Fig. 3.23) is a lidded, spouted jar variously considered a

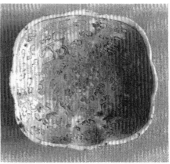

Figure 3.22. Porcelain ceramics purchased in China that duplicate items recovered in TUR research. *Left*, carp plate similar to that in Figure 3.21 was dated by an antique dealer to the Dao Guajg period (1821–1850) of the Qing Dynasty. *Right*, small, footed, scalloped sauce dish with green interior, similar to Nonya Ware in Figure 3.27, was dated by an antique dealer to a portion of the Qing Dynasty lasting from 1875 to 1908.

Figure 3.23. Wine pot or warmer with conical, knobbed lid. Its spout, handle, and upper neck are missing. A comparable, casually executed, underglaze blue decoration on clear white paste elsewhere has been termed Canton Ware, characteristic of the late nineteenth century. (Estimated height with lid, 14.5 cm; diameter of body 7.1 cm; TUR 2:1–L5b. Arizona State Museum photo by Helga Teiwes.)

Figure 3.24. Polychrome and blue on white teapots, spirits bottle, food container, and ginger jars. Tableware from TUR 3:4, 22:2; food containers from TUR 1:7, 3:4, 14:1.

Figure 3.25. Three cylindrical teapots with polychrome overglaze decoration are similar, although they came from refuse that could have been separated by as much as a half to three-fourths of a century. With only moderate size difference, all are cylindrical with low ring feet, have raised white attachments for paired wire-bail handles, and were constructed to hold knobless, sunken lids with rims extending over a brief vertical pot neck. Small-scale motifs of flowers, swooping birds, and bees or butterflies are outlined in black and filled with rose, green, blue, yellow, or orange. Patterns are crisper on the two ethnographic specimens, but little care was taken to keep filler pigments within defining lines. Spouts are undecorated. (Diameters, orifice diameters, and heights in cm: *left*, 12.6, 7.5, 14.7; *center*, 9.7, 5.0, 11.4; *right*, 13.3, 7.6, 15.8.) Provenience: TUR 3:4–2aL5 (*left*); TUR 22:2, Unit 2, Room 10 (*center*), Room 15 (*right*).

wine pot or warmer (Brott 1982: 57–59; Olsen 1978: 27–28; Praetzellis and Praetzellis 1979, Fig. 3b; Quellmalz 1976, Fig. 4) or a sauce pot (Pastron, Gross, and Garaventa 1981, Fig. 9.31; Willetts and Poh 1981, Figs. C9, 71). Brott further attributes it to funeral usage. It is a finely crafted white porcelain containing a hand-painted blue decoration of curved vines with attached pointed leaves and a blossom that some interpret as a sweet pea and others as a spray of prunus. More than any of the other Qing ceramics in Tucson, this pot recalls the Ming blue-on-whites of three earlier centuries. The Tucson specimen came from Level 5 of a trench at TUR 2:1. Chinese utilization of buildings at that location probably ended by 1904 (Figs. 1.3, 1.6, 1.8).

Five cylindrical lidded teapots are in the collection, three of which are covered with bright, small-scale floral and bird

patterns and two of which have a decoration of isolated, large, underglaze blue flowers (Figs. 3.24, 3.25). Shape and decoration are characteristic, as are paired wire bails that remain on three pots (Willetts and Poh 1981, Figs. 185–8, C12–3). The broken end of a spout on one blue and white teapot has a piece of copper pipe inserted into it so that it could continue to function. All but one of these vessels were recovered in or near Ying On rooms. The exception is a polychrome teapot, whose broken spout and cracked rim may have been why it was dumped into a latrine at TUR 3:4. A sixth teapot from TUR 23:8, with long-term Chinese occupation nearby, is unlike the other specimens in shape and decoration (Fig. 3.26). By tradition, generally oolong tea, a semifermented green variety, was prepared in earthenware or porcelain pots, never metal.

Figure 3.27. Nonya Ware mold-made serving bowls, some with faceted sides, are characterized by a green matte interior finish up to about one-fourth inch below the lip and by etched, colorful, polychrome-patterned exteriors. Stylistically descended from early twentieth-century exports, these bowls probably date to the 1920–1930 Ying On compound occupation and perhaps originally were part of the Chee Kung Tong equipment. (Diameters and heights in cm: *a*, 8.7, 3.6; *b*, 15.2, 5.0; *c*, 17.6, 5.0; *d*, 20.2, 5.2; *e*, 8.7, 3.6; *f*, 14.5, 4.2; *g*, 7.0, 3.6; *h*, 20.4, 5.5; *i*, 17.6, 5.6.) Provenience: TUR 22:2 (*c*, *g*, *h*), Unit 2, Room 19 (*a*, *b*, *e*), Room 14 (*f*), Room 11 (*i*), Unit 4, Room 10 (*d*).

A group of ten special serving bowls is distinguished by plain green glazed interiors and colorful overglaze patterns outlined by light engraving on exteriors (Fig. 3.27). Most exterior grounds are white, but one is green. Three of the exterior designs are chickens and foliage. Jenyns (1951, Plates 110, 3B, 3C) illustrates two cups with similar polychrome chicken motifs, which he assigns to the Dao Guajg period (1821–1850). A more typical specimen with symbolic motifs purchased in China was considered by local experts to date around 1875 to 1908 (Fig. 3.22 *right*). Both these dates are too early for the Tucson vessels, all of which came from inside or adjacent to post–1919 Ying On rooms. Few American archaeological reports to date mention more than occasional sherds of this ware (see Praetzellis and Praetzellis 1979: 151).

Figure 3.26. Distinctive teapot from TUR 23:8. The globular contour, squat spout, and arched ceramic handle suggest Euro-American styling, but the porcelain body and upper underglaze blue decoration appear of Chinese workmanship. The tan pebbled lower body and raised overglaze decoration are uncharacteristic of craftsmanship from either source. (Estimated height with lid, 12.6 cm; estimated maximum diameter, 15.2 cm.)

Figure 3.28. Fragrant Flowers and Calling Birds saucers from TUR 22:2. Designs are badly worn because of insufficient overglaze firing or rough use. All bases lack pattern or place of manufacture. (Diameters and heights in cm: *top*, 15.5, 3.0; *center* and *bottom*, 11.5, 2.3.)

Willetts and Poh (1981: 17–20) call the green interior type Nonya Ware, after Chinese women in the Penang, Malacca, and Singapore regions who were primary users of this kind of pottery. It was exported extensively to the China Straits in the decades spanning the turn of the twentieth century. The quality of workmanship seen in Nonya specimens declined thereafter, but these authors believe the ware remained a major trade commodity until the early 1930s. At that time the manufacturing kilns at Jingdezhen were destroyed by the Communists. The careless rendering of glaze and the stereotyped patterns on Tucson examples, in addition to peak occupation of the Ying On structure at that time, indicate a probable date in the 1920s and 1930s.

Modern Tableware or Houseware

Judging from styles and their continued availability in China and through export outlets abroad, the remainder of the ceramic collection from the Ying On rooms may be considered modern or, at least, dating from the post-World War II years.

A vessel series of six specimens has a decoration described by Olsen (1978: 21) from a four-character inscription as Fragrant Flowers and Calling Birds (Figs. 3.28, 3.29). Saucers, a plate, and two forms of bowls are present. An interesting international sharing of design is illustrated in Figure 3.29.

Rice-grain porcelain teacups, rice-soup bowls (Fig. 3.30), spoons and saucers and large, footed, rectangular, overglaze polychrome and underglaze blue bulb planters (Figs. 3.20, 3.31) are other ceramics from Ying On rooms that likely date to the final residency. Rice-grain porcelain is a thin well-potted ware with grain-size holes cut in the body at the leather-hard stage that subsequently fill with translucent glaze. The style is popular in China and in its export markets. In addition to shadows created by the cutting, deep cobalt underglaze diaper or scroll bands at rims and feet of hollow ware and rim bands and center medallions of flatware make a delicate ceramic recalling some Ming blue-on-whites but without the individuality.

Miscellaneous modern ceramics are represented by traditional bowl and spoon forms with diverse decorative treatment involving dragons and often incorporating gilt accents (Figs. 3.32–3.34 *left*). None is plentiful. Not only because of political and social factors was there less contact with Chinese homeland sources, but the number of tenants on the Ying On premises steadily decreased. For example, in 1952 there were 26 men residing there (Schweitzer 1952). By 1968, as demolition was imminent, there were just two elderly men left. Elsewhere, as the surrounding neighborhood

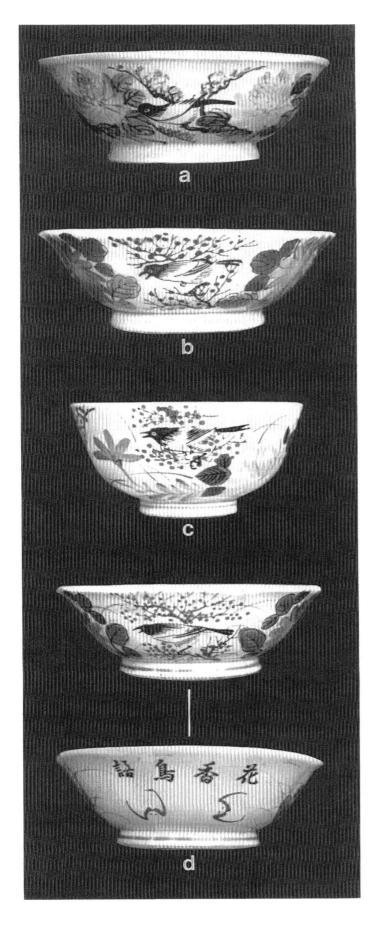

Figure 3.29. Modern Fragrant Flowers and Calling Birds export ware from the Ying On compound demonstrates trans-Pacific diffusion of style. *a*, Plain white interior; opposite exterior side bears a single stylized bat element and no Chinese characters; base marked *Made in China. b*, Interior flower motif; paste harder and colors colder than bowl *a*; opposite side bears two stylized bat elements and no characters; base marked *Japan. c*, Interior flower motif; opposite exterior side has no bat element but does have three Chinese characters; base marked *Made in Los Angeles. d*, Interior flower motif; opposite exterior side (at *bottom*) bears two stylized bat elements and four Chinese characters that translate Fragrant Flowers and Calling Birds; base marked *Made in Los Angeles*. (Diameters and heights in cm: *a*, 17.1, 6.0; *b*, 17.5, 5.7; *c*, 15.7, 5.3; *d*, 17.1, 5.7.) Provenience: TUR 22:2 (*b, d*); 22:2, Unit 1, Room 4 (*a*), Room 11 (*c*).

deteriorated into slums, more mobile Chinese Americans fled to the suburbs.

The final decadence of a long tradition in ceramic domestic vessels came with plastic rice bowls and soup spoons.

Existing records of Chinese-run grocery and general merchandise outlets in Tucson, dating from the early territorial days into the years just prior to the urban renewal efforts, mention Japanese goods being offered for sale. Some possible examples were found in Ying On refuse and in deposits at several Hispanic locales, but they were not common (Fig. 3.34 *center* and *right*).

Foodstuffs Suggesting Ethnic Preference

Much of the day-to-day diet of the Tucson Chinese cannot be reconstructed archaeologically but may be inferred from historical sources. For example, in addition to the commodities suggested to have been in the ceramic, metal, and paper containers, the sojourners surely depended for the major part of their meals on fresh produce, for which tangible evidence is lacking. It is known that during the late 1870s Chinese gardeners who had moved into the vicinity of Tucson began raising a large variety of vegetables, melons, and berries for the local market. They were shrewd enough to see opportunity in the limited amounts of chilies, potatoes, and beans being raised by some Hispanic families. The 1880 census for Tucson listed eight Chinese farmers and five peddlers who sold wagonloads of produce along the town's streets (*Arizona Citizen*, February 7, 1972; U.S. Federal Census 1880). Euro-Americans and Hispanics who did not have their own household gardens and the town's restaurants and saloons were their primary customers. But they also must have supplied their countrymen, some of whom no doubt were relatives, not only with vegetables commonly used by Westerners but kinds more typical of the Orient. By 1900 the number of such gardeners had increased to 36. Most of them were intensively working approximately 150 acres of land rented from Leopoldo Carrillo that were located west of the Santa Cruz River at the foot of Sentinel Peak (Sheridan 1986: 51; Sonnichsen 1982: 112; U.S. Federal Census 1900). After some twenty years, the draining of

Figure 3.30. With characteristic inflexible standardization of pattern and forms, three Rice-grain porcelain vessels from the Ying On compound (TUR 22:2) illustrate table service for a single individual. Such a set normally would include a footed saucer. *Left*, wine cup; *center*, teacup (Unit 2, Room 14); *right*, rice-soup bowl. (Diameters and heights in cm: *left*, 6.7, 5.3; *center*, 8.3, 5.7; *right*, 9.7, 6.8.)

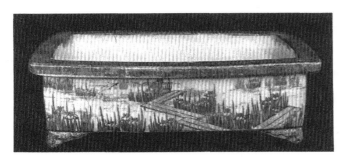

Figure 3.31. A blue underglaze modern bulb bowl with legs, one of three from the Ying On compound (TUR 22:2), is heavy, rectangular, and decorated with an appropriate landscape. Prominent cockspur scars on the interior resulted from stacking during glaze firing with vessels of similar size and shape. Tucson photographers taking Chinese subjects often made background use of such bowls. (Length, 32.1 cm; width, 20.7 cm; height, 10.0 cm.)

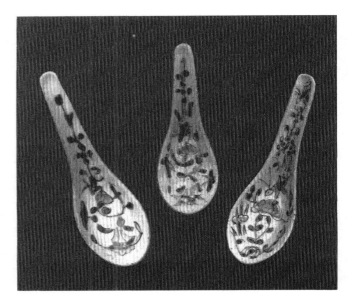

Figure 3.32. Spoons decorated in colorful overglaze floral patterns perhaps derived from Four Seasons. Their bowls, however, are oval, not faceted. (Lengths, 11.2 cm; bowl widths, 4.7 cm; TUR 22:2, Unit 2, Room 13.)

Figure 3.33. Assorted modern porcelains, most with overglaze decorations and a few with gilt accents, were stocked by barrio Chinese stories. *a*, Teacup with exterior dragon motif. *b*, Teacup with brown exterior and underglaze blue on white interior. *c*, Teacup with delicate figural pattern and Chinese characters. *d*, Serving bowl with moldmade, shallowly scalloped walls; interior is plain lustrous white; exterior is decorated in a dark green, blue, and pink floral pattern. *e*, Thin rice-soup bowl with plain white interior; exterior has an orange ground framing two panels containing figural elements, a dragon or phoenix with gold outlines. The base bears a seal translated as *Made in Los Angeles. f*, Rice-soup bowl with plain white interior and exterior decorated with four underglaze blue cormorant motifs. *g*, Rice-soup bowl with underglaze blue florals on exterior. (Diameters and heights in cm: *a*, 7.0, 5.0; *b*, 7.6, 5.6; *c*, 8.3, 5.6; *d*, 19.6, 6.3; *e*, 11.5, 5.7; *f*, 11.5, 6.0; *g*, 12.0, 5.0.) Provenience: TUR 22:2 (*a*, *b*, *e*); 22:2, Unit 2, Room 24 (*d*), Room 11 (*f*); TUR 20:2−2bL2 (*c*); TUR 14:1−2aL2 (*g*).

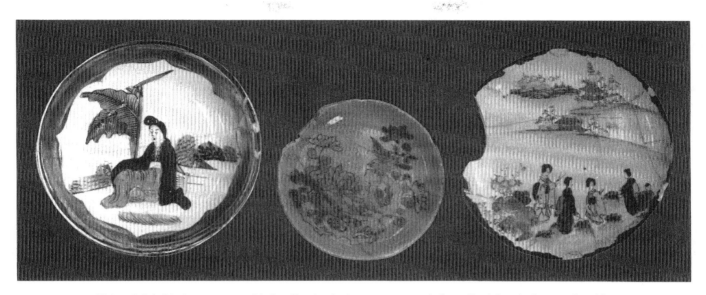

Figure 3.34. Modern saucers with fine-lined polychrome patterns. *Left,* stylized female figure painted in bright red, blue, and green sits under a banana tree, a plant known only to Chinese decorators with knowledge of the southern tropical parts of their country. The scalloped rim border is edged in gilt. The word *CHINA* in red on the base establishes place of manufacture. *Center* and *right,* two saucers with delicate asymmetrical patterns are possible examples of modern Japanese export ceramics; *center* is covered with a pale green glaze. Both came from Hispanic sites in a block where as late as the 1960s a Chinese-run store sold Oriental goods. (Diameters and heights in cm: *left,* 9.5, 2.5; *center,* 7.0, 1.9; *right,* 9.5, 2.5.) Provenience: TUR 22:2, Unit 2, Room 19 (*left*); TUR 38:1–2aL5/6 (*center*), 38:9H–2L4 (*right*).

a lake that stored water and the drop in volume of river flow curtailed agriculture in this area, but plots in the Elysian Grove district on the river's east bank south of town and westward out along the old road to Yuma had been cleared and planted by Chinese. The 1910 census indicated that of a total of 30 Chinese gardeners, 14 had shifted to these districts (U.S. Federal Census 1910). No data are available for Chinese gardening after this time, but it is not likely that the urban Chinese went without fruits and vegetables.

Although meat probably was not consumed daily by the Chinese, the records regarding meat are substantial and reflect food preferences and preparation techniques distinctive from those of the Euro-American and Hispanic host society. No explicit faunal analysis was done on this material, but relevant data were revealed through butchering studies by John Clonts that were undertaken concurrent with the TUR field work (Clonts 1969, 1970, 1971, 1983).

Fish was not a common or popular food among the indigenous population of this desert frontier. However, fish remains were abundant in TUR 2:1 and 69:2, together making up the area of densest Chinese occupation. This distribution is not surprising inasmuch as fish and shellfish, as well as such things as sea slugs, jelly fish, urchins, and eel, always have been a major source of protein in the southern Chinese diet. Myrick (1975: 20) writes that the Chinese railroad crews were so starved for fish that some of them left jobs grading Southern Pacific roadbeds so that they could fish the Colorado River at Yuma. The large size of many of the bones recovered in the above proveniences indicates that salt water fish somehow reached Tucson, stranded inland hundreds of

miles from the ocean. The most likely explanation is that, thanks to the Southern Pacific Railroad, seafood, dried or salted in the typical Chinese way or perhaps packed in ice if fresh, came from California. It is known that local restaurants received fresh oysters and clams by rail and such shells also were found in some proveniences yielding identifiable Chinese artifacts (Figs. 3.35, 3.36). Another immediate source was provided by merchant Chan Tin Wo, who leased nearby Warner Lake for the purpose of raising carp for his Chinese customers (*Arizona Daily Star*, November 1, 1889).

Also abundant in these two deposits were the bones of chicken, another staple in Chinese cuisine. Chickens were common also on Euro-American tables, but the excavated bones had been chopped into small pieces that allowed rapid cooking on a brazier-wok arrangement and easier eating with chopsticks. They were not the usual cuts for American-style fried chicken.

An estimated one-third of the faunal materials recovered in TUR 2:1 and 69:2 were pork bones. Pork is typical in Hispanic dishes such as *posole, chicharrones,* and *picadillo,* but again there were differences from Western methods in the butchering techniques by which these cuts of meat had been processed. Many bore cleaver marks where the pork had been cut into small segments similar to the chicken bones. It is likely that the same Chinese farmers who raised vegetables also raised fowl and pigs for other Chinese engaged in different occupations. Cat remains that had been butchered and land turtle carapaces (Fig. 3.35) suggest the local Chinese consumed other kinds of meat not considered edible by Westerners.

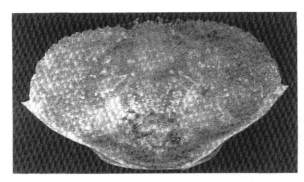

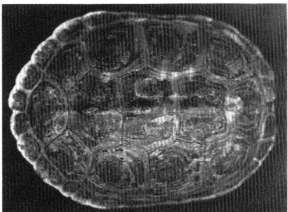

Figure 3.35. Remains of foodstuffs possibly used by Tucson's Chinese residents: *top*, crab shell; *center*, tortoise shell (both from TUR 22:2, Unit 2, Room 15); *bottom*, *left to right*, mussel shells (TUR 14:1–2bL12), clam shells (TUR 2:1–5L5), and oyster shells (TUR 3:4–2aL1, TUR 22:2–2eL2).

The range lands outside of Tucson were becoming an important cattle raising territory in the late nineteenth century, so expectedly there were numerous beef bones present in the deposits at TUR 2:1 and 69:2. Many of the recovered bones were from inexpensive cuts that could have been used in soups and stews suitable to the tastes and pocketbooks of the Chinese. A number of bones from larger cuts may have come from some communal kitchen in the tenement where both Chinese and Hispanics lived, although it is doubtful that the two groups would have eaten together. Perhaps a restaurant serving American-style dishes had been in the vicinity.

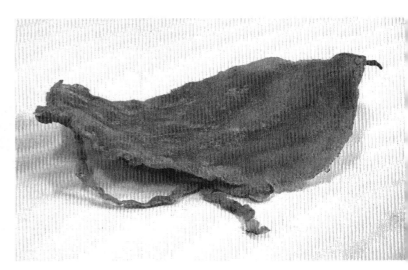

Figure 3.36. Dried jelly fish that may have been intended for a Chinese meal (TUR 22:2, Unit 2, Room 24).

In contrast to TUR 2:1 and 69:2, the various tests in the adjacent TUR Block 3 yielded little or no fish and chicken but quantities of pig bones, including feet. The animals had been butchered in a manner unlike usual Euro-American methods. There were beef bones that came from inexpensive cuts of meat, but also there were bones from the cuts demanding highest prices. Beef feet, a necessary ingredient for making Mexican *menudo*, were common. This assemblage points to both affluence and to a typical regional diet. It may be theorized that the acculturated Chan Tin Wo household had a liking for and could afford a more Westernized menu than the sojourners living in the nearby tenement and that Hispanic neighbors continued eating regional dishes that heavily depended on pork and beef.

Excavations conducted within the Ying On compound reveal similar distinctions. A trench cut through the courtyard yielded an array of fish, including some large salt water species. Finds within the rooms also produced seafood remains (Fig. 3.37). Pork bones, including six whole unborn or very young piglets, made up an estimated 90 percent of the total faunal remains. Suckling pigs were a ceremonial delicacy and could have been the centerpiece of tong functions. Inexpensive cuts of beef were represented, but none of the chops, steaks, and roasts typical of Euro-American or Hispanic diet were observed. On the other hand, latrines that had been sealed before the Chinese moved into the compound produced large amounts of beef bones and some pig bones. Clonts (1970) considers this grouping of remains typical of the barrio Hispanics.

The use of special Chinese seasonings continued to be important (Fig. 3.38).

CLOTHING AND TOILETRIES

Prior to current Westernization of dress, the basic costume for Chinese men and women of all ranks was similar and

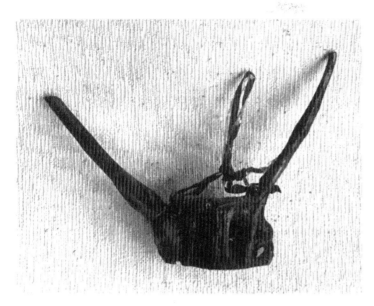

Figure 3.37. A large fish bone tied with red plastic ribbon may have been hung as an ornament (TUR 22:2, Unit 2, Room 15).

Figure 3.38. Brown soy sauce bottle bears the label of a local Chinese tong identified on a 1952 map as at 125 south Meyer Street, just a block south of the Ying On structures, where it was found. Perhaps the tong acquired special soy sauce in bulk and then bottled it for resale (TUR 22:2).

century the fibers used for the masses were hemp or rami; for the elite it was silk. After that time, cotton introduced from India or southeast Asia replaced more costly fibers for common cloth (Bluden and Elvin 1983: 209).

The chief outer garments were untailored, short, full, cotton trousers (*koo*) and a long tunic of cotton or felt buttoned or tied along the right side (*san*). Both were of dark color, most commonly indigo blue. Brighter colors or finer materials could be used for special occasions; such garments worn by women often were embellished by added embroidered or brocaded bands around the bottom of the garment or the sleeve or pant leg edges. Hip-length cotton jackets, frequently padded for warmth, fastened down the front with cloth frogs. Head covering for men was a skull cap with a lower band of contrasting material or, for both sexes, a broader, conical, rice-straw hat for protection from the sun while working in the fields. Footgear consisted of black, flat, white-soled, cloth slippers and white stockings. Special heeled slippers were worn by upper-class women with bound feet, but that deformation custom was outlawed in 1912.

Extensive collections of photographs taken in the late nineteenth century of Chinese at work along the streets of the American West show that for most men this unadorned, uniform set of clothing continued abroad as their typical outfit. This intensified the opinion of many Euro-Americans that since all Chinese dressed alike they all looked alike. However, as some Chinese found employment in rough or high-altitude terrain, they were forced to go to American markets for heavy leather shoes, tighter pants of firmly woven material, and wool coats. Black felt hats likewise added warmth and also allowed the universal, but troublesome, queue to be wound on top of the head under the hat.

Laborers, such as those in the late 1870s who worked their way to Tucson grading the Southern Pacific Railroad bed and laying its tracks, continued wearing traditional clothing, likely with the addition of sturdy footgear when it could be afforded. As the Chinese settled in town, their customary costume readily distinguished them from booted, denim-clad, Stetson-hatted Euro-American contemporaries. Since lower-class male Hispanic clothes also were of coarse cloth and were loose-fitting, the Chinese were less conspicuous among that population. As clothes wore out or the use of American goods became desirable, Chinese men gradually acquired diverse articles of Western dress, although the few women present surely continued to appear in their accustomed styles. At the turn of the twentieth century, many men pictured on required federal papers are outfitted in oddments of Western garb. Nevertheless, traditional clothes were requisite for festive occasions within the Chinese community; it was in these garments that a number of Tucson Chinese men had themselves photographed for family remaining in China (Figs. 1.7, 3.39). This was done to reassure their relatives of their prosperous well-being abroad.

The only articles associated with clothing retrieved from the TUR excavations in Chinese-occupied zones are unidentifiable tatters of leather shoes and some porcelain, shell,

changed very slightly over many centuries (Yarwood 1978: 86; Wilcox 1965, Plate 39; Williams 1960: 86–96). Only richer textiles and more careful construction distinguished the clothing of persons of high status. Until the fourteenth

Figure 3.39. An unidentified Tucson Chinese man in customary festive garb was photographed in the late nineteenth century by pioneer photographer Henry Buehman. He wears silken trousers tied at the ankles, silken hip length tunic, skull cap, cloth slippers, white socks, and holds a fan. A stack of Chinese booklets on the table was considered an appropriate prop. (Courtesy of the Arizona Historical Society, Tucson.)

bone, or metal buttons. All are thought to have been American products perhaps used by Chinese, although some of the buttons could have been on Asian garments. Generally, however, Chinese fasteners were of cloth.

Although many American work shirts and pants, all with telltale signs of hard and long-term daily use, were found draped on pegs, suspended on wire hangers in the Ying On rooms, or dumped with other trash, some diagnostic Chinese clothing was discovered packed away. Labels on a few of these articles confirm their manufacture either in China proper, in Hong Kong, or in Chinese American shops. It is possible that some articles were forty years old or more when retrieved; they had been infrequently used in association or tong functions and had been handled carefully. Expectedly, these customary garments were of somber colors or white, of silken blends or cotton materials, and generally were sewn by hand or had hand-finished detailing.

Two pairs of hand-sewn, light-weight Chinese trousers in the collection are of similar style and were fashioned from six pieces of fabrics that appear to be a combination of silk or synthetic fibers and cotton (Fig. 3.40c). Short, broad legs are attached to a pieced cotton crotch and wide waistband that likely was folded down over a cloth tie or girdle. They do not have a center placket. The trousers worn by the individual in Figure 3.39 are tied at the ankles, but the pants in this collection have no evidence of ties. In China, both pant versions were used contemporaneously by females and males (Yarwood 1978: 86). The lengths of these particular pants, including the wide waistband, differ greatly, one being 95 cm and the other only 76 cm. Whether that longer length indicates a taller user or a tied style is not clear. Waist widths are more similar, at 56 cm and 54 cm.

One short-sleeve, cotton-and-silk blend, white shirt and three long-sleeve, silk, white shirts with French cuffs represent an incipient adaptation of Western style, since shirts were not on earlier inventories of Chinese apparel. Of different cut than Western prototypes, their neat hand finishing with flat-felled seaming is characteristic. All have very narrow yokes. Long shirt tails could have been tucked inside trousers, but ordinarily Chinese upper garments were worn loosely outside of pant tops. The wide waistbands of different material and color on the Chinese pants suggest that when shirts were worn inside of trouser tops, the trousers most likely were Western.

Three shirts are finished at the neck with a modified horizontal band, or Mandarin collar, requiring a stud-button closure and are fastened two-thirds of the way down the front with four or five mother-of-pearl buttons. The yoke label on one reads *Manufacture Mee Woo Co*; the interior facing of the collar is stamped *26 539HK*, indicating a factory in Hong Kong. Except for being made of white brocaded silk with floral and bird patterns, the fourth shirt most closely resembles usual Western models, with pointed collar, a full placket with seven glass buttons down the center front, and a pair of flapped, buttoned pockets. It has a label reading *George Wing & Co. 627 Jackston St. San Francisco, Cal.* Modest size variation in the four shirts reflects the notable physical uniformity of the south Chinese adult male or perhaps a single owner. Shirts are from 39.5 cm to 44.0 cm across the shoulders. Full-sleeve length ranges from 60.0 cm to 67.5 cm; short-sleeve length is 38.0 cm.

Three light-weight cotton jackets and one hand-quilted cotton jacket were made by the same T-shaped pattern that called for two main pieces of fabric draped over, rather than stitched at, the shoulders (Figs. 3.40b, 3.41 *left*). Seaming occurs up the sides and out sleeve interiors and down the center back. The front is finished and equipped with frog closures. Sleeves are straight. All jackets have Mandarin collars, four patch pockets, and side vents. Two light jackets are shiny, dark brown, with lighter brown interiors; one is black with a subtle stripe. The quilted example is black, with a blue and white lining. Sewing was done by hand and interior seams were flat-felled. The four jackets vary in

Figure 3.40. Articles of Chinese male clothing from TUR 22:2. *a*, Black, silk skull cap made of six triangular pieces and a lower band. The lining is red cotton with a stamped label reading *6 Made in China*. The cap is believed to have belonged to one of the last tenants of the building (Unit 3, Room 2, in a box on the floor). *b*, Hand sewn, black, unlined cotton jacket, with Mandarin collar, patch pockets, seven frog closures, and side vents. (Length, 67.5 cm; length from center back to sleeve edge, 75.0 cm.) *c*, Hand sewn, blue-gray, silk pants. A wide waist band of white cotton folded over a separate tie. (Length, including waist band, 76 cm; width at waist, 54 cm.) *d*, Pair of fiber scuffs trimmed with wrapped cord and black edging and lined with fiber inner sole, cotton, paper, and pink silk; outer sole is leather. (Length, 26 cm; width, 9 cm; Unit 2, Room 14.) *e*, Typical, round-toed, flat-soled, black damask slippers reserved for dress wear are lined with white cotton and have a leather sole and low heel. Stamped inside each slipper is *Made in China*, accompanied by several Chinese characters. (Length, 26.5 cm; width, 8.5 cm; Unit 4, Room 11; Arizona State Museum photo by Helga Teiwes.)

Figure 3.41. Articles of Chinese male clothing from TUR 22:2. *Left*, hand sewn and quilted black cotton waist-length jacket, with blue and white striped lining, Mandarin collar, seven cloth frogs, four patch pockets, side vents, and tasseled cord tie. (Jacket length, 69 cm; length from center back to sleeve edge, 73 cm; cord tie length, 222 cm; Unit 4, Room 10.) *Right*, hand sewn, gray-blue silk, ankle-length robe with Mandarin collar, patch pockets, four frog closures at right side and two at neck, and side vents. Label with Chinese characters is sewn in neck. (Length, 124 cm; Unit 4, Room 12, trunk.) Three square white silk handkerchiefs with hemstitched edges (*on robe*) are 50 cm by 50 cm. Small, gray, brocaded silk coin purse with scallop-edged flap secured by a glass button is bound around edges with green piping and has a blue lined interior divided into three compartments (6.3 cm by 8.0 cm; Unit 4, Room 9). (Arizona State Museum photo by Helga Teiwes.)

length from 67.5 cm to 70.5 cm; center of back to end of sleeve is 73.0 cm to 75.0 cm. Again, the sizes hint of a prevailing physical uniformity of wearers.

One ankle-length (124 cm), hand sewn robe of grayish blue silk is made by the same uncomplicated T-shaped pattern as the jackets and represents a common counterpart to the richly embellished, but basically identical, robes favored by Qing court officials (Fig. 3.41 *right*). A single length of cloth reaches over each shoulder and is sewn together at the body sides and down the inside of the sleeves. The wider left side folds diagonally in front over the right and is closed with two frogs at the neck and four frogs under the arm at the right seam line. Side slits from hem line, Mandarin collar, and a right-side patch pocket finish this special garment. An untranslated neck-band label with Chinese characters may identify the maker.

Feet accustomed to soft cloth slippers must have regarded hard-soled, American leather shoes as binding and hot in Tucson's desert climate. It is not surprising to find that indoors Ying On tenants resorted to cooler, less restrictive, flat scuffs that covered only the toe area. Three badly worn, insect-eaten pairs were retrieved from Rooms 5 and 12 in Unit 1 and from Room 14 in Unit 2 of the Chee Kung Tong lodge. The pair from Unit 2 was of woven fiber, with inner sole of layered cotton, paper, and pink silk (Fig. 3.40*d*) and would have qualified as the specified grass slippers needed by recruits, according to Chesneaux (1971, Fig. 6) and Schlegel (1974: 120). Another pair has an imitation reddish leather upper portion, a lining of white cotton cloth, and a rubber sole. The leather inner sole is stamped *Hop Sang Shoes FTY 195 Fook Wah St. 4th FL Kowloon, Hong Kong*. The third pair of scuffs, with a single lower foot strap rather than a complete enclosed toe area, was homemade from diamond-treaded rubber boots that had been cut away and beveled to fit. Traditional stiff, brocaded, black silk slippers apparently continued to be used for rare dress occasions. One relatively unworn pair from Unit 4, Room 11 bears a *Made in China* stamp accompanied by some Chinese characters (Fig. 3.40*e*).

Two pillbox caps identical to the one worn by the Tucson Chinese man in Figure 3.39 were recovered in rooms of Units 3 and 4 of the Ying On compound (Fig. 3.40*a*). Made of six triangular panels and two exterior bands, they are of black polished cotton and silk. One is lined with red cotton and is stamped *6 Made in China*. The other sports a red band around the bottom and a red crown pompon, which, among upper-class men in the homeland, would have been replaced by an ornament and feather to indicate rank (Yarwood 1978: 88).

Among minor accessories in the TUR clothing collection are three square white silk handkerchiefs with hemstitched edges (Fig. 3.41 *on robe*). A small rectangular coin purse is of gray brocade with an embroidered floral pattern lined with blue silk (Fig. 3.41 *on robe*). Purses of this sort were cus-

Figure 3.42. Accessories and toiletries from TUR 22:2. *Top*, wooden back scratcher with long carved handle and five teeth has a cord tied through the distal end of the handle for suspension (length, 4.5 cm; width, 2.8 cm). *Center*, round comb carved from a single piece of wood had cracked and been mended by wire wrapped around an exterior groove. The circular shape of this comb may have made it useful for grooming the queue (height, 3.3 cm; diameter, 6.0 cm; Unit 2, Room 19). *Bottom*, black paper fan with narrow interior bamboo ribs and lacquered, heavier, outer bamboo ribs inset with three pieces of mother-of-pearl and carved with Chinese characters (length of ribs, 22.2 cm; Unit 4, Room 14). (Arizona State Museum photo by Helga Teiwes.)

tomarily a man's, rather than a woman's, dress article (Williams 1960: 95). A soiled, worn, 18-rib, folding fan also is similar to that in Figure 3.39. Peacock feather fans and stiff, circular fans are known in China from early dynastic periods, but the folding model, with outer guard sticks and inner ribs attached to a handle, is believed to have been a Japanese innovation reintroduced in the tenth or eleventh century (Williams 1960: 174). It became an immediate success with both sexes as a symbol of one of the Taoist Eight Immortals, as a device to emphasize speech, and as a practical way to stir the air. White fans were a recognition sign and occasional talisman among the Hong Men (Schlegel 1974: 220). Women's fans typically had more than 30 ribs, while those for men were coarser with 8 to 24 ribs (Williams 1960: 174). Fans were so important that eight different types of Chinese fans are on a list of items imported into San Francisco in the

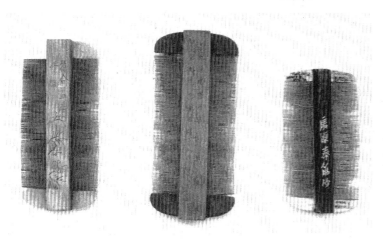

Figure 3.43. Double-edged wooden combs with incised or painted Chinese characters from TUR 22:2 (*left* and *center*, Unit 2, Room 10; *right*, Unit 3, Room 2).

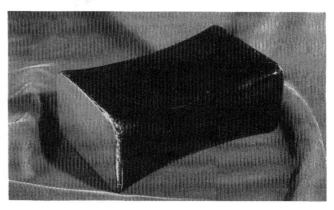

Figure 3.44. Pillow or head rest with a hard surface of black and red lacquer that had been damaged by rough usage and desert aridity. The slightly flexible pillow is rectangular with concave long edges to support the neck of the user. Labels on one end bear Chinese characters and the words *Made in China*. Several home-made wooden pillows in the shape of a low footstool were recovered in abandoned rooms. (Length, 20.7 cm; width, 13.4 cm; height, 9.0 cm; TUR 22:2, Unit 2, Room 13; Arizona State Museum photo by Helga Teiwes.)

decade of the 1850s (Giles and Layton 1986). Fans were carried tucked in voluminous sleeves or waistbands, but in photographs they were mere accessories denoting a cultured person.

Other diagnostic Chinese items for personal grooming are combs, and one round, large-toothed, wooden comb and five straight, double-edged wooden combs were recovered (Figs. 3.42, 3.43). Also found was a long-handled, wooden back scratcher (Fig. 3.42). Comparable articles still are readily available in modern China.

HOUSEWARES

Other than articles used for culinary purposes, characteristic Chinese house furnishings are notably absent from the Tucson collections. Undoubtedly such items are scarce because the occupants of the Ying On compound were impoverished single males just existing day to day with whatever furniture or substitutes for furniture were at hand. Their interest in orientalism may be presumed to have waned over the years. Three portable objects that had been acquired from Chinese sources are a lacquered pillow; a lacquered, canvas-covered trunk; and a painted, compartmentalized box (Figs. 3.44–3.46). Trunks and suitcases were necessary for men who were destined to travel periodically back and forth across the Pacific or who typically lived in quarters lacking storage facilities. The TUR trunk specimen seems too elaborate for the usual steerage passage taken by most of the sojourners. It probably was used by a later, more prosperous compound resident. The fact that the pillow and box came from the same room hints at a resident still emotionally attached to the culture of his homeland or one blessed with family or friends who gave him characteristic gifts to cheer him in his distant home-away-from-home.

Figure 3.45. Large, rectangular, wooden trunk covered with heavy paper that had been lacquered a reddish brown color. A fitted canvas cover encases the trunk, with slots for the brass handles and latch. The lid cover is secured by two buttons on the front and one at each side that fasten through buttonhole straps attached to the basal cover. A partial, illegible shipping label is glued to the top surface of the cover. Because of heavy use, age, and Southwestern aridity, the lacquered surface is in bad repair. (Length, 63.0 cm; width, 41.0 cm; height, 34.5 cm; TUR 22:2, Unit 2, Room 2; Arizona State Museum photo by Helga Teiwes.)

Figure 3.46. Wooden, octagonal box with fitted lid and eight removable, trapezoidal, inner trays surrounding a larger center tray. The exterior ground is painted with gold, over which are fine-lined motifs of two human figures seated in a pavilion, leaves, and scrolls executed in black. Interior compartments are red on interiors and black on exteriors. Such boxes may have been used for jewelry or other small personal items. (Diameter, 28.2 cm; height, 9.5 cm; TUR 22:2, Unit 2, Room 13; Arizona State Museum photo by Helga Teiwes.)

A brass padlock of the type still made to close dowry trunks of Chinese brides is one of the few nonceramic objects found in a Hispanic house, a two-story adobe at 114 south Meyer Street (Fig. 3.47).

ARTIFACTS ASSOCIATED WITH WRITING

The so-called four treasures of Chinese literary endeavors are paper, ink, ink-slab, and brush. The Chinese are credited with the invention of paper (C. Lee 1975; Nakata 1983; Williams 1960), and one of their interesting contributions is the development of a paper made of rice straw. Solid ink (*mo*) made of lamp black is mixed with varnish, gum, pork fat, musk, or camphor and is molded into flat cakes or round sticks. Its black color corresponds to the yin of the yin-yang dichotomy of Chinese cosmology. When needed, triturated ink was moistened with water in a well scooped in the middle of a smoothed stone or ceramic palette. Certain qualities of stone were preferred in order to enhance the beauty of the ink. More recently for routine writing or record keeping, the palette has been replaced by a simple glass plate inside the lid of a metal ink container. Calligraphic writing is executed with a brush of smooth, straight, animal hairs tied together and inserted into a length of bamboo. Brush thickness and pliability are determined by the intended type of message. For example, a wool brush held vertically makes a bold line suitable for posters or banners; a rabbit hair brush produces a more delicate line for letter writing. Other hairs used came from dogs, deer, foxes, mice, and camels.

The laborers who came to Tucson and continued to follow manual or domestic lines of work are believed to have been illiterate, but those who aspired to advancement through small businesses surely possessed some basic reading, writing, and accounting skills. Probably they served as scribes for uneducated countrymen, whose only means of remaining in touch with family and friends in China was through letters. It is assumed that as unskilled laborers gradually were eliminated from the immigration process, Chinese with writing abilities became more numerous. Literacy of at least some Ying On tenants and their continued use of painted calligraphic writing are demonstrated by finds of 11 camel's hair writing brushes with bamboo handles, 3 metal and 1

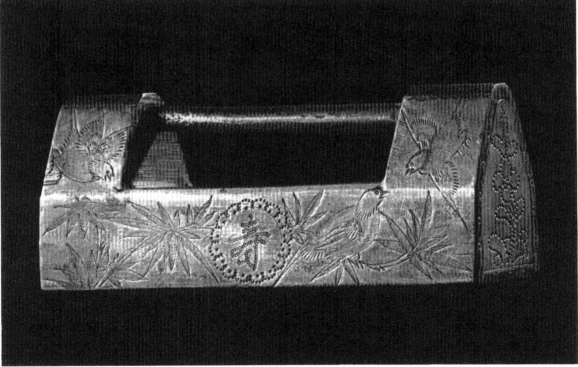

Figure 3.47. Padlock made of brass over a wooden frame in a style typically used to seal dowry trunks (shown enlarged). *Top*, engraved male and female courtly figures with three central inscription roundels meaning luck and double happiness. *Bottom*, opposite side bearing engraved motifs of three flying or perching birds with foliage and central inscription roundel meaning longevity. (Length, 8.2 cm; width, 2.2 cm; height, 3.5 cm; TUR 26:1, Room 12, on door of west wall; Arizona State Museum photos by Helga Teiwes.)

Figure 3.48. Writing tools and supplies from TUR 22:2. *a*, Seal with Chinese characters reading *Zu Sun Qi Gong Tang* (Tucson Chee Kung Tong) carved in relief on the face of a hard, fine-grained wooden block. The single Chinese character *Shang* (up) appears on the opposite surface. The worn carving and red and black ink smears confirm substantial usage. *b*, Tiny, lidded, brown-glazed stoneware jar for solid ink. The flat lid fits flush onto an upper unglazed flange of the base. Base of the jar exhibits molded Chinese characters. *c*, Oval brass box with copper base that contained solidified ink. The interior of the delicately etched, tightly fitting lid was equipped with a glass slab on which a bit of the black ink could be mixed with water to make a suitable writing medium. Some dried ink residue remains in the box bottom. Chinese characters and *China* are stamped on the base. *d*, Circular brass and copper box for solid ink. The fine-lined, etched, floral pattern on the lid exterior and the polished metal container reflect the Chinese high regard for writing skills. *e*, A small wooden seal with three Chinese characters carved in relief that translate as *Li Ye-Yang*, probably the name of an individual. The block surface is stained with red ink. Such personal seals are common accoutrements used to identify documents and other possessions. *f*, A squarish wooden seal with two carved characters on the face and a stamped *Shang* on the opposite surface to indicate orientation. The inscription characters are *Sheng Cai*, meaning Bear Wealth in archaic seal script. *g*, Two camel-hair brushes used for calligraphic writing. One has incised Chinese characters down the bamboo handle and an ink-hardened tip. A bamboo cap that fit over the distal end to protect the bristles was found in place on the brush at right. (Lengths, heights, and widths in cm: *a*, 10.7, 4.5, 3.4; *e*, 4.0, 4.1, 1.5; *f*, 2.5, 3.5, 1.6; *c*, length 5.3, height 3.9; *g*, average length, 21.4. Diameters and heights in cm: *b*, 4.0, with lid 3.1; *d*, 4.6, 2.0.) Provenience: TUR 22:2, Unit 2, Room 14 (*a*), Room 27 (*b*), Room 19 (*c*), Room 1 (*f*); Unit 4, Room 11 (*d*, *e*, *g*, one brush), Room 7 (*g*, one brush). (Arizona State Museum photo by Helga Teiwes.)

Figure 3.49. Bottle of liquid ink, used with pens for Western scripts, has a label reading *Writting ink   5½ ounces   Jab Tai Choom   Made in Hong Kong*. Only the Chinese name is visible in this photograph. (Height, 10 cm; TUR 22:2, Unit 3, Room 3.)

ceramic ink boxes (Fig. 3.48*b–d*, *g*), containers of liquid ink (Fig. 3.49), and three wooden seals possibly used with ink or a stamp pad to indicate ownership (Fig. 3.48*a*, *e*, *f*). Further supporting evidence for literacy is shown by the numerous personal letters, business and legal documents, and various medical tracts that were in the debris (Fig. 3.56).

ARTIFACTS ASSOCIATED WITH MEDICINAL PRACTICES

Chinese folk medicine is at the same time pharmaceutical, philosophical, and superstitious. More than three thousand remedial agents drawn from the full gamut of the faunal and floral environment comprise its inventory. Vegetal substances such as roots, herbs, leaves, berries, barks, and teas, processed in prescribed ways into powders, pills, salves, oils, or infusions, are regarded as efficacious for certain ailments. Fennel is considered good for hernias or eye catarrhs; soy bean curd for jaundice; teas (picked after the year's first thunderstorm) for colds, headaches, dysentery, or weak eyes; ginseng root (dug only at midnight of a full moon) for asthma, insomnia, dizziness, depression, impotence, or weaknesses of old age. Animal parts like deer antlers, shark fins, snake flesh, or cuttlefish ink are taken for other conditions. To further assure proper results, charms are written in blood, burned, and the remains are swallowed in tea.

Despite a diet generally regarded as comparatively nutritious, crowded unsanitary living conditions of the peasantry and high infant mortality make concern with health universal. Medicines, however, generally are viewed as preventive rather than curative, and they are involved with balances requisite to the yin-yang concept. Yin is associated with the body's interior, yang with the body's surface (Melzer 1969; Wallnofer and von Rottauscher 1965).

Inevitably as Chinese went abroad, they took along the medicines on which they heavily depended. If they did not personally carry these substances, they acquired them through suppliers, such as the three Chinese doctors and three druggists present in Tucson in 1900 (U.S. Federal Census 1900). Glass medicine vials recovered through excavation and a wide assortment of other glass containers, tins, jars, and paper packets, as well as various plant materials considered to have medicinal properties, were found at the Ying On house. They indicate the local Chinese remained loyal wherever possible to the traditional remedies (Figs. 3.50–3.56, Table 3.1).

Glass medicine vials of comparable style to those illustrated in Figure 3.51 have been reported from Aptos, Donner Summit, Riverside, San Francisco, and Ventura in California and Virginia City in Nevada (Evans 1980: 93; Pastron, Prichett, and Ziebarth 1981, Vol. 3: 317, Fig. 7.27; Whitlow 1981: 48, Fig. 14).

The recovery of ginseng root and branches (*Panas ginseng*) shows that the plant continued to be popular among the elderly men at the Ying On compound. When made into an extract with dried orange peel, also found in Ying On refuse, ginseng was the basis for a common sedative. Ginseng was therapeutically valuable in other ways and was also prepared into powders, broths, extracts, or pastes mixed with honey.

It may be significant that the living quarters of the final two occupants yielded only one example of these medicinal containers. The remainder were scattered throughout rooms in all units that had been lived in earlier.

ARTIFACTS ASSOCIATED WITH RECREATION

Games

As long as foreign observers have been allowed in China they have commented on the fondness of the Chinese for a variety of games. Still today, while bicycle, cart, and truck traffic swarms by, groups of men may be seen huddled around sidewalk tables intent upon some such group activity.

The Chinese sojourners and settlers in the American West, lonely and with time on their hands, found games accompanied by betting a major recreational outlet. Financial losses suffered may have contributed to extensions of time overseas, but the companionship and intensity of feelings engendered by the activity reinforced the common ethnic bonds of the participants, while further isolating them from their surroundings. Because the Euro-American world around them was similarly engrossed in games of chance, Chinese transfer of their own gambling behavior from the homeland to the new environment was not suppressed. In fact, it was a frequent source of municipal tax revenue. However, when gambling was outlawed in 1907 for the Arizona citizenry at large (Bret Harte 1980: 89), Chinese secret continuation of this pastime, often carried on in places with illegal opium smoking, became a source of trouble for police. The *Tucson Daily and Weekly Citizen* of July 26, 1909, reported a raid on a "gambling den" in the Chinese quarter and the arrest of 26 men. However, games and betting associated with them continued through the period of this study.

According to Culin (1891: 196), the usual gambling games of the overseas Chinese were dominoes, fantan, and a lottery called in Cantonese *pak hop siu*. Possible evidence for all three, plus playing cards, mah-jongg markers, and Chinese chess (or elephant checkers) were found during the TUR research (Figs. 3.57–3.60). Also noted were pieces of dried orange peel that, in addition to their use in medicinal preparations, were kept in boxes with buttons serving as gambling tokens to bring good luck (Culin 1891: 15).

Recovered related documents include gambling account books for unidentified games from 1924 through 1926, an unidentified Chinese chess account book for 1935 and another dated 1937 from the Yeh Yeh Company, and eight domino receipt books for 1934. A notation in one of the books states that proceeds from the games were earmarked for the making of a bronze idol (University of Arizona Library, Special Collections, TUR manuscript collection).

Figure 3.50. Containers of Chinese medicinal preparations: *a*, cardboard box and packet of a mixture of red tea, spearmint, and licorice; *b*, glass bottle with cork; *c*, glass bottle of pills with wood stopper; *d*, cardboard box that had contained a plastic medicine vial; *e*, cardboard box with identical English and Chinese inscriptions; *f*, glass bottle of brown powder with wooden stopper; *g*, glass bottle of red pills with wooden stopper; *h*, small pressed metal can; *i*, cardboard box. Table 3.1 identifies contents, manufacturer, and provenience. (Arizona State Museum photo by Helga Teiwes.)

Figure 3.51. Chinese glass medicine vials that were made as tubes, then were dipped into molten glass and shaped on a hard surface to produce a rectangular form in the gather. Sheared necks of various lengths resulted from the vial being snapped off the tube (Brott 1982: 58). Bottles appear to have been sealed with corks. Color varies from aqua to off-white. Contents were probably linaments, nose and ear drops, and other liquid medicines. (Heights in cm: *a*, *c*, 6.4; *b*, 6.5; *d*, 6.3; *e*, 5.7; *f*, 4.3.) Provenience: TUR 69:2–L2 (*a*), 69:2–L1 (*f*); TUR 22:2–2bL2 (*b*); TUR 3:4–3aL6 (*c*), 3:4–3aL11 (*d*), 3:4–3aL2 (*e*).

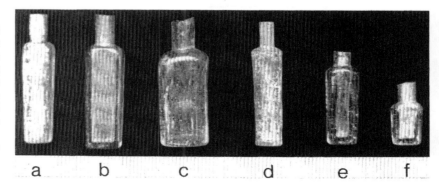

Table 3.1. Identification of Containers of Medicinal Preparations shown in Figure 3.50
(Translations by John W. Olsen)

Item	Name	Manufacturer or owner of pharmacy	Purpose of medicine	Provenience
Figure 3.50:				
a	*Luk Wo Char* (Spring of Dragon Tea)	Mee Chun Tea Co., Ltd. Lau Tak Chee, Toy Shan City, Canton (Guangzhou), China, distributed through Hong Kong	Sedative, relief of coughs, throat irritation	TUR 22:2, Unit 2, Room 22
b	*Er Liu Er* (Two Six Two)	Yao Hua Pharmacy, Shanghai, China	Cures "72 dangerous diseases," particularly plague, tuberculosis, and various infants' diseases	TUR 22:2, Unit 3, Room 2
c	*Sha? Qi Wan Ling Dan* (Sunstroke Efficient Pills?)	Ma Bai-liang, Fozhen, Guangdong, China	Relief of sunstroke, cholera, fever	TUR 22:2, Unit 2, Room 11
d	*Bao Ji Wan* (Pills of Relief)	Packed in Taibei, Taiwan province, China	Summer cold, vomiting, fever, headache, travel sickness, cholera, drunkenness, cure-all	TUR 22:2, Unit 4, Room 11
e	Longjing Tea* (Before rainwater, second solar period tea)	Referred to as Lung Chin Tea on box, selected by Tack Kee and Co., no place of packaging		TUR 22:2, Unit 4, Room 8
f	(Illegible first character) *Zhi Tong San* (? Stop-ache Powder)	Yong Shou Tang, Guangzhou and Shanghai, China. Owner of pharmacy: Su Rui-sheng		TUR 22:2, Unit 2, Room 18
g	*Li Zhi Du Tong Wan* (Pills for Immediate Cure of Stomach Ache)	Yong Shou Tang, Guangzhou and Shanghai, China. Owner of pharmacy: Su Rui-sheng		Unknown
h	*Wan Jin You* (Tiger Balm)	Inscribed "Made in China"	Relief of symptoms of rheumatoid arthritis, colds, general cure-all	TUR 22:2, Unit 3, Room 3
i	*Zhu Po Hong Ling Yao Gao* (Pearl and Amber Red Efficient Medicinal Salve)	Ji Chun Tang Pharmacy, Guangzhou and Hong Kong, China; Luo Zhi-ting, owner	For skin irritation, "muscular rot," to relieve aches, remove poison, regenerate muscle	Unknown

*Longjing refers to Dragon Well tea, a particular variety from Hangzhou, Zhejiang, China.

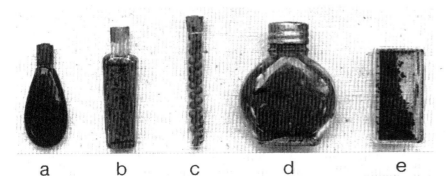

Figure 3.52. Containers for various Chinese medicines from TUR 22:2: *a*, dark green, tear-shaped, glass bottle and stopper, dry powder inside; *b*, empty, green, rectangular, glass vial with label; *c*, tube with cork containing red seeds; *d*, globular, clear glass bottle with metal cap containing dark granular substance; *e*, black granular substance found in a cloth pouch bearing name of Huie Bean Yuen Co., Vernon, Texas. (Heights in cm: *a*, 5.0; *b*, 6.3; *c*, 6.5; *d*, 6.3.) Provenience: Unit 4, Room 6 (*a*), Room 1 (*b*); Unit 2, Room 17 (*c*), Room 19 (*d*), Room 16 (*e*).

Figure 3.53. Paper boxes that had contained Chinese medicinal products, from TUR 22:2. *Left*, box for tiny pills with ingredients described as gallstone, musk, pearl, toad secretions, and other effective Chinese drugs (Unit 3, Room 3). *Center*, box of China Products Company containing Chon Lee, a pill prepared from pressed tangerine and said to be effective for tiredness and as an appetizer (Unit 2, Room 21). *Right*, box of Lam Chon Char tea from the Tin Fook Tong (Unit 3, Room 3).

Figure 3.54. Plant materials thought by Chinese to have medicinal properties, from TUR 22:2: *left*, dried opium poppy pod (Unit 2); *center*, dried orange peel (Unit 2, Room 5); *right*, ginseng root (Unit 4, Room 11).

Figure 3.55. Lidded, footed ginseng steamer of opaque porcelain with exterior underglaze landscape decoration in two shades of blue. The stand of strap metal appears to be homemade. Its three supporting legs and open basal area permitted the pot to be warmed above an open flame. Whether its recovery in the former Chee Kung Tong room has any sociological significance is unknown. (Diameter, 7.4 cm; jar height, 10.1 cm; TUR 22:2, Unit 2, Room 14.)

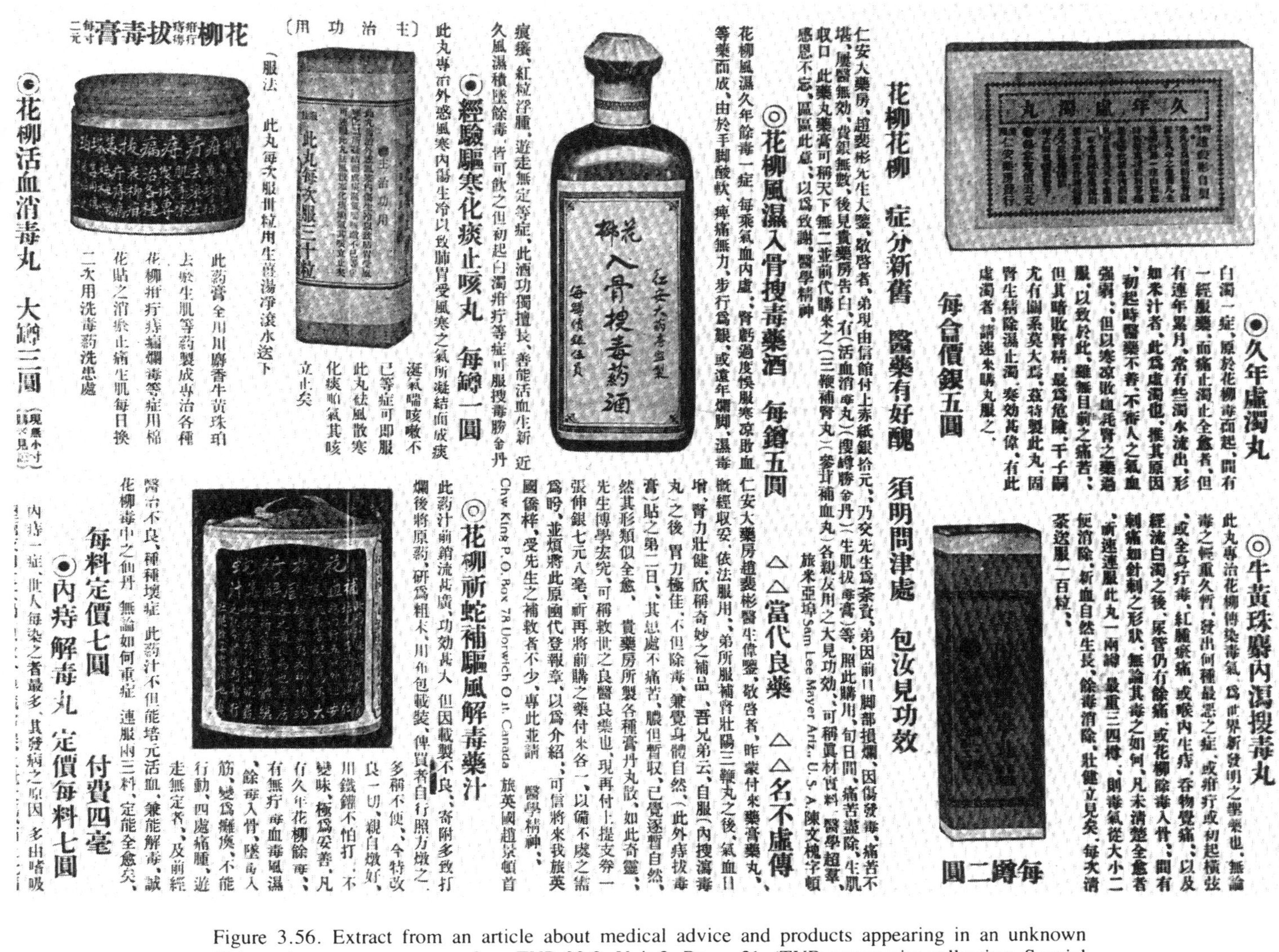

花柳花柳　症分新舊　醫藥有好醜　須明問津處　包汝見功效

◉久年虛濁丸

白濁一症，原於花柳毒而起，間有一經服藥，而痛止濁止全愈者，但有連年累月，常有些濁水流出，形如米汁者，此爲虛濁也，推其原因，初起時醫藥不善，不審人之氣血強弱，但以寒凉敗血耗腎之藥過服，以致於此，雖無目前之痛苦，但其暗敗腎精，最爲危險，千子嗣尤有關系莫大焉，茲特製此丸，固腎生精除濕止濁，奏効甚偉，有此虛濁者，請速來購丸服之、

每合價銀五圓

◎牛黃珠麝內瀉搜毒丸

此丸專治花柳傳染毒氣，爲世界新發明之聖藥也，無論毒之輕重久暫，發出何種最惡之症，或疳疔或初起橫弦，或全身疔毒，紅腫瘀痛，或喉內生瘡，吞物覺痛，以及經流白濁之後，尿管仍有餘痛，或花柳餘毒入骨，間有刺痛如針刺之形狀，無論其毒之如何，凡未清楚全愈者，祈速速服此丸一兩罇，最重三四罇，則毒氣從大小二便消除，新血自然生長，餘毒消除，壯健立見矣，每次清茶送服一百粒、

每罇二圓

仁安大藥房，趙裴彬先生大鑒，敬啓者，弟現由信館付上赤紙銀拾元、乃交先生爲茶資，弟因前日脚部損爛，因傷發毒，痛苦不堪，屢醫無効，費銀無數，後見貴藥房告白，有（活血消毒丸）（搜毒勝金丹）（生肌拔毒膏）等，照此購用，旬日間，痛苦盡除，生肌收口 此藥丸藥膏可稱天下無二，並前代購來之（三鞭補腎丸）（蔘茸補血丸）各親友用之大見功効，可稱眞材實料，醫學超羣，感恩不忘，區區此意，以爲致謝，醫學精神

旅米亞埠 Sam Lee Mayer Ariz., U.S.A. 陳文槐字頓

◎花柳風濕入骨搜毒藥酒　每罇五圓

花柳風濕久年餘毒一症，每乘氣血內虛，腎虧過度，恢服寒涼敗血等藥而成，由於手脚酸軟，痺痛無力，步行爲艱，或遠年爛脚，濕毒瘡瘍，紅粒浮腫，遊走無定等症，此酒功獨擅長，善能活血生新 近久風濕積墜餘毒，皆可飲之，但初起白濁疳疔等症可服搜毒勝金丹

△△當代良藥　△△名不虛傳

仁安大藥房趙裴彬醫生偉鑒，敬啓者，昨蒙付來藥膏藥丸、概經收妥，依法服用，弟所服補腎壯陽三鞭丸之後，氣血日增，腎力壯健，欣稱奇妙之補品，吾兄弟云，自服（內搜瀉毒丸）之後，胃力極佳，不但除毒，兼覺身體自然，（此外痔拔毒膏）貼之第二日，其患處不痛苦，膿但暫收，已覺逐暫自然，然其形類似全愈，貴藥房所製各種膏丹丸散，如此奇靈，先生博學宏究，可稱救世之良醫良藥也，現再付上提支券一張伸銀七元八毫，祈再將前購之藥付來各一，以備不虞之需爲盼，並煩將此原函代登報章，以爲介紹，可信將來我旅英國僑梓，受先生之補救者不少，專此並請 醫學精神，

Chw King P.O. Box 78 Uorwich O it. Canada 旅英國趙景頓首

◉經驗驅寒化痰止咳丸　每罇一圓

（主治功用）此丸專治外感風寒內傷生冷以致肺胃受風寒之氣所凝結而成痰涎氣喘咳嗽不已等症可即服此丸祛風散寒化痰順氣其咳立止矣

（服法 此丸每次服卅粒用生薑湯淨滾水送下

花柳 疳疔 痔瘡 拔毒膏 每寸二元

此藥膏全用川麝香牛黃珠珀去腐生肌等葯製成專治各種花柳疳疔痔瘡爛毒等症用棉花貼之消瘀止痛生肌每日換二次用洗毒葯洗患處

◉花柳活血消毒丸　大罇三圓（現無小寸）

◎花柳祈蛇補驅風解毒藥汁

此藥汁前銷流甚廣，功効甚大 但因載製不良，寄附多致打爛後將原葯，研爲粗末，用布包載裝，俾買者自行照方燉之，多稱不便，今特改良一切，親自燉好，用鐵罐不怕打，不變味，極爲妥善，凡有久年花柳餘毒，有無疔毒血毒風濕，餘毒入骨，墜毒入筋，變爲癱瘓，不能行動，四處痛腫，遊走無定者，及前經醫治不良，種種壞症 此藥汁不但能培元活血，兼能解毒，誠花柳毒中之仙丹 無論如何重症 連服兩三料，定能全愈矣、

每料定價七圓　付費四毫

◉內痔解毒丸　定價每料七圓

內痔一症，世人每染之者最多，其發病之原因 多由嗜吸

Figure 3.56. Extract from an article about medical advice and products appearing in an unknown Chinese language newspaper, from TUR 22:2, Unit 2, Room 21. (TUR manuscript collection, Special Collections, University of Arizona Library, Tucson; Arizona State Museum photo by Helga Teiwes.)

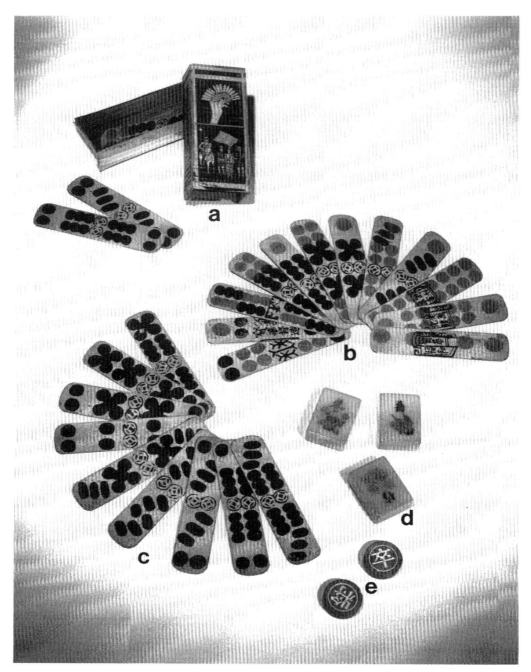

Figure 3.57. Gaming pieces, from TUR 22:2, Unit 2. *a*, Thin, compound paper and wooden box for playing cards has an outer case with open end and an inner topless tray that slides into it. The label on the box bottom is divided into an upper panel depicting a hand holding fanned out cards and a lower panel showing one horse-mounted and three standing human figures. The top label (not illustrated) is decorated with a picture of a child playing cards. One side label depicts two birds on a branch; the other has a Chinese inscription identifying the brand as Swallow, made by Jin Hua Zhai, and stating that the paper used was changed in 1933 to distinguish these cards from imitations. *b*, *c*, Fanned playing cards, 21 from a deck of 84. The long rectangular cards with rounded corners are made of stiff paper. The deck is divided into 21 sets of 4 identical cards. Markings consist of red and black spots of different contours that are placed singly or in various combinations; reverse sides are solid black. These cards appear relatively new and were found in a room next to the Ying On Association rooms, perhaps the property of a Chinese Club known to have occupied the room in 1958. *d*, Three plastic mah-jongg tiles inscribed with a decorative motif appropriate to the accompanying Chinese character: bamboo, Buddha's hand, and chrysanthemum. All tiles were recovered in the Chee Kung Tong lodge, confirming social activity carried on there. *e*, Two dark green plastic Chinese chess markers, also known as elephant checkers (Williams 1960: 10). The character etched in one signifies "general"; in the other, "soldier." (Length and widths in cm: *a*, 9.5, 3.8, height 2.5; *b* and *c*, 8.6, 2.0.) Provenience: Room 1(*a–c*), Room 14 (*d*), Room 21 (*e*). (Arizona State Museum photo by Helga Teiwes.)

Figure 3.58. Keno cards, account slips, and individual tickets may have been deliberately hidden in the attic of a patio latrine at the Ying On compound, perhaps because the gambling associated with the game had been illegal in Arizona since 1907. (TUR 22:2, Unit 2, attic of latrine east of Room 16; Arizona State Museum photo by Helga Teiwes.)

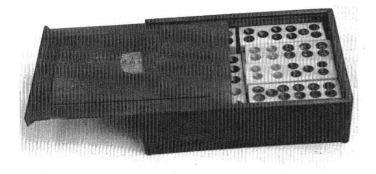

Figure 3.59. Set of 31 large ivory dominoes, with red and black or all black dots, in a labeled wooden box. (Length of dominoes, 6.3 cm; TUR 22:2, Unit 2, Room 16, west wall cupboard.)

Figure 3.60. Glass counters of black to dark blue or white color used in fantan. The "white pearls" counted as 100; the "black pearls" counted as 500 (Culin 1896: 154). (Average diameter, 0.75 cm to 1.20 cm; thickness, 0.5 cm; TUR 22:2, Unit 4, Room 11.)

The recovery from Room 11, Unit 4, of glass fantan counters, domino receipt booklets from the 1930s, and 10 Chinese and 2 Japanese coins suggests that one occupant had entertained himself and a friend or two by gambling. The documents reveal the name of only one tenant of this particular room, although there surely were a number of others. Gin Gay Yen (or Gin Fong) had come to the United States in 1913. For an unknown length of time he worked at the Chinese-operated Richelieu Cafe in downtown Tucson. He began drawing social security in 1941 and received correspondence until 1948, when it is presumed he died. His term of residency coincides with the domino booklets, but whether he was responsible for the other gaming items remains unknown.

Coins

For editorial convenience, Chinese coins are included with artifacts associated with recreation because of their presumed use for gambling activities that might well have endured long after other usage ceased. Culin (1891: 5–6) states that not only were coins imported to the United States by late nineteenth-century Chinese, but he speculates that some of the mintages in circulation as much as 300 years prior to that period actually may have constituted reproductions made specifically for use in wagering. Such replication has not been authenticated. However, Culin describes how coins were cleaned in vinegar and then polished with damp sawdust on a cloth bag so they would gleam on the gaming tables.

Notwithstanding this role of cash in the sojourner communities, it is likely that familiar, small denomination, metal coins from the homeland may have been used within Chinese enclaves on the western frontier primarily for the purchase of native goods from Chinese-operated stores (Farris 1979: 48–52). So long as they operated within their own communities, immigrants and retailers who worked through a network of wholesalers from their country might have continued their own economic practices and the currency to sustain them without much regard for the divergent monetary system of the alien land around them. Simply put, Chinese cash bought Chinese groceries from Chinese importers to be stocked in Chinese stores for Chinese customers—all on American shores, but only until such time as historical events made the process obsolete.

Superstitious, lower-class Chinese also are known to have considered coins from certain periods in their country's history to be lucky (Farris 1979: 60; Olsen 1983: 43, 45). The central square holes in metal coins, a function of the minting process, enabled groups of them to be strung together as gifts or charms. One such set of six coins braided together with red cord was recovered in an unidentified Ying On compound room. Coins stacked on an iron rod were hung at heads of beds to keep away evil spirits, and others were fashioned into jewelry to be worn for the same purpose (Burkhardt 1953: 176).

Another possible explanation for the presence of Chinese metal currency in the western United States is its former use as a viable and traditional medium of exchange within the brotherhood of secret societies. Fees assessed for observances of the god Kuan Kung's birthday, initiation rites, burning of prayer slips before an oracle, Chinese New Years celebrations, and other similar functions emanating from Chinese cultural content may have been satisfied only with customary Chinese currency. Moreover, for verification of membership all Hong Men were obliged to have three pieces of Hong cash on their persons at all times (see below, *Artifacts Associated with the Chee Kung Tong Organization*; Davis 1971: 137). Whether this custom was carried to America by Chinese immigrants is unknown but certainly likely, at least through the Qing period when adherence to past concepts was most intense.

Chinese cash coins (described by Olsen 1983: 41–45) were concentrated in two primary localities in the TUR district. Trenches and a well in the first Chinatown area (TUR 2:1, 69:1, and 3:4) produced 23 coins dating approximately from 1880 to 1910 (Fig. 3.61). Some 50 other coins were in the later (1919–1968) refuse of the Ying On compound rooms. Eight coins had been accidentally dropped into latrines there. Seven of these were in the top two feet of latrine C, located at the rear of intermittent Chinese businesses on south Meyer Street around 1883 but abandoned some time between 1904 and 1919. The other coin was in the upper two to four feet of latrine E, which might have been open until a shed was erected over it some time after it was recorded on a 1952 Sanborn map. Two additional coins came from the upper two feet of a trench dug through the use-compacted earthen surface of the compound patio. Other East Asian coins retrieved from the rooms in the Ying On compound included three from Japan, two from Hong Kong, and one from Vietnam, all presumed to have been in possession of local Chinese after World War I. Three additional Chinese specimens came from the presidio cemetery, from Block 23, and from Block 38, all areas associated with nearby Chinese occupation. No Asian coins were encountered in any purely Hispanic or Euro-American context. A greater percentage of coins dating from the early Qing periods (1662–1820) was found in quarters believed last used by downtown Tucson Chinese than in places where they had first settled, but 11 excavated specimens from the early deposits could not be identified because of severe corrosion. Only five of the recovered coins had been minted within the time of the TUR district occupation, just one of which was an example of pre–1949 Republican coinage.

The presence of Chinese coinage in Tucson and elsewhere in the American West stems from a large-scale reservoir of small-value coins held for centuries and dispersed over a period of time wherever Chinese went. It is hypothesized, but unproven by TUR research, that the local stockpile diminished through time because of loss, the impossibility of replacement due to separation from the motherland, and de-

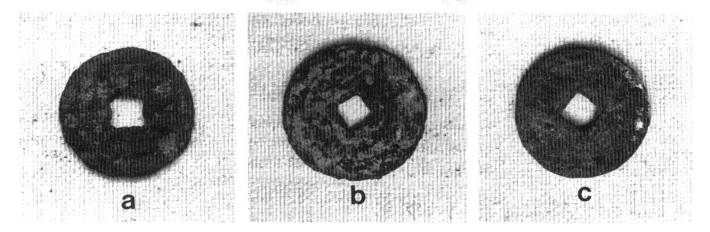

Figure 3.61. Three heavily corroded Chinese metal coins, probably manufactured during the Jia Qing period from 1796 to 1820 (Olsen 1983, Table 1), were recovered from Tucson's oldest Chinese quarter. (Diameters in mm: *a*, 23, TUR 2:1L4b; *b*, 25, TUR 2:1; *c*, 21, TUR 2:1L5.)

monetization of Qing Dynasty cash coins following the establishment of the Republic of China. At the same time, overseas Chinese communities in the West were experiencing greater adaptation to and assimilation of American culture. In the end, the main use of the coins was as intrinsically worthless gambling tokens. Even that usage was doomed. In the dreary compound rooms, inevitably cash ante surely converted into penny ante.

Tobacco Pipes

Chinese men were known as inveterate pipe smokers (Culin 1890b: 198). Only two traditional, long-stemmed pipes were found during TUR research (Fig. 3.62), but a territorial reporter confirms their common presence.

> When visited this morning Ling Kee, owner of a grocery at Simpson and Convent streets, proved to be a fat, good natured looking chap and was smoking one of those long-stemmed queer looking Chinese pipes with a bowl about the size of a shallow thimble and a mouthpiece like the neck of a beer bottle (*Arizona Citizen*, May 16, 1893).

Some nineteenth-century Euro-American white clay pipes recovered during the TUR project also might have been used by Tucson Chinese, as they were elsewhere (Society for Historical Archaeology 1987: 17–18).

Prince Albert and Velvet tobacco cans, a plastic pail lined with a Chinese newspaper containing cigarette butts and ashes, crushed empty packages of cigarettes, bills in the Ying On accounts for Lucky Strike cigarettes, and ash trays show that some compound tenants had taken up the use of American smoking products.

Ceramic Spirits Bottles

The production of grape wine began in China before the Christian Era, but was banned more than 41 times because consumption of it was excessive. Appeals for temperance appear in records from the Zhou period onward (Hahn 1968: 143). Brandy was introduced in the thirteenth century. In more recent times, northern Chinese have made use of sorghum as a base for spirits, and southern Chinese have developed a potent alcoholic beverage from rice or sugar cane (Grosier 1981: 60–61). A liquor called *pai-chiu* or *bai-jiu* is

Figure 3.62. Homemade tobacco pipes, copying more elaborate commercial Chinese pipes, from TUR 22:2. Chemical tests suggest that traces of opium, with tobacco, may have been smoked in them. *Top*, pipe with bowl of meerschaum-lined hard wood on wooden stem (Unit 3, Room 3); *bottom*, pipe with brass bowl and connector on wooden stem (Unit 2, Room 27). (Bowl diameters and stem lengths in cm: *top*, 3.2, 31.5; *bottom*, 1.9, 29.0.)

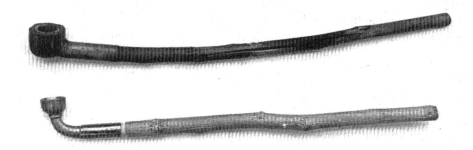

Figure 3.63. Ceramic spirits bottles, generally believed to have contained *Ng Ka Pi* (or *Mei Kuei Lu Chiew*) liquors of 96 to 106 proof alcohol content: *a*, early style (TUR 3:4–3aL9); *b*, middle style (TUR 3:4–3aL10); *c*, base of late bottle shown in *e*; *d*, potsherd of jar interior revealing juncture of molded basal and upper body sections; *e*, late style (TUR 22:2, Unit 2, Room 14). Estimated capacities are about 30 ounces (Pastron, Gross, and Garaventa 1981: 402); average height is 16.3 cm; average maximum diameter is 13.3 cm.

similar to vodka (Anderson and Anderson 1977: 342). Thus, for a very long time drinking games and clubs have been an important part of Chinese social life and constitute one expression of the celebratory behavior for which the southern Chinese are particularly well known (Clayre 1984: 120; Spence 1977: 278).

Homesickness, social alienation, sordid living conditions, and physical demands suffered by Chinese on the American frontier are suspected of having reinforced an already long tradition of heavy drinking. More stoneware bottles (Fig. 3.63) once filled with 96- to 106-proof *Ng Ka Pi* spirits imported from China were recovered through TUR research than any other kind of ceramic containers, but their numbers are relatively inconsequential when compared to American glass liquor bottles. Following a typological chronology suggested by Olsen (1978: 26–27), one complete and five shattered specimens of the earliest style Chinese spirits bottle were found in a well in the first Chinatown area (TUR 3:4). These specimens have exterior glaze only on the upper two-thirds of the vessel. A molded double triangle pattern appears on the side of one of these presumably early bottles that is similar to others in the West (for example, see Chace 1976: 515 and Praetzellis and Praetzellis 1979: 253, Fig. 1a). Twelve middle-style examples, with glaze to the ring foot, came from excavations in two localities north of Congress Street occupied to about 1912 (TUR 3:4, 69:2) and in another that remained the scene of Chinese dwellings and businesses possibly into the 1920s (TUR 14:1). Two came from non-Chinese deposits, TUR 18:1 and 38:7, the latter in a block with Chinese grocery stores from 1896 on, if not earlier. The Ying On tenement (TUR 22:2) yielded seven late-period bottles among the litter left in the dwellings, some with paper labels of distilleries such as Wing Lee Wai and Kie Fung Yuk still operating in Tientsin and Hong Kong. Four of the modern bottles came from the headquarters room of the Chee Kung Tong. The impressed English message stating *Federal Law Forbids Sale or Reuse of this Bottle* refers to a United States regulation enacted following the repeal of prohibition in 1933. Although some spirits bottles are handmade, both they and mold-made counterparts are of the same clay and are covered with the same deep brown glaze as the other food containers. Doubtless, they were made in similar factories making low-grade containers.

Spirits bottles or their fragments comparable to those from the TUR district have been recovered from nearly all Chinese sites so far studied in western states. However, the length of the continuum at Tucson remains unique. Through an estimated eight decades represented by these finds (about 1880–1960), the only stylistic change in the spirits bottles came late as a coarsening of the glaze and molded bilingual inscriptions on side and base.

No stoneware liquor bottles of the westernized so-called Euro-American shape reported for the San Francisco waterfront sample are among either the archaeological or ethnographical collections from Tucson (Pastron, Gross, and Garaventa 1981, Fig. 9.13b, opposite 398).

Considering the size of the Tucson Chinese population for almost ninety years, the number of Chinese spirits bottles is minimal. These data suggest that from the beginning of the Chinese colony in Tucson native liquor was reserved for special occasions, and day-to-day consumption depended on the easily obtainable American products. To judge from modern practice, green tea also was consumed throughout the day, as well as with meals.

ARTIFACTS ASSOCIATED WITH OPIUM USE

After its introduction by the British in the early 1800s, the use of opium in China was at an all-time high level by the 1880s. Although imperial rulers had banned its importation at least six times from 1729 to 1853 (Clayre 1984: 257; Gernet 1982: 534), economic and social factors continued to produce widespread smuggling, corruption, and consequent physical ravages of all levels of the population. Then, to all intents and purposes, the 1858 Treaty of Tientsin with the British, which allowed free importation, canceled good intentions of stamping out the drug problem (Courtwright 1982: 66). Needing revenues derived from either opium's increasing importation into China or from local cultivation, the Chinese government in the wane of the nineteenth century was unable or unwilling to take action against its use. As a result, the nation achieved the highest rate of opiate addiction in the world.

Many of the south China peasants and lower-class urban dwellers who made up the bulk of the migrants then coming to America were common users. They initially brought small supplies of the drug across the Pacific in their gear (Courtwright 1982: 68–69). However, it was the vastly greater volume of opium regularly shipped by Cantonese suppliers that fueled the overseas Chinese markets and kept supplied the commonplace opium dens that appeared in virtually all Chinatowns in the western United States. According to Kane (1976: 16), 77,196 pounds of opium prepared for smoking, with a value of $773,796, came into the United States in 1880. With such large-scale trade in the drug and potentially huge profits to be made from its distribution, it was just a matter of time until the fighting tongs that had spread to the New World got involved. Soon they edged legitimate shopkeepers out of the opium market. Even before the 1880s, crimes associated with this traffic and what were seen as the harmful effects of smoking opium led West Coast municipal authorities to enact ordinances against its sale, possession, or use. Most bans proved ineffective because of clever evasion by Chinese and lax enforcement of the laws.

It was at this time of greatest opium use by the overseas Chinese and a concomitant rising American resistance to it that the first sizable increment of Chinese came to Tucson. There was some immediate, albeit minor, trouble. Myrick (1975: 57) reports that in 1880 five of the Chinese engaged in leveling the Southern Pacific Railroad yards were arrested and fined from $7.00 to $10.00 for smoking opium. Two years later seven more individuals were arrested for the same offense (*Arizona Citizen*, February 3, 1882). Any town ordinance that may have been violated apparently soon was overlooked because Sanborn mappers in 1883 indicated two opium dens located in the Chinese quarter to the west of north Main Street. A map prepared in 1889 failed to designate similar usage of any structures in the area, but this may have been mere oversight. At some time in the same general period the Chee Kung Tong organization was established nearby and, to judge from its activities elsewhere, it likely controlled the drug's local distribution and benefited from its profits.

Many of the Chinese men in Tucson in the last decades of the nineteenth century fit the profile usually given for opium users (for example, see Felton and others 1984: 98–106). They were young, poor, uneducated, uprooted, without families, perhaps both physiologically and psychologically battered. However, not all Chinese smoked opium, and those who did were not necessarily addicts. Figures on use of opium by nineteenth-century Chinese in America vary from 10 to 50 percent; an undetermined number of those users are suggested to have indulged only as part of special occasions (Courtwright 1982: 69–70).

During the first decade of the twentieth century, worldwide public outcry against the evils of opium gradually created a new atmosphere of cooperation in China. In 1906 the Qing regime began to apply excessively high taxation on its importation and banned its cultivation at home. Two years later the British government, chiefly responsible for earlier flooding of China with Indian opium, agreed to decrease its export to the Empire of China. Just prior to the fall of that empire, all governments having treaties with China signed an agreement to control the rampant global smuggling of the drug. Meanwhile, in 1909 the United States Congress passed the Smoking Opium Exclusion Act prohibiting importation of opium for other than medicinal purposes, with $50 to $5,000 fines and possible sentences of imprisonment up to two years if convicted of sale, possession, or nonmedical use of the drug (Clyde and Beers 1966: 22–23).

Thus, as the Arizona territorial era was ending and Tucson's first Chinatown was slated for demolition, the acquisition and enjoyment of opium became illegal and consequently clandestine. The dens had disappeared long before, but opium smoking was acknowledged to have continued. Perhaps local officials were not overly concerned so long as it was only the Chinese who were abusing themselves, but when participation by non-Asians became known, action was taken because there was some evidence that Euro-Americans were more apt to become addicts than were the Chinese (Dai 1964). At the end of the nineteenth century there were a reputed 5,000 Euro-Americans in San Francisco alone who had fallen victim to the drug (Ch'en 1979: 244). The Tucson press reported one raid on a parlor where such mixed company had gathered.

The city officials cleaned out a "hop joint" and gathered in a whole cageful of "birds". The raid had

been planned previously, but an opportune time to carry it out never arrived until last night.

The joint is located in Chinatown, and the police have had it under suspicion for some time. There are the usual number of fiends in the old pueblo, who make a business of hitting the pipe quite regular, but the police have been unable to corner a large bunch of them together. The smokers of little brown pills are not confined to "chinks" either, not even to white men. A few women are also addicted to the habit, and it is this traffic that the authorities have been endeavoring to break up.

Sing Lee is the proprietor of the joint which was raided last night. His bunch of guests had not taken the usual puff last night when the officers burst in upon them. Officers Flannigan and Hopely made the raid, and gathered in the following: Chip Long and William Green, two colored men, Gaggie Wall, Pearl Andrews, and six Chinamen, Joe Ching, Kee Lyue, Lung Vaw, Ling Yung, Ling Kee, and Sam Kee. The whole bunch was unloaded at the city hall and they made a wild scramble for bail. A few of them had to be locked up.

They were arraigned before the city recorder this morning and each of them was fined $6.

The government officers have been watching the opium traffic in this vicinity for some time, but no arrests have been made as yet. It is thought that the drug is being smuggled across the line (*Arizona Citizen*, October 11, 1902).

Archaeology undertaken in the original Chinatown confirmed an impressive use of opium by pioneer residents. TUR 69:2 and 2:1, yielding a number of opium related artifacts, probably were at or near the site of one and possibly both of the early dens and a major tenement occupied by single Chinese. Expectedly, TUR 3:4, the location of an outstanding merchant's property, was not as productive.

Inasmuch as the opium related artifacts have been dealt with elsewhere (Ayres 1988; Matter 1969), detailed descriptions will not be repeated here. Suffice it to say that approximately 55 fragments and a few complete ceramic or stone opium pipe bowls came from the first two proveniences, with just two from the third. Basing an opinion on the number of fragments, as well as on complete specimens, Ayres (1980: 11) estimates that 120 opium pipe bowls were recovered archaeologically and ethnographically. A well at TUR 3:4 did produce part of a lamp used in heating opium. Fourteen additional bowl specimens were recovered from features in four blocks south of Congress Street (TUR 22, 23, 30, and 38) that had experienced Chinese occupation. The bowl remains represent the range of forms and styles known in other Western sites (Etter 1980: 97–101; Wylie and Fike 1986). No temporal differentiation is apparent in characteristics of those recovered from Chinatown proper and of those from the possibly later barrio sites.

The second kind of opium related materials recovered from excavations were many pieces of small cans in which the substance was packed and sold. These metal objects are so heavily corroded and fragmented that no accurate estimate of their number can be made, although Ayres (1980: 11) apparently thought the total of excavated examples was approximately a hundred. They were concentrated in TUR 69:2 and 2:1, with a few stray pieces found in TUR Blocks 23 and 29. Several of the privies on TUR Block 22, which had been sealed by new construction prior to 1919, also produced can fragments.

The official suppression of opium in China and America did not end the demand for the drug. Instead, it drove the traffic and consumption underground, where the tongs were the pushers and the users generally were those most resistant to acculturation. At the same time, there was a growing body of more integrated American-born Chinese with families and alien small businessmen intending to make America a permanent home who spurned the morale crutch that opium was supposed to provide.

Tucson illustrates these trends. TUR researchers recovered few opium paraphernalia in the southern barrio Chinese establishments of the statehood period outside the confines of the Ying On compound, TUR 22:2, where the evolving Chinese business community had lived while experiencing a slow dissolution of their ancient subculture.

The Chinese Ying On tenement on south Main Street afforded an environment conducive to continuation of the opium habit. That was where those who are thought to have lacked the resources or resolve to adjust to the American way congregated. Some likely had been unsuccessful sojourners. The Chee Kung Tong, a chapter of which maintained a lodge in one room of the structure, was reputed to have been active in opium smuggling in northern Mexico (Fong 1978, quoting *El Ejemplo de Sonora* 1932: 227–232). There is little doubt but that the Tucson Chee Kungers were another link in the secret opium distribution network reaching from the Mexican border to the interior of the West. Most of the occupants of the compound until World War II likely were tong members, and the drug probably was available to them although at prices steadily rising in proportion to the risks. The men staying in the compound can be presumed to have been particularly susceptible to the drug's temptation for a variety of reasons. First, the tong itself was a tie to the past and sanctioned opiate bliss. A reactionary clientele at hand reinforced that tie. The desire for ethnic identity, companionship, psychological escape, and freedom from physical pain, as well as the peer pressure attendant to communal living in marginal circumstances, contributed to the habit's perpetuation (Ball 1966: 68–72). The occurrence of this practice in spite of financial drains must have deepened the prevailing poverty of the tenement dwellers. And, of course, there may have been addiction. It is not suggested, however, that all compound tenants used opium.

Although there is no way now of determining the exact age of many of the trash litters that filled parts of the abandoned Ying On compound, the opium related articles seem to fall into two temporal groupings centering on the World War II years. They were more varied than the opium equipment recovered archaeologically. The full kit that smoking required (Figs. 3.64–3.66) included scales to weigh raw opium, (two small ones were recovered in adjoining rooms), parts of lamps fueled with peanut oil used to warm the substance, needles to insert the malleable opium into the upper aperture of the pipe bowls, pipe bowls and portions of stems and fittings, hooks for cleaning out encrusted bowl interiors and tampers for crushing residue for reuse, and pump drills to enlarge bowl openings. The traditional ceramic pipe bowls did not differ from those associated with the territorial era.

A group of what surely must be objects in use late in the occupational sequence reflects the years after World War II, when the Chee Kung Tong had moved on and opium and its associated material goods were not readily obtainable. Then it was necessary to create opium smoking paraphernalia out of objects designed for other uses (Fig. 3.65). The fact that many such objects came from Room 16 of Unit 2 and Rooms 2 and 3 of Unit 3 of the Ying On compound, rooms still being used near the time of demolition, supports this notion. There also were customary articles in use in the same rooms. One pipe was found on a table in a Rainbow Bread wrapper.

The most intriguing find connected with opium use was a cache of approximately 73 brass, copper, or galvanized steel opium cans that had been tossed up into the attic above the gable-roofed toilet-bath structure in the Ying On compound courtyard (Fig. 3.67). Most cans were intact, some with lids and labels in place, but others had been smashed deliberately (Fig. 3.68). Lee Yung, Yick Kee, Lin Wee, and Yee Kee companies are identified on labels that occasionally were in English as well as Chinese. One label notes, "The Lin Wee Company has taken up the use of Anglo script to certify the original product because there are some shameless companies who want to imitate it." The steel cans are believed to have originated in northern Mexico, where they had been recycled from containers originally made for other uses (Ayres 1988), thus strengthening the probability of a Mexican-based smuggling network.

The cache of tins reveals a matter of conscience on the part of the Chinese. Had an open privy been available, it likely would have received this incriminating evidence of illegal activity. With a flush toilet in use, the attic space was the next best hiding place. Certainly the police were aware of the opium smokers at the compound. According to the *Arizona Daily Star* (Rodeo Edition, February 22, 1935), they raided the house occasionally, confiscated opium pipes, and brought offenders to the police station. The severe penalties allowable under the law were not applied.

ARTIFACTS ASSOCIATED WITH THE CHEE KUNG TONG ORGANIZATION

Secret societies (tong) were deeply rooted in the Chinese cultural matrix, but they became especially numerous following the collapse of the Song Dynasty. The origins of the society that was to have the greatest impact in America are confused. Robertson (1977: 162) categorically states that this secret society was formed in 1674, just thirty years after

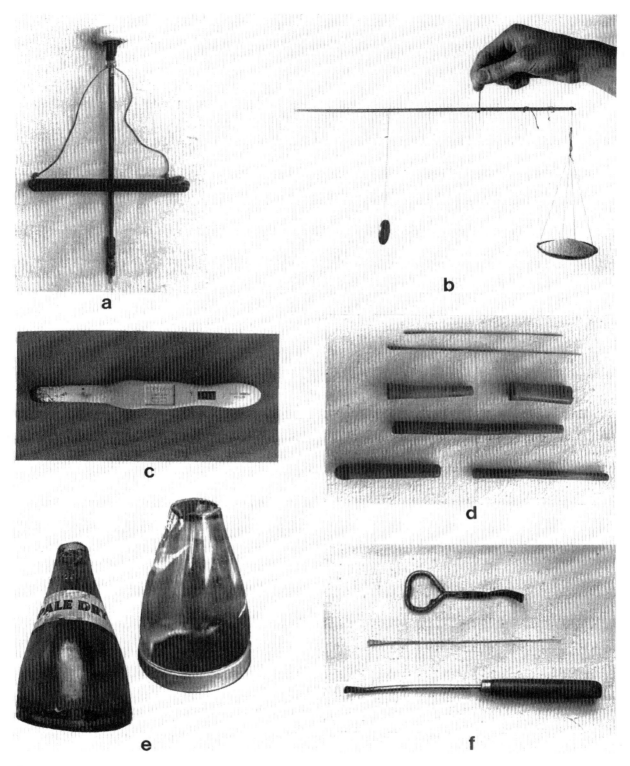

Figure 3.64. Opium-smoking equipment from TUR 22:2. *a*, Home-made pump drill used to redrill clogged openings of the bowls of opium pipes, consisting of white porcelain door knob, a metal shaft with metal bit, and wooden crosspiece with strings attached (Unit 4, Room 1). *b*, A traditional, commercially made, tiny scale used to weigh opium consists of a calibrated balance beam, brass pan suspended at one end by four cords, and a brass weight hanging from the opposite end. Kisch (1965, Fig. 25a, b) illustrates a typical violin-shaped case for such a scale, but none was found in the Ying On compound refuse (Unit 3, Room 3, fireplace mantle). *c*, White plastic fruit ribbon peeler and knife has a blackened end, suggesting its use in applying opium to the bowl aperture or in cleaning bowl interiors. The object bears a prominent molded inscription reading *Old Stagg Kentucky Straight Bourbon* (Unit 3, Room 3, desk). *d*, *Top*, darning needles used for inserting malleable opium into small hole on upper surface of enclosed pipe bowl, lower one has one flat end (Unit 3, Room 3 and Room 1); *center*, bamboo pipe stem fragments (Unit 4, Room 1 and Unit 3, Room 2); *bottom*, wooden tampers or pestles probably used to crush opium residue for reuse (Unit 4, Room 6, and Room 15 *bottom left*). *e*, Upper portions of two quart-size beverage bottles that had been cut to function as lamp chimneys over which opium is softened (Unit 2, Room 16 and Room 20). *f*, Metal bottle opener (*top*), metal darning needle, and ice pick with flattened end used to insert opium into pipe apertures or in cleaning away residue (Unit 2, Room 16, and Unit 3, Room 3 (darning needle). (Lengths in cm: *a*, 30.0; *b*, 38.0, pan diameter 6.9; *c*, 17.7; *d top*, 15.1, 18.4; *d center*, 8.0, 5.5; *d bottom*, 15.7, 9.5, 12.6. *e*, Base diameters in cm: 8.2, 8.8; heights in cm: 13.8, 14.5. *f*, no measurements.)

Figure 3.65. Makeshift opium pipe bowls created from household objects, from TUR 22:2. *Left*, brass door knob with small hole drilled into its upper surface, the shank serving to attach the knob to a pipe stem with the aid of tape and glue (Unit 2, Room 20). *Center*, Mexican earthenware jar, with hole drilled in base and jar neck fitting into a pipe stem and secured in place with cloth strips (Unit 3, Room 2, fireplace mantle). *Right*, oil squirt can with hole in base and threaded neck that could be fastened into a pipe stem (Unit 2, Room 22). (Maximum diameters and heights in cm: *left*, 5.6, 4.4; *center*, 6.3, 7.5; *right*, 6.3, 4.0.)

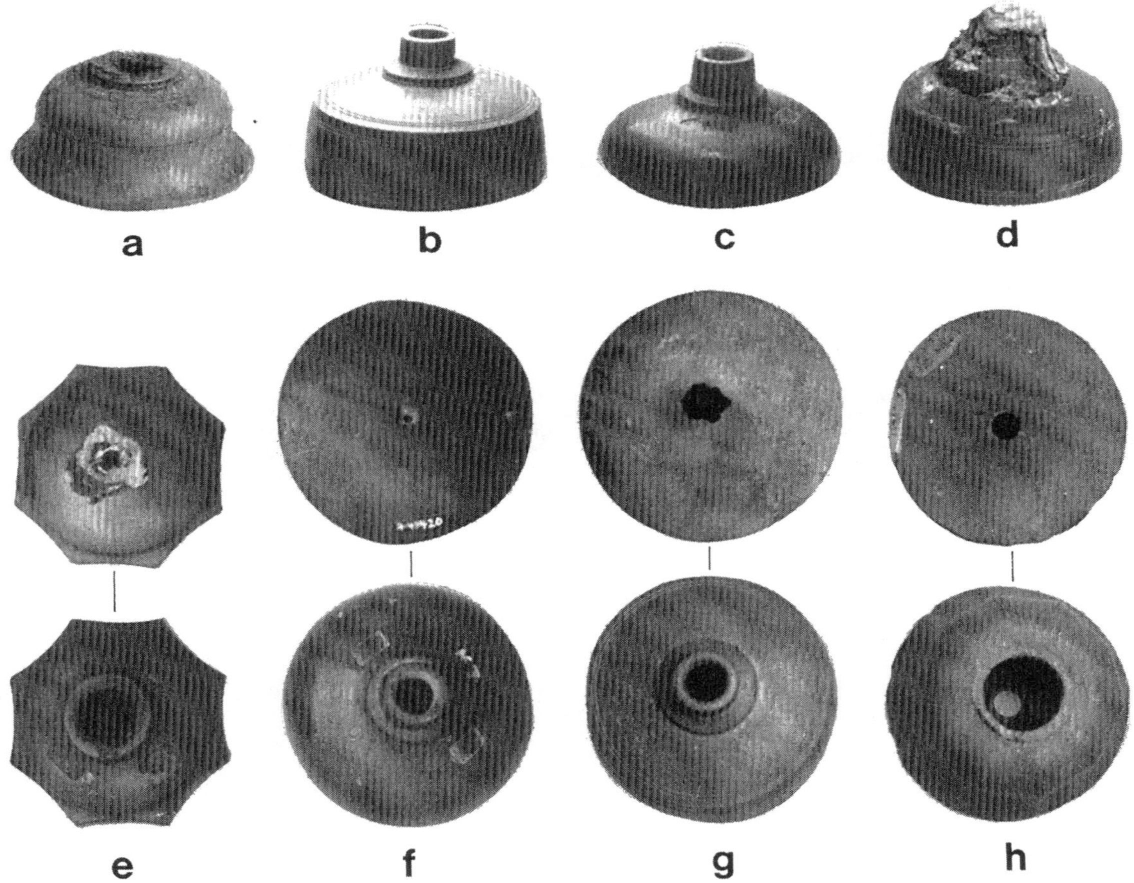

Figure 3.66. Sample of ceramic opium pipe bowls. Average base diameters are 5.8 cm to 6.4 cm; average heights are 3.8 cm to 4.2 cm. Provenience: TUR 29:5–A2 (*a*); TUR 22:2, Unit 3, Room 3 (*b, e*); 22:2–2fL2 (*c, f*); 22:2–2fL1 (*d*); TUR 2:1L5B (*g, h*).

Figure 3.67. Latrine building in the Ying On compound courtyard. Room to *left* (7 feet by 7 feet) housed a flush toilet; room to *right* (8.5 feet by 8.5 feet) contained a bath. For an unknown number of years, perhaps almost half a century, the gable-roofed loft above the rooms had been used as a hiding place for emptied opium cans. (Arizona State Museum photo by James E. Ayres.)

Figure 3.68. Metal cans once containing opium that were recovered from the attic of a latrine building in the Ying On compound courtyard. The cans at *left* and *right* in the top row may have been of Mexican manufacture, but the others were of Chinese derivation.

the Manchurians, who were not ethnically Chinese, swept down out of the northeast to establish themselves as the Qing Dynasty. DeBary and his associates (1960: 649) see an aborted beginning of the society somewhat earlier. Davis (1971: 61) records the society's first participation in a public demonstration in China as late as 1814. Regardless, and although strongly influenced by ancient mysticism, morality, and fraternal assistance to members, the avowed purpose of the society initially was to lead an underground resistance against the Manchu conquerors in order to reinstate the Ming ruling house. The determination of the society to meet that goal intensified when the subversion of some sympathetic monks at the temple of Shaolin in Fujian Province was discovered, causing the temple to be destroyed by imperial troops. Davis's interpretation is that the monks cooperated with the Manchurians in helping drive out invaders, only to be persecuted by those they had helped. It was this injustice that led to the rise of the secret society (Davis 1971: 13).

To proclaim its purpose, the group took the name of the first Ming ruler, Hong We (1368–1398), and organized itself along paramilitary lines, with commanders, vanguards, soldiers, and recruits (Gernet 1982: 546). Among the variations of the name were Family of Hong, Hong Party, Gate of Hong, or Elder Brothers (Chesneaux 1971: 15). The members created a secret cant; composed cryptograms illegible to nonmembers; adopted modes of dress for ceremonies; devised a set of secret recognition signals such as how to offer tea, liquor, or a pipe to a stranger to determine his possible affiliation; and followed elaborate rituals, including blood oaths, to spiritually unite sworn Brothers (Schlegel 1974: 167–222). A common logo was a triangle, the three sides representing heaven (father), earth (mother), and man (Fig. 3.69). This insignia caused later English speakers to refer to the group as the Triad Society (typical of Guangdong Province) or the Heaven-Earth League (typical of Fujian Province).

Figure 3.69. The mystic triangle or seal of the Triad Society, also known as the Heaven-Earth League. The sides of the triangular pattern represented heaven, earth, and man (Schlegel 1974: 30, center of diagram).

Once formed in Fujian Province, the Hong Men movement spread widely. Its stronghold was centered in south China. Attracting a throng of the customarily disadvantaged, its membership was composed of small tradesmen, farmers, boatmen, miners, beggars, bandits, women, youths, and others at the bottom of the social scale (Chesneaux 1971: 68; Robertson 1977: 163). The Hong Men leadership imposed upon the members a range of political, social, and religious conduct diametrically opposed to that of the orthodox society, which for two centuries kept dissent and lawlessness brewing (Chesneaux 1971: 30, 61). Davis (1971: 4) characterizes the society as un-Confucian, nonfamilial, democratic, voluntary, parasitic, parochial, and criminal.

On four occasions during the first half of the nineteenth century, as oppression, corruption, and ineffective dealings with encroaching foreign powers swamped China in turmoil, the Hong League unsuccessfully engaged in fierce peasant uprisings against imperial authority. The most devastating was the Taiping Rebellion (1850–1864) with political and heretical religious goals; it ravaged most of southern China and killed millions of citizens. Scores of embittered, homeless, defeated Hong Men, and disbanded army units who joined their ranks, fled into exile. Doubtless many escaped in vessels carrying law-abiding sojourners to California (Robertson 1977: 163).

The south China affiliation of this organization ensured its spread to the United States. Therefore, almost on the heels of the first diasporas, an unsettling facet of Chinese life was transferred to the West Coast. By the 1860s Hong Men in San Francisco, particularly those speaking a Sze Yap dialect and emanating from the Toishan district of Guangdong Province, had regrouped to form the first American lodge. Their leader was a man named Low Yet, who had taken part in the failed Taiping Rebellion. Probably the most well-known member of the San Francisco chapter, although not in residence, was Sun Yat Sen, destined to be the father of the Republic of China (Dillon 1962: 177, 180). From San Francisco, the society spread to virtually all Chinese settlements in the West, most of which were predominately composed of Sze Yaps. By the late decades of the nineteenth century, it is believed that two-thirds of all Chinese in the United States belonged to this organization (Culin 1970).

On the surface, the political orientation of the Triad Society continued. However, the need for mutual moral and financial support in a foreign land that was becoming more hostile with each passing year attracted large numbers of displaced migrants more interested in survival than in politics. Voluntary membership was open to all, whereas clan and territorial associations were restricted to persons with necessary surname or residential credentials. The more powerful of the residential groupings usurped control of certain occupations and limited participation, by force if necessary, to their own members (Light 1972: 91–92). Thus, those only eligible for small uninfluential clan or territorial associations found strength through numbers among the Hong Men, or

I'Hing (Patriotic Rising) as the society also is known (Culin 1890a: 39; 1970). In the western states the new overseas branch adopted the Cantonese name Chee Kung Tong, meaning Active Justice Society, and set itself up as a subrosa government for the overseas Chinese (Dillon 1962: 92). In time, up to thirty splinter groups, or tongs, proliferated, but all essentially owed their existence to the group that had had real power in China, the Triad Society. To most Euro-American observers, Chee Kung Tong members were identified as Chinese Masons because of what were perceived as comparable secret rites derived from "mysteries of the East." In actuality, there was no connection between Freemasonry and the Chee Kung Tong. Nevertheless, after years of hearing themselves called Masons, some Chee Kungers came to believe themselves a legitimate part of that international brotherhood and consequently entitled to use the official Masonic seal and slogan (Culin 1890a: 42–43; Lyman 1970: 34–38). With many lines of work open to the Chinese limited by peer pressures to specific associations, some of those on the outside who sought refuge in the Chee Kung Tong turned to preying on countrymen through extortion or blackmail or to carrying on illegal rackets involving them such as opium smuggling, prostitution, gambling, robbery, or hired killings. This behavior was a transfer from Asia to America of an established mode, but in many ways the United States Exclusion Act played into their hands by exacerbating an already explosive internal situation within Chinese racial ghettos. The so-called tong wars of the 1880s and 1890s resulted, and the Chee Kung Tong was deeply involved (Dillon 1962: 71). In the late nineteenth century the criminal element within the society was largely restricted to the cover provided by densely occupied urban Chinatowns, where its activities subverted the avowed goals of the organization and gave American police a giant problem.

A chapter of the Chee Kung Tong is documented as present in Tucson by 1895, although quite possibly it had become established some years earlier. A contemporary newspaper account described a huge red flag flying over the headquarters of the Chinese Masons at 67 Pearl Street, opposite the residence at 88 Pearl Street of prominent merchant Chan Tin Wo (*Arizona Citizen*, October 25, 1895). The Sanborn map of the following year indicates Chinese occupation at the site and the 1900 census lists two residents, but the building is not labeled as a meeting place until 1901. Then it is called joss house number two, as if perhaps the first building had burned or been otherwise destroyed. The term "joss house" came from the use of incense sticks or idols, both being called josses. Commonly, the same structure was regarded by Euro-Americans as a temple, because religious and secular observances were intertwined in Chinese secret society practice. Furthermore, the Masonic hall frequently was known as a temple. No Confucian, Taoist, or Buddhist temple as such is known to have existed in Tucson, making it obvious that the Sanborn joss house was, in fact, the meeting hall for the Chee Kung Tong. Mappers wrote "ruins" across the area in 1909, at a time when the first urban renewal program in that sector was being contemplated.

With the original Chinatown leveled, another joss house appeared in 1919 in a room of the west arm of a formerly Hispanic structure on south Main Street that thirty years later became known as the Ying On compound. The city directory for that year and for 1920 noted its presence at 93 south Main Street, but the numbering later was changed so that 85 south Main Street remained the post-territorial Chee Kung Tong headquarters to at least 1940. It should be noted that the city directory for that year mistakenly listed the address as 75 south Main Street, which would have put the lodge in a vacant lot to the north. In these last days of the Tucson tong a 90-year-old man, who apparently had been one of the first sojourners in Tucson, served as caretaker (*Arizona Daily Star*, Rodeo Edition, February 22, 1935). It seems appropriate that he and the tong faded together.

The participation of the American lodges of the Chee Kung Tong in the political and social dissidence that consumed the homeland membership was called into doubt by no less a personage than Sun Yat Sen. After a visit to San Francisco in 1896, he wrote:

> At that time, however, there were fairly widespread amongst the Chinese migrants the so-called 'Hung-men' societies although by my time they had been reduced to little more than mutual aid clubs. . . . The watchwords: 'Down with Ch'ing' and 'Long live Ming!' were near and dear to many Chinese. But the same cannot be said of our many Chinese emigrants, as they, being abroad in free country, had no necessity to organize societies of fighting character. Therefore in America the 'Hung-men' societies naturally lost their political colour, and became benefit clubs. Many members of the 'Hung-men' societies did not rightly understand the meaning and exact aims which their society pursued. When I approached them, during my stay in America, and asked them why did they want to overthrow the Ch'ing dynasty and restore the Ming dynasty, very many were not able to give me any positive reply (Chesneaux 1971: 135, 146).

There are no available records of Chee Kung Tong participation in Tucson in either political agitation or the kinds of bloody internecine warfare as occurred in the California Chinese slums. Inasmuch as crimes committed usually were confined to those against other Chinese, it is presumed that American authorities often were inclined to look the other way and not to interfere. However, participation in illegal smuggling operations that involved United States laws probably did occur in Tucson, considering the city's location astride major smuggling routes from Mexico. By the time the tong move was made to the southern barrio, World War I had ended large-scale illegal entry into the United States of Chinese laborers, but there remained a trickle of immigrants docking in north Mexican ports who sought enrichment by fair means or foul in the United States. These unlawful newcomers may have found help and shelter within the bosom of the Chee Kung Tong. Opium, by then outlawed both by China and the United States, still managed to seep across the permeable Mexican border, undoubtedly with some Chee Kung Tong help. Moreover, abundant evidence was

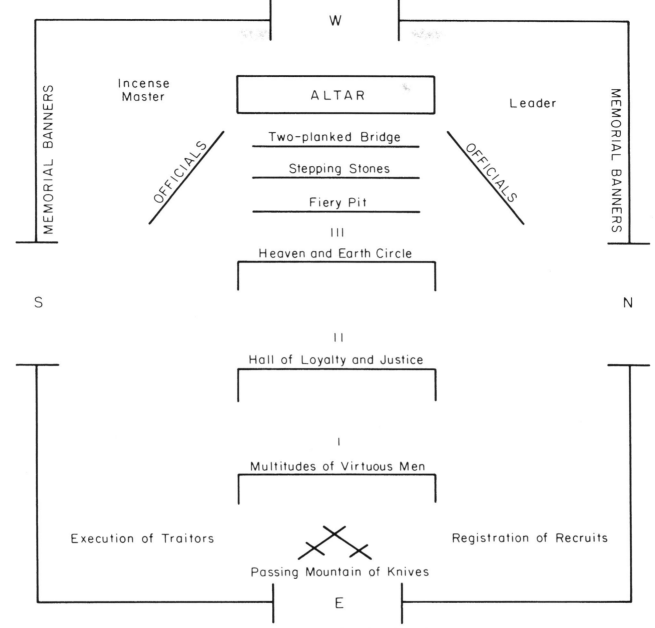

W

ALTAR

Incense
Master

Leader

MEMORIAL BANNERS

MEMORIAL BANNERS

OFFICIALS

OFFICIALS

Two-planked Bridge

Stepping Stones

Fiery Pit

III

Heaven and Earth Circle

S

N

II

Hall of Loyalty and Justice

I

Multitudes of Virtuous Men

Execution of Traitors

Registration of Recruits

Passing Mountain of Knives

E

Figure 3.70. Ideal plan of a Triad lodge. The orientation of the affiliated Tucson Chee Kung Tong meeting room on south Main Street may have been reversed so that the entrance was the west, or outside, door. Recovered banners, one of which is illustrated in Figure 3.80, may have been used at stations I, II, and III, with other banners of an instructional or historical nature hung on side walls opposite the altar. The feature where traitors were executed is thought to have become an anachronism in twentieth century America. (Modified from Davis 1971, Fig. 6.)

uncovered within the compound for the continued use of opium right up to the time of abandonment.

With the Qing ruling house out of China in 1912 and the supremacy of the Nationalists more or less assured despite a civil war that raged for years, any political activism on the part of the Chee Kung Tong subsided. Particularly away from large centers of Chinese population, such as in small inland communities in Arizona, interest in past causes faded with eroding ties to the motherland. Unquestionably, the local chapter slowly reverted to being solely a fraternal order that emphasized chivalry and morality and that provided a

social outlet for a shrinking membership.

In China, Triad meeting places were hidden in order to avoid disruption by government forces, but in America derivative chapters generally gathered in buildings in the midst of densest Chinese occupation without any attempts being made to conceal their whereabouts. Ideally, a Chee Kung Tong meeting room was square in plan to represent a walled Chinese city and contained different elements symbolizing both a beleaguered encampment and phases of a mythical journey that initiates had to make (Fig. 3.70; Chesneaux 1971: 32; Davis 1971: 152; Schlegel 1974: 20). Doors on each of the four walls were considered gates to the cardinal directions guarded by society officers against intrusion by enemies.

At the location in Tucson on south Main Street, the society settled for a large rectangular meeting room in a row of similar rooms (Fig. 2.18). At the time of demolition, interior doorways on three walls had been sealed, but perhaps that had happened during remodeling of the early 1950s after the Chee Kung Tong no longer met in the room (Ayres 1968a). Traditionally, the east door was most important, which in this lodge would have brought participants in rites through the seclusion of the central patio and a living room. It is possible that the typical plan was reversed in this case so that the back of the altar would not face the most public door on the west. Outside over that western double-door to the street was a sign giving the organization name in English and Chinese. Above that was a vertical flagpole that at some unknown time acquired a finial made from a toilet tank float. The 10-foot long (3.05 m), triangular flag and its emblazoned crest of the lodge floated from the pole on special days, as if to announce to the world that the society had at last achieved public recognition by Sun Yat Sen's government.

If that brilliant Chinese-red banner wafting over a sleepy Hispanic neighborhood along the old Spanish Royal Road seemed incongruous, the interior of the meeting room was more so. A 1935 local paper provides the only known description of its appearance, thereby stripping away the last semblance of secrecy.

In the Chee Kung Tong rooms more of the China of the story books is in evidence. All the decorations . . . came straight from China. The altar before which the neophyte stands to take his vows of brotherhood is a great, gilt, rococo affair, handcarved of wood, and bristling with heraldic Chinese gods, goddesses, animals, vegetables, jewels, and fruits. If traditionally correct, the altar would have been square, that form meaning the world and righteousness. So many things are symbolized on this altar that not even the members of the tong can explain them all. Out of an incalculably ancient past came these deities and hieratic fauna and flora, and much of their significance has been lost.

The center motif of the altar is the dragon. He is a Confucian dragon, a symbol of the good and virtuous life. [The Hong Men rejected orthodox Confucianism in favor of a blend of heterodox Buddhism and Taoism, and it is probable that the Chee Kung Tong adopted the same philosophy.] Below his mouth, not quite touching it, is affixed a pearl. This jewel represents the unattainable state of perfection the dragon is forever trying to achieve, but never quite does. In a larger sense, the dragon is China herself, and the pearl is that state of righteousness and virtue for which the Chinese must endlessly strive.

Elsewhere on the altar are storks feeding their young, rural Chinese carrying heavy burdens, lions and lionesses, curious fish, donkeys, roosters, peacocks, griffons, golliwogs, imps, devils, gods, maidens, and emperors, and vegetables fancy and staple. This altar is gilded in some places, lacquered in others, and is inset with tiny mirrors. The artist who made it was Huey Son Yueh of Canton. The time it took him to make it is not even guessed at by its present owners.

Another example of the same Huey's artistry hangs from the ceiling of the center of the tong room. This is another handcarved affair illumined with gold paint. It represents a scene in China 4,000 years ago. At that time there occurred a sort of convention of six of the seven historic Chinese nations: these six being known as Tai, Ch'ou, Yien, Chiu, Yueh, and Han. The seventh nation, Man, was so powerful that it never deigned to attend conventions of the lesser nations. Huey Son Yueh has represented this convention by carving six sets of people, each set carrying a distinctive banner, gathered around a throne upon which is sitting the great emperor of China. So many people are in the carving, and so closely packed together are they, that they seem to move about as one looks at them.

Tables and chairs of teakwood, old and mellow, make up the furniture of the room, plus several cuspidores of frankly American manufacture. A bowl for incense burning [an incense burner of white porcelain has been described for other Triad lodges by Schlegel (1974: 120)] and vases of artificial flowers stand before the altar, as does an intricate device for fortune-telling [probably a bamboo tube inside of which were slips of paper bearing numbers corresponding to known fates (Wells 1971)]. The walls are covered with pictures of gatherings of Chinese freemasons in different cities (*Arizona Daily Star*, Rodeo Edition February 22, 1935).

Judging from other known joss houses, the principal god displayed over the altar was Kuan Kung, generally believed in the West to be the red-faced, scowling god of war and an appropriate symbol of the warlike attitudes of the Chee Kung Tong. DeBary and others (1960: 651) contradict this notion by pointing out that Kuan Kung, who died in the early third century, was a hero who joined with two sworn Brothers to defend the Han Dynasty. The god was regarded as an oracle, who gave guidance about propitious dates for certain undertakings, including burial of a departed Brother (Culin 1891: 40; R. Lee 1948: 1–11). A red bucket (*t'ao*) of approximately a bushel capacity shown in Figure 3.71 originally may have been filled with up to thirty sacred objects, including an array of pennants. Among the other articles were incense, foodstuffs, cash, mirrors, abacuses (Fig. 3.72), and writing materials (Davis 1971: 184; Schlegel 1974: 41; Ward and Stirling 1925, Vol. 1: 49). This particular bucket was an American object that the tong members had used, pasting their own label over an original one from the United Indurated Fibre Company. After the Chee Kung Tong ceased to function in the Ying On compound, a later resident used the container for domestic purposes, perhaps to hold fireplace wood.

Schlegel (1974: 45) records the Hong quatrain about the abacus:

On the golden board are myriads of thousands
   of changes;
We compute the multiplication and division
   before Ming.

Figure 3.71. A bushel-size, reddish brown container made of hardened fiber material originally had been part of the altar furnishings in the Chee Kung Tong meeting room. It bears a red label with the secret characters of the lodge reading *mei li feng gu*, but the meaning is unknown. The flat base is stamped *United Indurated Fibre Co Patented Lockport, NY USA*. Metal handle attachments are bolted to the container walls just below the rim, but the handle is missing. Wax dripped on parts of the exterior probably came from altar candles. (Diameter, 29.7 cm; height, 23.8 cm; TUR 22:2, Unit 3, Room 2, fireplace top; Arizona State Museum photo by Helga Teiwes.)

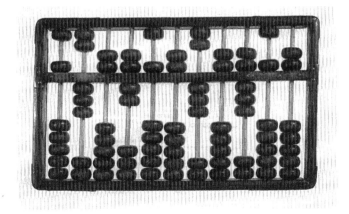

Figure 3.72. Abacus, characteristic Chinese calculating board composed of 11 bamboo rods, each holding 7 wooden balls, set within a wooden frame. Working from right to left, each rod represents a designated unit. Below a horizontal divider, one ball moved up equals one; above the divider, one ball moved down equals five. (Length, 26.5 cm; width, 16.5 cm; TUR 22:2; Arizona State Museum photo by Helga Teiwes.)

We'll multiply and divide till the Tsing-dynasty
   is finished in this world;
Gentlemen! Quickly restore the kingdom to Ming.

Large red candles, a pair of scales to symbolize justice, packs of Hong paper money to be burned so that their plumes of smoke could carry messages to the gods, and other items also should have been present on the altar (Wells 1971).

Some of this ceremonial gear may have been in Tucson since the 1890s or earlier, but unfortunately little of it could be identified in the refuse on the Ying On premises when the researchers arrived in 1968. The bucket was recovered from living quarters, where it was being put to secondary use. Two abacuses and two brass pans from balance scales, also found in living rooms, could have been Chee Kung Tong furnishings. However, inasmuch as some of the Ying On compound residents through the years had been small tradesmen who would have used similar objects in the course of their work, the association of those items with the secret society cannot be positive.

Banners

Of special significance was the recovery of a stack of 39 colorful banners used by the society for various purposes. The importance of the banners is not in their extrinsic value, for they are of poor quality and workmanship. They do, nonetheless, reaffirm the Hong League affiliation of the group. They also reaffirm the love of pageantry and of what Chavannes (1973: 21) terms the shadow language of symbolism by even the humblest Chinese and provide a glimpse of their inherited attitudes toward rectitude, discipline, and structured behavior. The fact that such important once-secret material was abandoned rather than destroyed further supports the idea that interest in undercover, esoteric activity based on an outmoded world-view embedded deep within the Oriental psyche had vanished with Western liberating circumstances.

The Chee Kung Tong banners are of four general types. All had particular roles in initiation rites for recruits and probably in other programs as well. Two may be considered charter banners; the one shown in Figure 3.73 is the more elaborate and conceivably could have been brought from China. That its age is greater than the accompanying banners is suggested by the exclusive use of cryptogrammatic characters to form a text that may extol the glories of the Ming Dynasty. The painted border dragons and phoenixes symbolize the royal house, and the remaining design elements have other abstruse significance. The textile likely was hung on one of the walls when rituals were performed.

The second charter or instructional banner, a translation of which appears in Appendix A, seems an updated, expanded version created in the United States. It is fashioned from two pieces of polished cotton cloth, is machine-stitched, hemmed, and has corner tabs for hanging (Fig. 3.74). Its central section contains the Hong character on a red circle and an allegorical passage in reference to purposes of the society and the need to enlist soldiers to carry out its program. Brushed texts to each side are ethical rules and prescribed punishments for infractions (Appendix A). This banner would have played a prominent role in initiation rites, during which the officer termed Vanguard read the oaths to kneeling initiates. The 36 oaths appearing on this

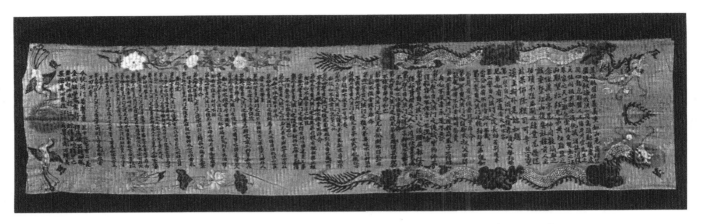

Figure 3.73. Large, tan, cotton banner with painted, polychromatic, symbolic dragons at the upper and lower right representing the Emperor, a pair of phoenixes at the left border representing the Empress, floral sprays, and a sun motif surrounding a painted text of illegible, black, Chinese characters. The text presumably relates the virtues of the Ming Dynasty. (Length, 320 cm; width, 76 cm; TUR 22:2, Unit 2, Room 14; Arizona State Museum photo by Helga Teiwes.)

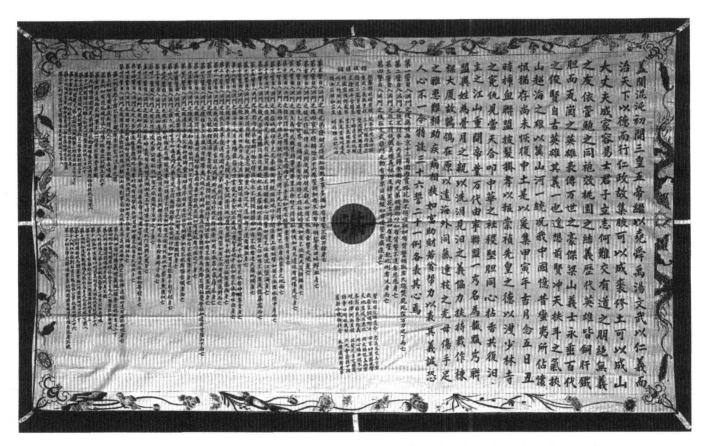

Figure 3.74. Large, yellow, cotton Chee Kung Tong banner itemizing the oaths and regulations of the lodge and punishments to be meted out for infractions of them. Painted, symbolic, imperial dragons, phoenixes, and flowers form the border. The Hong Men seal in red with a central black character (the name and color sounding identical when verbalized) forms a centerpiece around which are black calligraphic texts in legible Chinese, translated in Appendix A. (Length, 230 cm; width, 140 cm; TUR 22:2, Unit 2, Room 14; Arizona State Museum photo by Helga Teiwes.)

banner represent the 36 gods in heaven and are characteristic of other chapters, although wording differed (Chesneaux 1971: 13–35; Davis 1971: 146; DeBary and others 1960: 651–657; Schlegel 1974: 135–144; Ward and Stirling 1925, Vol. 1: 64–70).

The yellow color of the cloth on which the inscriptions are brushed may refer back to the imperial rulers, the only ones allowed to use that color in clothing, tiles, and other possessions. Inasmuch as yellow is noted in other Hong Men banners, the color might have been adopted either as a signal of defiance against ancient authority or perhaps to recall the former symbol of a military commander (Franke 1974: 171). Yellow also was regarded as the center from which the four cardinal directions radiated, its use in this case enhancing identification of the society as the center of each member's universe (Davis 1971: 119). A pre–1912 date for the formulation of these particular oaths, although not necessarily for the banner itself, is suggested by Oath 36 concerning establishment of a new government. Regulation One is puzzling in its reference to loyalty to the king, but perhaps a more accurate translation would have been loyalty to the lodge leader, who had supreme authority over members.

Primarily, the oaths deal with the interdependence of sworn Brothers and stress the internal solidarity critical to the group's survival. In the old days, undivided loyalty to the society was demanded over family loyalty. In fact, the Hong Men disavowed traditional familial ties in favor of surrogate kinship among sworn Brothers. Oaths 3 and 24 underscore caution against incest within this artificially defined relationship. On the other hand, a clue to softening of former sanctions against family bonds is found in oaths of the Tucson lodge that commend such allegiance. Other modern standards are prohibitions against kidnapping of women and children, which run counter to the nineteenth-century society's heavy participation in prostitution and slavery rackets.

Penalties for breaking lodge laws reflect fears of backsliding or betrayal and invoke determination to keep members in line through threats of arcane, severe types of punishment. One officer was assigned the task of administering prescribed blows with a fearsome Red Staff, a fir pole three feet, six inches long (106.7 cm), which surely amounted to a death sentence regardless of the number of hits inflicted as determined by the severity of the offense (Schlegel 1974: 42). Other officers are said to have carried out verdicts calling for decapitations or drownings. In the freedom of twentieth-century America, such sentences remained on the books to ensure group unity.

The walls, altar, and urns of the lodge room were enlivened further with banners that were scarcely more than bright, generally unhemmed, frayed lengths of cotton cloth bearing boldly brushed inscriptions meant to remind observers of moral credo. One series recovered from the lodge room at TUR 22:2 (Unit 2, Room 14) consists of narrow strips, varying from 94 cm to 169 cm in length and 21 cm to 30 cm in width, meant to be hung vertically. Five of them are of red cotton with a single row of black characters. Four of the passages have been translated as follows.

> Since the separation of heaven and earth [since the beginning of time], there has been war.
> There are lots of flowers blooming outside the temple [the organization is healthy and growing].
> There are three Buddhas and a Sage to show the dignity of the temple [Buddhas are gods of happiness; Sage is punisher of evil].
> Love and virtuousness can be found anywhere.

Four similar, but slightly smaller, banners are of pink cotton with black inscriptions of uplifting symbolic phrases. In addition to the one in Figure 3.75, other messages read:

Figure 3.75. One of a series of four pink cotton banners belonging to the Tucson lodge of the Chee Kung Tong, which likely were displayed in pairs above the altar or on the walls. The inscription of this specimen states *The phoenix in the mountains* [happiness]. (Average length, 127 cm; average width, 28 cm; TUR 22:2, Unit 2, Room 14; Arizona State Museum photo by Helga Teiwes.)

Figure 3.76. Banner and flag, from TUR 22:2, Unit 2. *Left*, an elaborate banner, hung in a prominent place during special ceremonies to which only sworn Brothers of the Chee Kung Tong were privy, is made of reddish polished cotton cloth, edged with a broad black band overlaid with a narrow yellow trim ribbon. The upper part has four large appliquéd black Chinese characters; the lower panel is elaborated with a large green circle and glued and painted black characters. A pair of pale blue pennons hangs to the right side. (Length, 104 cm; width, 68 cm; Room 4.) *Right*, one of two commercially made flags of the Republic of China, believed to have belonged to the local chapter of the Guomindang, or Nationalist Party, for nearly three decades. It was hoisted over the front entrance to the meeting room to announce Chinese political holidays to the local Asian community. (Length, 195 cm; width, 72 cm; Room 7; Arizona State Museum photos by Helga Teiwes.)

The oceans and sacred turtle [provide good luck].
The pavilion [lodge] never covered by clouds
    [evil].
The rain drop on the flower [appreciation of
    natural phenomena].

Another banner found in the Chee Kung Tong collection that fits into this grouping of specimens with inspirational or historical connotations is a roughly square piece of white cotton cloth (91.2 cm by 88.5 cm) with two selvage edges, two unfinished, raveled edges, and three vertical columns of characters beneath a heading. The inscription translates:

The temple of good fortune and virtue [top].
The place of good fortune is cleaned by wind [left].
The door of virtue does not have a lock on it [right].
The god of good fortune of Shao Lin temple
    in Fu Zhou county of Fu Jian state [middle].

A rectangular banner of comparable purpose and style was retrieved from TUR 22:2, Unit 4, Room 12, where it may have been taken by a tenant residing in the compound after the Chee Kung Tong ceased its activities in the adjacent building. Its nine vertical rows of characters have not been translated.

A third grouping consists of two well-made, machine-stitched banners of the type seen in China on home altars. Inasmuch as they were stored with other Chee Kung Tong materials, their use on the society altar is assumed. Schlegel (1974, Table 10, right) depicts a comparable specimen. One example (68 cm by 104 cm) has three red braid loops sewn along the top by which it could be suspended from a rod or hung against a wall (Fig. 3.76 *left*). It is of reddish polished cotton cloth, over which black, yellow, blue, red, and green elements of cloth or ribbon are added, along with appliquéd, glued, and painted black characters. Blue pennons hang at one side. A pair of nearly identical specimens of different dimensions and made of pink cotton were retrieved from the same room of Unit 2 in the Ying On compound. Their passages of text, possibly from the Confucian classics, read:

The greatest accomplishments can be achieved
through considering all the possibilities.
In virtue one must strive for constant increase.

The second altar banner is attached to a thin bamboo stick that has a carved knob and red tassel at its top and two side pennons (Fig. 3.77). It is yellow with tan, maroon, and blue elements and black characters translated as:

The law of heaven: benevolence, justice,
etiquette, intelligence.

The martial hierarchy of the Chee Kung Tong is demonstrated by another set of banners. A small orange U-shaped one mounted on a bamboo stick is edged in blue and has a black inscription stating:

Supreme Commander of the military forces.

This banner may have been carried in certain rituals by the leader of the tong or thrust upright into a bowl of sand at his place of honor. Two large rectangular yellow polished cotton cloths (67 cm by 46 cm) with a lower curved edge have identical pictures in black of the leering humanoid head of a mythological creature accompanied by some untranslated Chinese characters. Their significance has not been determined, although they vaguely correspond to flags of tiger generals noted elsewhere.

An assortment of 16 serrated, triangular pennants, some attached to thin bamboo poles, are of particular interest inasmuch as they all contain brief inscriptions, including the name Ding with or without the title *Sichuan Supreme Commander*. Names given are Ding Zheng-tian, Ding Han-fu, Ding Xia, Ding He, Ding Si, Ding Shan, Ding Yen, Ding Nian, Ding Hua, Ding Xuan, and Ding Long, Ding with no personal name, and a Ding general.

On the banner in Figure 3.78, Ding appears to be an ordinal rank. On the other banners of this type it is a surname. No persons having the Ding surname appear in the 1910 federal census, the last tabulation for which personal names are available, and no Dings are mentioned in the translated surviving documents left in the building. These facts suggest that the surname may have been a borrowed one to sustain the members' fictional fraternal relationship. The reference to Sichuan stems from a lodge custom of considering itself affiliated with one of the provinces of south China. During the nineteenth century Sichuan was a center of the Hong Men resistance and the refuge during the 1930s and 1940s of the Nationalists. Two banners are red edged in white, seven are maroon, two are blue, three are orange, one is white, and one is black. In the Qing military organization there

Figure 3.77. A machine-stitched altar banner attached to a thin bamboo pole is made of yellow cotton cloth bordered with tan. At the upper edge is a secondary maroon band edged with blue. Tan pennons hang from either side. The pole by which the banner could have been carried or held upright in a basal container is topped with a carved knob and a red tassel. (Pole length, 63.5 cm; banner length, 19.0 cm; width, 17.0 cm; TUR 22:2, Unit 2, Room 14; Arizona State Museum photo by Helga Teiwes.)

Figure 3.78. Cotton pennant used during certain rites by an officer of the Chee Kung Tong to mark his station. The right edge of the triangular piece of cloth is folded over and machine stitched to form a casing to fit around a staff; the two remaining edges are deeply cut in a saw-toothed manner. The supporting pole is missing. The black painted inscription reads *Under Sichuan Supreme Commander Ding Zheng-tian.* (Lengths of the six banners in the set, 28 cm to 53 cm; widths, 29 cm to 37 cm; TUR 22:2, Unit 2, Room 14 assumed; Arizona State Museum photo by Helga Teiwes.)

were units of troops known as Banners, who were distinguished by the color of their flags (Davis 1971: 18; Gernet 1982: 464). Possibly the Tucson Chee Kung Tong banners were used similarly in ceremonies to distinguish companies of "soldiers," as well as to indicate guard posts at the lodge entrances (Schlegel 1974: 20).

In accord with a military organizational format, a small, red-orange, triangular, straight-edged banner (28 cm by 42 cm) with a single character meaning *Order* signified the highest rank used in the army of ancient China. A larger triangular pennant (115 cm by 113 cm) of red polished cotton cloth with a serrated white border and attached green cloth and red braid pennons displays a circular green element and characters meaning *Vanguard* (Fig. 3.79). Vanguards ranked second in the tong hierarchy and were responsible for putting initiates through a complicated ritual. Three long nar-

Figure 3.79. Large, triangular, serrated banner of white-bordered, red, polished, cotton cloth with green and red pennons, showing proper display position (after Schlegel 1974, Tables 12, 13). An appliquéd circle of green cloth bears painted Chinese characters identifying this as the banner of the Chee Kung officer called the Vanguard. (Length, 115 cm; width, 113 cm; TUR 22:2, Unit 2, Room 14.)

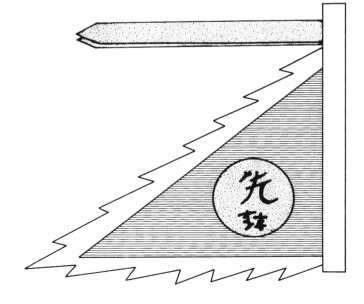

Figure 3.80. Rectangular, red cotton banner with black painted characters meaning *First Door.* This and two similar banners marked symbolic stages through which initiates had to pass toward the final ceremonial station before the Chee Kung Tong altar. (Average lengths, 64.0 cm; average widths, 21.5 cm; TUR 22:2, Unit 2, Room 14; Arizona State Museum photo by Helga Teiwes.)

row strips of red cotton have inscriptions translated as *First Door, Second Door*, and *Third Door*. These either refer to successive formalized phalanxes in the ancient Chinese army through which the enemy had to break in order to achieve victory or, more probably, they marked symbolic entrances arranged down the half of the lodge room leading up to the altar (Fig. 3.80; Davis 1971: 130, Fig. 6).

Musical Instruments

Music is an integral part of Chinese ceremonial and social life. People of all levels are encouraged to participate in it, but for those low in the societal hierarchy, it always has been on a group basis rather than for individual enjoyment. As in the West, music serves to arouse the emotions. But, additionally, Chinese music is overloaded with a pervasive symbolism conveyed by the playing on a 9-note Qing scale of some 72 different instruments, combined with nasal singing and posturing (Wiant 1965; Williams 1960: 143). Instruments made of stone, metal, bamboo, wood, skins, gourds, strings, or clay are thought by the Chinese to imitate human or animal voices, mythical creatures or demons, or the sounds of nature. The results often are too explosive, too highly pitched, or too discordant for Western tastes, which are cultivated to value harmony. Frontier newspaper reports describing various Chinese events frequently commented in derogatory terms on the accompanying music. A defensive Tucson Chinese is quoted as having responded to such lack of appreciation.

Our music is good—beautiful. It is yours which is bad. Your music is false—not like nature. Music is color. You take all your pots of paint and let them run together. You make confusion. The wind doesn't make music the way you say it does! A bird doesn't sing that way! A wave tumbles on the shore and makes one note

and only one. Yours is a music that is only noise. You play so soft that if I want to hear something I have to strain my ears. . . . We are a simple people and we are not going to change our music . . . founded on rules which are 4000 years and more old (*Arizona Daily Star*, May 21, 1889).

Four ubiquitous kinds of Chinese instruments confirm the continuation of traditional music at the Ying On compound (Fig. 3.81). All are low quality objects befitting the economic standing of users and listeners. They are included with ceremonial artifacts because it is believed their primary usage had been in affairs at the Chee Kung Tong room. Typically they were played to ward off evil spirits, to announce worshippers to the gods, and to create moods for theatricals and an atmosphere of exaggerated excitement. Two large brass gongs (*tam tam*) probably once had been suspended on a wooden stand in one of the group meeting places. Two bowl-shaped drums were not of a size and shape to have hung on the same rack but, instead, may have been hit with hard wooden mallets while supported on a tripod stand. Although more than twenty variations of drums are in the Chinese repertory, from very small to several feet in diameter, drums of this style and ones of comparable scale but flatter profile were most common in ordinary bands. A pair of brass cymbals and a possible odd single cymbal were held in the hands of seated performers. The fourth object is a typical wooden percussion instrument in which two hollowed slots in a solid block of wood produced distinct tones when struck. This kind of instrument was particularly favored for funeral dirges in beating out a rhythm to help coffin bearers keep in step and in recalling for all mourners the solemnity of the occasion (Wiant 1965).

A wire brush has been included tentatively with the small assortment of musical instruments, but its specific purpose

Figure 3.81. Chinese musical instruments, from TUR 22:2. *a*, One of two large brass gongs recovered appears to have been hammered to a round contour, then spun on a lathe and scraped while spinning. From a central concavo-convex area, it flattens out toward a slightly upturned lip. A raised central knob has a ragged strap of pink silk by which the instrument could have been suspended. Large and small black Chinese characters appear on the obverse, small ones on the reverse. Several large characters read *CANTON* [Guangzhou]. *b*, Pair of brass cymbals made in the same manner as the gongs, each had a suspension strap of white cotton cloth looped through a central knob. *c*, Rectangular percussion instrument made from a solid block of fine-grained hardwood that had been hollowed out from a slot opening along the two long sides. When struck, each face of the block yielded a different tone. A pair of holes drilled through one end permitted the insertion of a cotton suspension cord. *d*, Brush with fine wire bristles and wooden handle that may have been used to play a drum. *e*, One of two conical drums made of a thick wooden frame covered by heavy rawhide that was secured by three rows of metal studs. Painted red and black Chinese characters indicated this drum was made by the Ta Chang Company, Canton. A stamp on the second specimen shows it was the product of Chuan Shing, also of Canton. (Diameters in cm: *a*, 59.0; *b*, 24.2; *e*, 20.3. Lengths in cm: *c*, 23.8, width 10.0, height 6.6; *d*, 39.0.) Provenience: Unit 2, Room 7 (*a*), Room 19 (*b*, *c*, *e*); Unit 4, Room 11 (*d*). (Arizona State Museum photo by Helga Teiwes.)

admittedly is uncertain. It resembles metal brushes used occasionally by American drummers; it also could have been a more mundane tool for scouring woks or pans.

One square of bow resin of the sort used on violin strings was recovered from refuse in Unit 4, Room 11, but, even though such instruments were part of the usual Chinese musical ensembles, no violin had been discarded.

Only one of the instruments, a gong, was retrieved from the lodge room. The second gong was left in a more southerly room of the same unit of the building complex. The drums, cymbals, and percussion instrument were found in the room to the north. It is surmised the instruments were carted off by later residents after the Chee Kung Tong had no further need for them.

Initiation Materials

The procedure by which persons became full fledged Chee Kung Tong members was generally the same as it had been for the Hong Men of the previous century. In the nineteenth century the first step had been to cut off the mandatory queue demanded by the hated Manchus. By the time the tong was ensconced in the barrio, the wearing of the queue already had been discontinued universally. Next, initiates had their faces ceremonially washed and were dressed in suitable garb consisting of straw sandals, loose-fitting, long, white garments, and a red kerchief around the head. A pair of fiber slippers recovered in the lodge room is believed to have been such required footgear (Fig. 3.40*d*). There followed successive movements from an initial arch of wooden swords past iconographic obstacles toward the altar, pledges of fidelity, burning of incense, ritualistic consumption of wine, lighting of the Hong lamp, recitations, prayers, and reading of the 36 oaths. There remains no tangible clue to these actions, with the possible exception of a bill among Chee Kung Tong records for $5.00 to cover the cost of a Tucson-made oil lamp, which may have been a necessary replacement for the sacred lamp (Schlegel 1974: 41; University of Arizona Library, Special Collections, TUR manuscript collection). Finally, each person pricked a finger so that drops of blood would flow into pots of tea, which were sipped by all present. Formerly a cock was sacrificed to provide additional blood, but it is not known that this practice continued overseas. Following all this, the initiated received books of the oaths and recognition signs and badges of membership, such as the pin in Figure 3.82. They paid established fees for clothes, instruction, and foods to be served in a culminating meal.

Within the drab adobe walls of the lodge room, air heavy with odors of incense, charred paper money, hot candle wax, and body heat created an essence of ageless China. The flowers on the altar had become artificial ones, but at least for a few hours each month the Flowery Kingdom lived on on south Main Street.

Figure 3.82. Octagonal metal membership pin given a Chee Kung Tong initiate. The form and elements of design probably have symbolic significance (Chesneaux 1971, Fig. 1). The fact that it was recovered amid the attic debris in the courtyard latrine structure suggests that it was a part of the accoutrements of a secret society that someone felt should not fall into nonmember hands. (Width, 3.50 cm; thickness, 0.13 cm; TUR 22:2, attic of latrine; Arizona State Museum photo by Helga Teiwes.)

Business Records

As for any club, record keeping was a necessary part of the Chee Kung Tong management. In the nineteenth century this probably was accomplished with the aid of scribes, since the membership was drawn from the illiterate plebian classes. By the time the society was in its second headquarters on Main Street, some officers may have become functionally literate in several languages.

An assortment of objects left from their activities is intriguing but woefully incomplete. It includes a document said to be an official edict to the Chee Kung Tong branch in Tucson from the Supreme Lodge, Chinese Freemasons of the World, 36 Spofford Alley, San Francisco, California, USA. It had been mounted on a sheet of metal that, judging from corner holes, had been nailed to a wall. Another item indicating a presumed affiliation with the Masons was a rubber stamp bearing the Masonic seal, Chee Kung Tong name, and address at 85 south Main Street. A set of by-laws confirmed a second affiliation, this one to the Red Door branch of the Triad Society. Among other documents were a membership roster for 1920; a cloth-bound ledger with entries in Chinese for the decade 1914 to 1924; a general account book dated from 1920 to 1934; notes regarding monies owed and received by the society, including fees assessed for the reading of the 36 oaths; bills from the local utility company, from contractors who had made repairs to their quarters or done remodeling, and from newspapers from Vancouver, Havana, and San Francisco; and a group photograph of a 1923 conference (Fong 1978; University of Arizona Library, Special Collections, TUR manuscript collection).

Figure 3.83. Congratulatory banner of white silk bearing large black Chinese characters reading *Congratulation of Dai-Shan Ning Yang   Guild Hall completion   Club ideas and group effort   From comrades of trade union of Da-Fu.* (Length, 54.5 cm; width, 27.5 cm; TUR 22:2; Arizona State Museum photo by Helga Teiwes.)

YING ON MERCHANTS
AND LABOR BENEVOLENT ASSOCIATION

The Ying On Merchants and Labor Benevolent Association was an entirely different kind of organization than the Chee Kung Tong. However, in 1950 when it moved into new quarters on the southwest corner of the tenement block, its large meeting hall was graced with some of the same kind of furnishings as the Chee Kung Tong had used. A reporter from the *Arizona Daily Star* on April 18, 1950, commented on a gilded teak shrine said to be 150 years old and a statue of Kuan Kung that had been transported from the Association's former headquarters across Main Street. An accompanying photograph reveals the presence also of traditional vertical banners with inscriptions and a brass urn, as well as the United States flag and seal of the organization. The secular nature of the group precluded other accoutrements such as were found in secret society rooms.

Inasmuch as the Ying On association remained active in the civic affairs of the community after the TUR project, nearly all its decorative objects were removed from the building prior to demolition. Two exceptions were congratulatory banners that had been presented by other organizations on the completion of the building on south Main Street. One of these was a length of pink polished cotton painted with characters translated as:

> The opening ceremony of the Ying Rui showing completion of the new business building.

The other similar congratulatory message was on a length of white silk from the trade union of Da-Fu (Fig. 3.83).

CHAPTER FOUR

Euro-American Artifacts From Chinese Proveniences

Ayres (1980: 10) reports that 19 excavated proveniences produced Chinese artifacts. In the area of the first Chinatown, some tests concentrated on the zone where tenements, a grocery store, an opium den, and a wash-house were shown variously on maps from 1883 to 1896 (Figs. 1.3, 1.6). Other tests on or adjacent to the property of the leading Chinese merchant explored features that probably had been associated with a second opium den, a store, and a dwelling (Fig. 2.1). Immediately to the east in the triangular block between Pearl and Main streets there had been a joss house and some businesses.

Although Ayres considers these localities to be exclusively Chinese, all localities had been occupied previously by Hispanics and Euro-Americans. Some of them had been property owners who later rented facilities to Chinese. According to the 1898 Tucson Block Book (Arizona Historical Society), the area the TUR engineers designated Block 2 (Block 185 in 1898) had been owned then by Frank Hereford (later sold to W. Paulson) and F. S. Romero. Block 3 (Block 188 in 1898) was owned by Chan Tin Wo, A. Caballero, R. Pacheco, J. Pacheco, and S. W. Whitside (Fig. 4.1). Chan Tin Wo had acquired his home from Euro-American pioneer, William S. Oury (Peterson 1966: 166; Smith 1967: 150), who had purchased it from Francisco Torano in 1857, just three years after the Gadsden Purchase. The 1898 Block 189 across the street from TUR Block 3 was divided between Zechendorf, Johnson, and Warner.

An unknown number of Hispanics and Euro-Americans continued to live among the Chinese until the area was closed. The Hispanics were sufficiently significant in number for mappers to indicate the largest rooming houses as "Mexican-Chinese tenements."

Similarly, south of Congress Street, Euro-American and Hispanic businesses and domiciles had come and gone on blocks of known Chinese occupation both prior to and coeval with it. A hotel catering primarily to Euro-American customers was erected on one block that at various times also contained a Chinese wash-house, restaurant, and dwellings. The confused history of Block 22, the hub of the second Chinatown, is recounted elsewhere in this study.

With this documented mixed occupation, it was to be expected that the artifact collection retrieved from exploration of these localities would represent something of the material culture of all three ethnic groups, as well as earthenwares

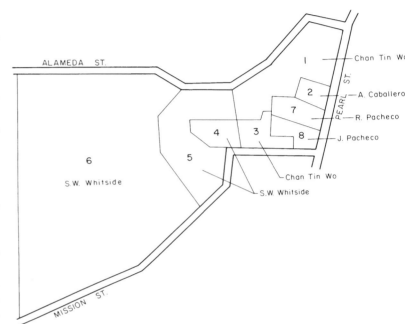

Figure 4.1. Parcels of Block 188 of the 1898 Tucson town site were owned by three Hispanics, one Euro-American, and the Chinese merchant Chan Tin Wo. Some structures on these properties may have been rented occasionally to other Chinese. Engineers for the Tucson Urban Renewal project numbered the eastern portion of this area Block 3. Excavations in four latrines, one well, and two trenches at TUR 3:4 provided cultural materials left from all three ethnic groups. (Tucson Block Book, 1898, Arizona Historical Society.)

and basketry of Tohono O'odham Indians who resided in two places nearby and were known to have sold their products to town dwellers (Fig. 1.2). It seems safe to assume that most of the recovered Chinese goods had been used by Chinese residents. The American goods utilized by both Euro-Americans and Hispanics present another problem. The gaps and inconsistencies in the available property records, directories, and maps, and the sometimes unclear associations of artifacts, as well as the excavation in arbitrary rather than natural levels, makes user attribution debatable. Still, from the beginning of their presence in Tucson, some Chinese acquisition of American items is plausible because of marketing circumstances and a slowly emerging Americanization of part of the Asian community. Comparable associations of American and Chinese goods have been noted in other places in the West.

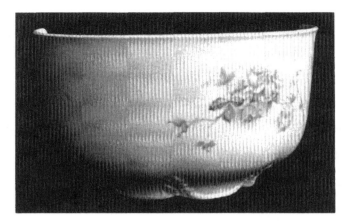

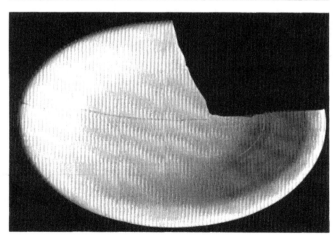

Figure 4.2. Euro-American ceramics possibly used by Chinese. *Top*, small bowl with undecorated interior and floral motif on exterior. (Diameter, 12.6 cm; height, 7.5 cm; TUR 3:4–2aL4.) *Center*, Granite Ware shaving mug with gold lettering and rim and basal bands. (Base diameter, 7.5 cm; height, 8.2 cm; TUR 2:1–5b.) *Bottom*, small, undecorated, oval dish. (Length, 13.3 cm; width, 9.5 cm; height, 2.7 cm; TUR 3:4–2bL2.)

Figure 4.3. Hallmarks on bases of ceramics illustrated in Figure 4.2. *Top*, dog head, *Vitreous   P & G*, unidentified. *Center*, *Dresden Stone China   1894*, mark of Brunt, Bloor, Martin, and Company, East Liverpool, Ohio, open from 1875 to about 1900 (Gates and Ormerod 1982: 214). *Bottom*, *Ironstone China*, Royal Crest, *Alfred Meakin Tunstall   England*, produced between 1879 and 1896 (Pastron, Prichett, and Ziebarth 1981, Vol. 3: 693).

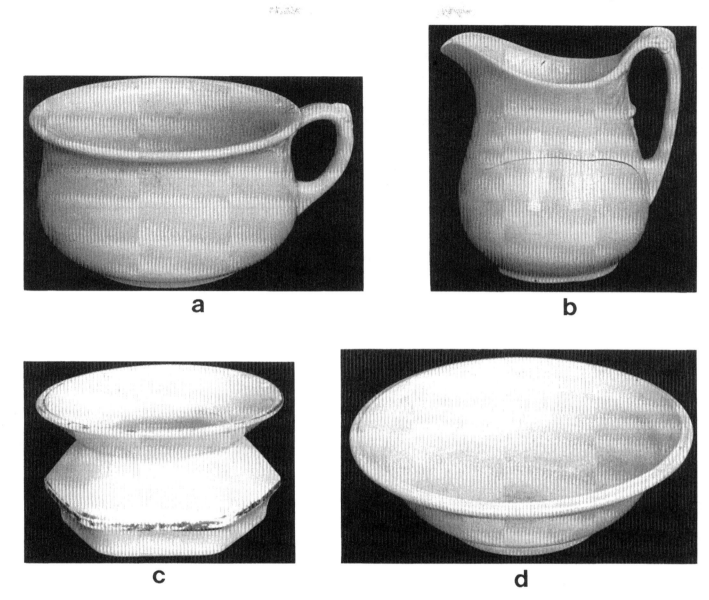

a   **b**   **c**   **d**

Figure 4.4. Victorian-era Euro-American personal household furnishings typically used by Tucson Chinese. *a*, White improved earthenware chamber pot is marked on base *Powell Bishop*. *b*, Heavy white pitcher of sort used with wash basin is marked on the base *Royal Ironstone China Charles Meakin England*. *c*, White glass spittoon representing accommodation to American habits by Chinese men notoriously given to expectorating in public. A reporter noted similar objects in the Chee Kung Tong room (Arizona Citizen, February 22, 1935). *d*, White improved earthenware wash basin marked on base *Pearl White Goodwin Bros*. (Diameters and heights in cm: *a*, 22.1, 14.0; *b*, 12.0 by 17.0, 18.0; *c*, orifice diameter 17.7, 10.0; *d*, 25.1, 12.0.) Provenience: TUR 3:4–3aL6 (*a*), 3:4–5bL2 (*b*); TUR 22:2, Unit 2, Room 26 (*c*), Unit 3, Room 3 (*d*).

Although need for tablewares in addition to those from China was limited, a few random pieces of Euro-American ceramics likely were put to use by Chinese settlers (Figs. 4.2–4.5). In the territorial period most items are unidentifiable whitewares and ironstones that formed the basic outfitting of contemporary Euro-American households. A few pieces, such as those in Figure 4.3, bear hallmarks. The Charles Meakin factory, located in Staffordshire, produced these kinds of wares from approximately 1870 to 1890 (Pastron, Prichett, and Ziebarth 1981, Appendix D, Table 10.01), and Meakin wares are known in Chinese contexts at Sacramento and Fort Ross, California. Wares from the Goodwin Brothers factory, operating in East Liverpool, Ohio, between 1876 and 1893 (Gates and Ormerod 1982: 52, Fig. 43a), have been recorded from Sacramento and Lovelock (Praetzellis and Praetzellis 1979: 167, 170). The disparity of twenty or thirty years between manufacturing dates and occupation-use dates can be attributed to retainment or acquisition of older ceramics at reduced costs.

Through time a diverse assortment of cheap objects used for cooking and eating was acquired by the Chinese bachelors on south Main Street. An inventory of things left in

Figure 4.5. Small brimmed plate with a handpainted pattern of an Apache Indian woman and baby in a typical cradleboard executed in dark brown, tan, blue, and light purple against a white ground. A gold band runs around the scalloped edge. The human figures likely were copied from a photograph, as Indians were especially popular with Arizona photographers in the late nineteenth century. The hallmark indicates the plate was made in Germany for a Euro-American distributor. Use of this plate by Chinese reflects the cultural cross currents at work in the American West. (Diameter, 15.6 cm; height, 1.8 cm; TUR 22:2, Unit 2, Room 1.)

Unit 3, Room 2 (Table 2.1), includes ceramic dishes, bowls, and cups of unknown kinds; tumblers, cups, and bowls of glass; a tin mug; and several styrofoam cups, showing that the room's occupant had the same array of things as his low-income Euro-American and Hispanic neighbors.

Another example of Chinese use of non-traditional items might be found in writing materials. None of the calligraphic brushes or brass boxes of solid ink such as were recovered in the Ying On rooms were unearthed in the excavations, but undoubtedly they were standard equipment in some households. When solid ink was unavailable, locally obtained ink in liquid form may have been substituted (Fig. 4.6). That rare person attempting to write in the languages of non-Chinese neighbors would have used liquid ink with pens, which require a different set of motor habits.

A slate board and slate pencils found in TUR 22:2 and 69:2 possibly were associated with Chinese contexts. They were common writing accessories of Euro-American Tucsonans during both the territorial and early statehood eras, and they may have been introduced to the Chinese in the church-sponsored schools offering instruction in English and in the Scriptures.

Not illustrated but noted in the Ying On compound refuse were such commonplace American stationery supplies as writing paper, envelopes, ballpoint pens, and stamp pads, which verify a crossover to contemporary Western habits.

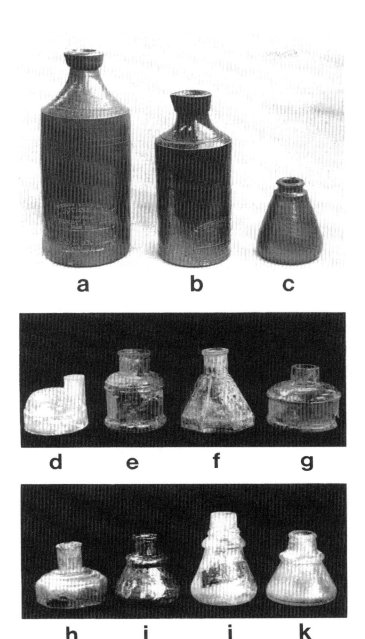

Figure 4.6. Ink and mucilage containers possibly associated with Chinese contexts of the territorial era. *a*, Brown, cylindrical, narrow-mouthed, heavy bottle bearing an impressed inscription reading *Vitreous Stone Bottles   J. Bourne & Son   Patendees   Denby Pottery   Near Derby   R & J Arnold   London*. *b*, Similar bottle and inscriptions. *c*, Small, pear-shaped bottle of same composition but lacking an inscription, described by Wilson (1981) as a cone stand style. *Middle row*, glass ink bottles: *d*, inkwell; *e*, *Thomas Inks* molded on base; *f*, eight-sided specimen; *g*, *L. H. Thomas Co   Chicago* molded on base. *Bottom row*, glass ink and mucilage bottles: *h*, blue glass, eight-sided; *i*, *Carter's   Made in U.S.A.* molded on base; *j*, bears label reading *Thomas   Mucilage*; *k*, mucilage bottle. Bottles comparable to some of these are identified and dated in Wilson (1981): *a*, pages 409, 412, dated 1863–1890; *c*, page 390, 1865–1890; *d*, page 420, 1880–1890; *f*, page 379, 1870–1890; *i*, page 385, 1875–1890; *k*, page 383, 1875–1890. (Heights and base diameters in cm: *a*, 18.3, 7.5; *b*, 15.0, 6.3; *c*, 7.0, 5.5; *d*, 4.3, 5.6; *e*, 6.9, 5.1; *f*, 6.9, 5.1; *g*, 5.6, 6.4; *h*, 5.0, 5.5; *i*, 6.3, 6.0; *j*, 8.2, 6.0; *k*, 6.3, 6.3.) Provenience: TUR 3:4–5bL3 (*a*), 3:4–5bL2 (*b*, *k*), 3:4–3aL10 (*e*, *g*); TUR 2:1–L5b (*c*, *d*), 2:1–2f5b (*h*); TUR 22:2–5bSecE–L2 (*f*), 22:2–2fL2 (*i*), 22:2–2bL1 (*j*).

Figure 4.7. Chemical and proprietary medicine bottles possibly associated with Chinese contexts of the territorial era. *Left*, long-necked, collared, rectangular bottle of clear glass. *Hegeman & Co New York   Chemists* molded on side panels. *Right*, short-necked, collared with lower ring, clear, light green glass bottle. *Dr. Kilmer's   Swamp   Root   Kidney   Liver & Bladder Cure* molded in oval center panel on front; *The Great Specific* molded above and below center panel. *Binghamton N.Y.   Dr. Kilmer & Co* molded on side panels. (Heights and lengths of bases in cm: *left*, 25.4, 7.5; *right*, 21.5, 7.4.) Provenience: TUR 22:2–2bL1 (*left*), 22:2–2aL3 (*right*).

The Chinese arrival on the Arizona frontier coincided with the height of the American craze for proprietary medicines and cure-alls. Since the Chinese already had an ageless respect for herbal medicines and their mode of life subjected them to a variety of common ailments, they may have been ready consumers of Western preparations. However, all the examples of medicinal bottles illustrated in Figures 4.7 through 4.10 were recovered from latrines in the Ying On compound where exclusive Chinese utilization cannot be demonstrated (Figs. 2.15–2.17). In the later years of Chinese residency in the TUR district, the bottles formerly containing proprietary medicines were replaced in their trash by common nonprescription products such as Listerine and Bromo-Seltzer.

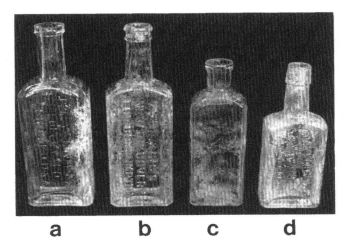

a   b   c   d

Figure 4.8. A sample of glass proprietary medicine bottles possibly associated with Chinese contexts of the territorial era. *a*, Long-necked, thickened lip, rectangular bottle of clear glass. *Foley's Honey & Tar Foley & Co Chicago USA* molded on front panel. *b*, Long-necked, double-collared, rectangular bottle of clear, light blue glass (Wilson 1981: 110, ginger panel style, dated 1865–1890). *Dr. King's New Discovery For Consumption* molded on front panel. *Chicago Ill H. E. Bucklin & Co* molded on side panels. *c*, Short-necked, thickened lip, rectangular bottle of clear glass. *C. W. Cole Co "Three in One"* molded on side panel. *d*, Long-necked, collared, rectangular bottle of clear, light green glass (Wilson 1981: 161, dated 1885–1890). *Chamberlain's Cholic and Diarrohea Remedy* molded on front panel; *Chamberlain Med. Co. Des Moines IA U.S.A.* molded on side panels. (Heights and lengths of bases in cm: *a* and *b*, 17.1, 5.6; *c*, 14.0, 4.7; *d*, 14.0, 5.2.) Provenience: TUR 22:2–2fL1 (*a*, *b*), 22:2–2fL2 (*c*), 22:2–2aL4 (*d*).

Figure 4.10. Florida Water bottles. Although generally regarded as a toiletry preparation to perfume and soothe the body in summer heat, Florida Water may have been used by some Chinese to reduce the effects of sunburn. For that reason, these examples are included with medicinal bottles. *Left*, long-necked, collared, cylindrical bottle of clear, light blue glass. *Florida Water Murray & Lanman Druggists New York* molded on front. A comparable specimen is illustrated in Wilson (1981: 229) dated 1870–1890, although Pastron, Prichett, and Ziebarth (1981: 630) place the introduction of the product between 1837 and 1847. *Right*, long-necked collared, cylindrical bottle of clear, light blue glass. *Solon Palmer's Florida Water New York* molded on front. (Heights and lengths of bases: *left*, 22.9, 5.6; *right*, 15.8, 3.6.) Provenience: TUR 22:2–2fL2 (*a*), (*left*), 22:2–2fL1 (*right*).

Figure 4.9. Proprietary medicine bottles possibly associated with Chinese contexts of the territorial era. *Left*, short-necked, collared, rectangular bottle of clear glass. *Sciroppo Pagliano* molded on front panel. *Right*, short-necked, lipped, pear-shaped bottle of dark amber color (Wilson 1981: 130, dated 1871–1890). *Valentine's Meat Juice* molded on front. The Valentine Meat Juice Company, of Richmond, Virginia, claimed the product was good for fever, exhaustion, and critical conditions before and after operations (Awald 1968). (Heights and lengths of bases in cm: *left*, 11.4, 3.5; *right*, 8.2, 4.4.) Provenience: TUR 22:2–2cL3 (*left*), 22:2–2eL3 (*right*).

Figure 4.11. Ale and beer bottles. *Left*, two-toned, salt-glazed, stoneware bottle with wire bail, used to contain ale. Wilson (1981: 17) illustrates a similar specimen dated 1863–1890 and indicates (page 7) that ale bottles appeared earlier than beer bottles on the western frontier because ale could be shipped without pasteurization. *Center*, blue bubbly, glass bottle for beer with tapered collar and molded ring below it. *A.B.Co B16* molded on base refers to American Bottle Company, in operation from 1905 to 1919 (Ayres and others 1986). *Right*, clear, bubbly glass bottle bearing raised numerals *934* on base. (Heights and base diameters in cm: *left*, 21.5, 7.3; *center*, 24.0, 6.3; *right*, 24.0, 6.4.) Provenience: TUR 22:2–5bSecE–L1 (*left*), 22:2–2cL3 (*right*); TUR 3:4–3aL9 (*center*).

Figure 4.12. Heavy, thick-walled soda-water bottles. The thick, rounded collars were needed to hold wired-on corks in place. *Left*, bluish glass bottle; *Acme Soda Works Ventura Cal* molded in oval frame on front indicates a date later than 1880, when the Southern Pacific Railroad made feasible ready shipment of such products. *Center*, clear, light green glass bottle with *J.F.I. Tucson* molded on front. The John F. Innis Company, a local bottling works, was in business until 1881. It was sold to the Pioneer Soda and Ice Works, which may have continued to use the stock of bottles of its predecessor until 1896. Part of a wire bail is caught inside the bottle. *Right*, clear glass bottle that might have contained root beer; *Hires* is molded on the base. (Heights and base diameters in cm: *left*, 17.5, 6.0; *center*, 17.7, 5.6; *right*, 23.4, 6.1.) Provenience: TUR 3:4–2aL4 (*left*), TUR 2:1L3 (*center*), TUR 22:2–2fL3 (*right*).

An entrenched habit of beverage consumption, the aridity of the Sonoran Desert, the traumas associated with the self-imposed way of life, added to the local availability of liquors and soda waters, account for the association of more of these kinds of bottles than any other with Chinese occupation. Native Chinese liquor of one type was imported in such limited quantity that it gradually was reserved for special celebrations.

Similar spirits and nonalcoholic beverage bottles have been reported commonly from other overseas Chinese sites. In this report most, but not all, of the illustrated examples (Figs. 4.11–4.14) were found within the trenches and latrines of the Ying On compound, where ethnic attribution is uncertain (Figs. 2.15–2.17). However, the few dates available coincide with the period when the latrines were in use and various Chinese establishments were in the immediate vicinity.

According to Wilson (1981: 7), ale bottles such as that in Figure 4.11 *left* appeared earlier on the western frontier because ale could be shipped without pasteurization. Although ale likely was consumed by Chinese, at the turn of the twentieth century beer was becoming a popular beverage in China because of the efforts of German brewmasters (Clayre 1984: 120). A taste for this drink either may have been acquired during home visits of sojourners or as a result of interaction with local Euro-Americans and Hispanics.

a   b   c   d

Figure 4.13. Beverage bottles. *a*, Clear, cylindrical flat-based, glass bottle with tapered collar and ring below it, for wine or brandy. *b*, Light green, cylindrical, glass bottle with tapered collar and ring below it, for wine or brandy. Base is kicked up. *c*, *d*, Cylindrical, flat-based, glass bottles, each with collared neck and molded ring below it (for bitters?); *c* is dark green, *d* is amber. (Heights and base diameters in cm: *a*, 28.3, 7.4; *b*, 29.7, 7.4; *c*, 26.8, 8.2; *d*, 28.9, 8.0.) Provenience: TUR 3:4–2aL1 (*a*), 3:4–2aL3 (*d*); TUR 22:2–2bL2 (*b*), 22:2–2aL2 (*c*).

Cheap and plentiful on the Arizona frontier, the bottles in which it came littered Chinese deposits.

Since the Chinese population was predominately composed of men whose household chores can be assumed to have been limited, the sort of bottles containing domestic supplies recovered in possible association with Chinese contexts is relatively negligible. Other than soap and starch, these immigrants were not interested in Western-style cleaning, bleaching, or dyeing preparations. Their traditional cloth slippers did not require polish, and work boots probably did not get any. In later years when low-cut leather shoes became the usual footgear, some polishing became routine. The Chinese food habits did not entail prepared bottled condiments, extracts, or sauces, such as Euro-American or His-panic housewives used. What the Chinese may have purchased in bottles were products needed to keep small tools functioning. One long-necked, double-collared, greenish glass bottle from TUR 3:4 was labeled *Crown Sewing Machine Oil*, and a short-necked, lipped, clear glass bottle had molded on the base *Special Battery Oil Thomas A. Edison Incorporated Primary Battery Division Bloomfield N.J. U.S.A. Reg. U.S. Mark Pat. Off. Made in U.S.A.* (TUR 22:2).

Small Euro-American toilet articles such as combs, razors, and toothbrushes likely were acquired by local Chinese (Fig. 4.15). Only the combs had identifiable Chinese counterparts.

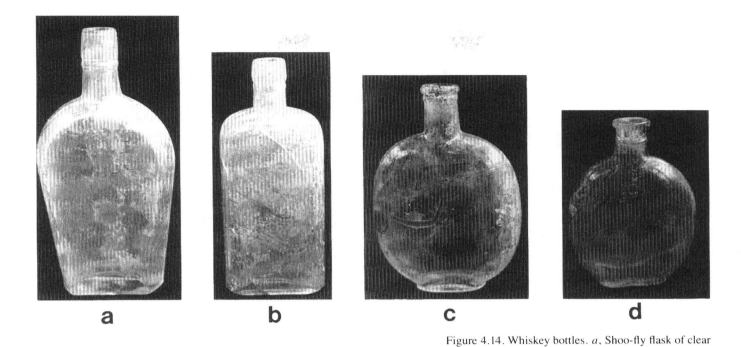

Figure 4.14. Whiskey bottles. *a*, Shoo-fly flask of clear glass, one of four from the same provenience. Wilson (1981: 36) describes similar flasks as having a brandy neck finish, dating 1865–1890. *b*, Clear glass, collared bottle termed by Wilson (1981: 32) a picnic flask, dating 1865–1890. *c*, *d*, Handmade, colorless, round-bodied, glass picnic flasks for whiskey. Because they do not have labels or molded distillery names, they are presumed to have been filled in a local saloon from bulk supplies. Wilson (1981: 31, 33, 39) dates similar bottles 1863–1890. They are estimated to have held approximately 16 and 8 ounces respectively of sour mash. (Heights and length of bases in cm: *a*, 20.0, 7.5; *b*, 17.2, 7.0; *c*, 14.0, base diameter 4.4; *d*, 11.2, base diameter 4.8.) Provenience: TUR 22:2–2eL3 (*a*, *c*, *d*), 22:2–2aL3 (*b*).

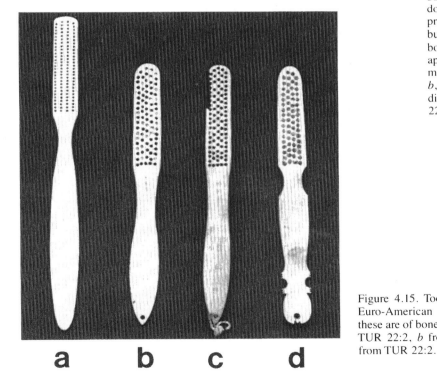

Figure 4.15. Toothbrush handles are frequent items of Euro-American derivation in Tucson Chinese refuse; these are of bone: *a*, handle marked *The Conqueror*, from TUR 22:2, *b* from TUR 2:1–3, *c* from TUR 2:1–4, *d* from TUR 22:2.

CHAPTER FIVE

Accommodation, Assimilation, and Social Stratification

Archaeology accomplished during the TUR project fails to elucidate many details relevant to the important anthropological questions of accommodation, assimilation, and social stratification. The 20-year-old archaeological data were gathered with other goals in mind. Nor is it known with certainty that material things, the stuff of archaeology, necessarily reflect those conditions in regard to the overseas Chinese.

During the first half century of their presence in the western states, the Chinese continued to use traditional items wherever possible. That preference underlies accumulations of Chinese trash in proveniences in the first Tucson Chinatown. However, subsequent political unrest, from the fall of the Manchus to the rise of the Communists (corresponding to the time of Arizona statehood until after World War II), periodically interrupted trade and distribution of desired goods from China to her citizens abroad. Although Hong Kong and Taiwan took advantage of that situation, this cutting off of usual sources of supply brought a greater volume of American goods into the hands of overseas Chinese than otherwise might have happened. Even so, perhaps until the 1930s it would stretch credibility to claim that substantial utilization of American items necessarily equalled assimilation.

THE ARCHAEOLOGICAL RECORD

The distinctive Chinese articles that substantiate occupation within the boundaries of the first Chinatown were stoneware food and spirits containers, stoneware and porcelain tableware, opium containers and smoking paraphernalia, coins, and glass medicine vials. During excavation all articles of possible Chinese derivation were saved, whereas large amounts of Euro-American goods from the same deposits were discarded. It is notable that all Chinese items within any category were of the same kinds and calibers, making it impossible to distinguish "capitalist" Chan's discards from those of the lowliest sojourner who lived across the street in a crowded tenement. Doubtless the more luxurious items in Chan's household were removed when the family departed. Quantitative data are not meaningful for comparative purposes because the exploration of one block was limited to trenching several trash pits, whereas in the second block four latrines, two trenches, and a well were dug. The well may have been the one described in an 1870 real estate

advertisement as having "the best well water in town" (*Arizonan*, June 18, 1870), but it did not produce an abundance of articles tossed into it by later users.

Chinese preference for their native material culture enabled excavators in the southern barrio to confirm later occupation recorded by contemporary mappers. Again, inasmuch as the goods recovered matched items from the first Chinatown in style and quality, no social stratification or substantial temporal distinction can be verified through retrieved artifacts. Because sampling concentrated on areas of potentially the greatest density of Chinese (that is, the locale of the sojourner masses), there was a homogeneity within artifact categories that thwarted socially oriented research.

Notwithstanding these drawbacks, items recovered archaeologically in the barrio indicate that the Chinese there were successful in maintaining some of their dietary and recreational habits. One exception was the consumption of spirits, which generally had to be acquired from American sources. Attribution of Euro-American things is not positive because of conditions noted earlier, but the impression is that their use by Chinese did rise over time, first, as substitutes for commodities not available from China or to supplement them and, later, out of preference. A few articles, such as leather shoes, were accepted quickly as being more practical for certain situations. Whether the steady increase in utilization of American goods can be interpreted as growing assimilation is a moot point, but it is at least suggestive. There is no evidence for a comparable absorption of Hispanic material culture, and it appears that the Chinese made only rare use of friable Mexican earthenwares. Otherwise, most articles in circulation in Tucson were common to both Euro-American and Hispanic users and therefore cannot be markers for cultural affiliation.

THE ETHNOGRAPHIC RECORD

Expectedly, the ethnographic collection from the Ying On compound fills many gaps in the repertory of material goods known to have been used commonly by overseas Chinese and provides proof of production into recent times of some styles of imported items. It strongly suggests a situation of coping through moderate acceptance of American products, although perhaps without any fundamental assimilation of the American life style itself. However, recognition must be made of a bias in the data resulting from the fact that *all* identifiable Chinese items were saved, whereas those thought to be of Euro-American, Hispanic, or other derivation were retained more selectively. Photographs and several inventories taken of vacated rooms substantiate this field practice (Figs. 2.25–2.31; Table 2.1). It is obvious that from the time of the move into the Ying On compound, the basic outfitting was low-caliber American. Additionally, a veneer of Chinese articles related to personal habits of diet, costume, diversion, ceremonialism, and written communication enabled their users to successfully maintain their Asian identity and a group cohesiveness that, in their eyes, set them apart from "others." There is no way now of determining which, if any, of those things were residuals saved for sentimental reasons through a lengthy occupancy that eventually were used less often as time passed. Moreover, the specialized use during the 1920s and 1930s of certain rooms as headquarters for two highly characteristic late Qing and early Republican organizations, the Chee Kung Tong and Guomindang, also may unduly influence the notion of accommodation. The discarded belongings of these two groups, associated with reaffirmation of political, philosophical, and sociological values peculiar to the homeland from which members or their forebears emanated, are sufficiently distinctive to distort interpretation. That is to say, to Euro-American observers the print of George Washington reported to have been on the Guomindang wall pales before a comparable print of Sun Yat Sen and the flag of the Republic of China simply because of their novelty in Tucson (*Arizona Daily Star*, Rodeo Edition, February 22, 1935). On the other hand, members of the post-World War II Ying On Merchants and Labor Benevolent Association, which acquired the compound and erected a two-story meeting lodge at one corner, epitomized the new breed of enfranchised civic and business leaders of the Chinese community. The trappings they left in their hall are recognizably Chinese but can hardly be used as evidence for nonassimilation.

Another facet of the evaluation of the Ying On compound material is that most, but not all, of the single male tenants who paraded through the premises for half a century in actuality represented an aberration from, rather than the norm of, the coeval barrio Chinese. Further, any clue to social stratification within the compound enclave was lacking in the materials recovered because most residents apparently were in the lower economic levels.

The character of the boarders in the compound changed through the years. At times they were transients looking for jobs and lodging elsewhere. In early days one suspects some were escaping the eagle eyes of United States marshals, inasmuch as the Chee Kung Tong was thought to have engaged in smuggling both illegal entrants and opium into the United States via Mexico. Other residents were indigents provided for by the associations. These organizations were known to take care of their own and keep Chinese off the public

dole, an activity that was particularly strong in the 1930s when three dozen unattached Chinese men crowded into the compound's meager rooms (*Arizona Daily Star*, Rodeo Edition, February 22, 1935). Together they cooked, ate, slept, smoked opium, gambled, and carried on the Chee Kung Tong rituals much as the sojourners of a previous generation. Outside the compound, the atmosphere was Depression America for the Chinese families (composed of American-born father, mother, and children or alien father and one or more alien sons brought in under his sponsorship). Inside the compound life was more apt to reflect Old China, in spite of the use of American utensils, hand tools, clothing, or furniture. Although the evidence is uneven, it does suggest that for most of these pre-World War II residents, the line of least resistance kept them in the comfortable, familiar tracks of the Chinese lifeway, with minimal help from American resources when necessary or affordable. But the lack of their unqualified acceptance by the broader community kept the Chinese informally segregated.

The two organizations that shared the compound exploited the conservatism of its residents and may have obstructed or slowed the integration process, but the organizations themselves also changed with the times. Much of the Chee Kung Tong ritualism, for example, was anachronistic in the Tucson of the 1920s and 1930s, but it appears to have been carried out regularly with due solemnity. The obsolete revolutionary goals were forgotten, and the strict tenets of blood brotherhood behavior were softened to conform to more modern points of view. The lodge was transformed into purely a social center, as confirmed by a visiting Chinese writer (L. Lee 1938). The most intriguing change, revealed by documents recovered during the TUR research, was that the once-secret society restricted to Chinese had begun to accept non-Asian members. In 1920 all six such new recruits were Euro-Americans, only one of whom lived near the Chinese quarter (University of Arizona Library, Special Collections, TUR manuscript collection). Aside from a mellowing of Chinese behavior, that fact points to a continuing tolerance on the part of some Euro-Americans and perhaps a continuing resistance on the part of some Hispanics.

Some time in the 1920s the Guomindang, or Nationalist Party, set up headquarters next to the sympathetic Chee Kung Tong (Wong 1982: 22) in a large room that opened to south Main Street. A vertical flagpole was raised over its entrance (Fig. 2.21 *bottom*). Tucson's layered history was such that few individuals were startled to see the brilliant red flag of the Republic of China (Fig. 3.76 *right*) flapping in the breeze over the surrounding Hispanic neighborhood along what some 150 years earlier had been Spain's Royal Road to the northern borderlands.

The Guomindang had evolved out of a revolutionary band led by Sun Yat Sen. By 1929 it had become the dominant political party of China, controlling the government through an organizational structure similar to that of the Russian

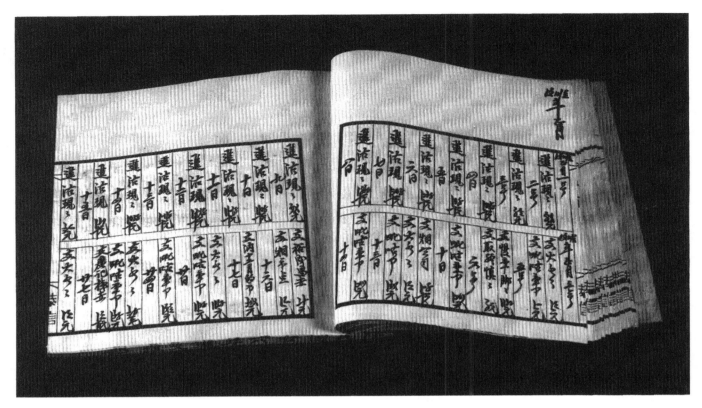

Figure 5.1. Ledger of the Chung Hsing Company, bearing a date of 1937, from TUR 22:2. The book, made in China, is bound in dark blue cloth laced together with red cord. Pages are doubled sheets with black vertical lines and red borders imprinted on them. (TUR manuscript collection, Special Collections, University of Arizona Library, Tucson; Arizona State Museum photo by Helga Teiwes.)

Communist Party (Wang 1982: 19). Overseas cells in all areas where the Chinese had settled and their financial and moral support were vital cogs in the party mechanism for several important reasons. First, persons of Chinese racial extraction were regarded as citizens of China regardless of place of birth, and there was an undercurrent of concern that they not slip away from their cultural moorings. Second, those Chinese who had had enough courage and ambition to move abroad permanently often had gained greater resources and political awareness. From the perspective of Euro-Americans, on the other hand, the Guomindang was another linkage to the Old Country that potentially might delay integration.

Recovered documents in the Main Street tenement indicate that borderline poverty did not prevent local Chinese from dispatching monies to China through the Guomindang to help political causes there. At one point sufficient donations were collected that Sun Yat Sen himself responded with a foot-long letter of thanks and encouragement. Proudly, it was framed and hung on the chapter wall (*Arizona Daily Star*, Rodeo Edition, February 22, 1935). It was difficult, nonetheless, for men living in peace halfway around the world to maintain any sense of involvement in a stream of chaotic events in China that seemed never to improve the lot of most of their homeland relatives. Apathy slowly ate away

interest, until by the mid 1930s the meeting room had become mainly a social hall where men met to talk, play games, or enjoy refreshments. Even so, some residue of anxiety for what was transpiring in the Old Country continued, as evidenced by receipts recovered of contributions to help fight the Japanese or the Communists and by sheets in various denominations of Nationalist liberty bonds.

At the same time that interest in what was taking place in the homeland slowly faded, other documents show a rise in concern about civic affairs relevant to Chinese in the United States. Dues cards from the American-Chinese Citizens Alliance were retrieved from rubbish in a number of compound rooms, suggesting the duality of allegiance that had arisen as a result of Chinese births in America.

Most of the collected personal papers of men who called the Ying On compound home date from the two decades after World War II. Earlier documents had been such things as ticket stubs for steerage passage from Hong Kong or Yokohama to San Francisco, United States Certificates of Identification as required under the Exclusion Act, medical papers, business ledgers kept in the traditional manner (Fig. 5.1), and ration coupons issued during the war. But postwar materials were Social Security cards, Selective Service notices, tax receipts, automobile registrations, dog licenses, give-away calendars dating from 1949 to 1957, family photographs and letters, records of international cash transfers, bank statements, receipts for rent paid to the Ying On Association that had purchased the property, papers from the Arizona Department of Public Welfare for old age assistance, and bills for cemetery lots and future burial. Indeed, even though they may have eaten with chopsticks, enjoyed an occasional game of Chinese checkers, puffed on an opium pipe now and then, and written in calligraphic script, most of these men of the 1950s and 1960s had become full-fledged participants in the American system. The papers show that some Chinese successfully had made their way through the years in various local mercantile and food service businesses but, at advanced age, alone, and with no compelling reason to go elsewhere, had settled in Ying On rentals to live out their remaining allotted years.

The modest inventory of material possessions used by these late residents was overwhelmingly American (Table 2.1): tools and hardware to keep objects functioning or to improvise others if needed; brooms, brushes, linens, and mops with which to keep house; utensils to prepare and eat a variety of foods that apparently had expanded to include dishes that were not traditionally Chinese; clothes that were indistinguishable from those of other lower class barrio residents; and a gamut of over-the-counter medicines and toilet articles.

Lacking funds, some Ying On bachelor tenants left behind a number of examples of how they coped. A fireplace poker with a U-shaped end had been bent from an iron rod. A dustpan had been cut from the base and sides of a five-gallon tin can. Wire clothes hangers had been twisted into trivets. A piece of copper tubing had been inserted into the broken spout of a teapot so that liquid could continue to be poured from the vessel. A metal door knob, an oil squirt can, and a small Mexican earthenware jar had been drilled to substitute for the ceramic bowls of opium pipes. Pump drills likely used for enlarging bowl apertures had been made from porcelain door knobs, metal tubing, wood strips, steel bits, and abrading stones. Pipes for smoking tobacco had been created from parts of commercial bowls and long, hollowed, wood tubes or bamboo. Scuffs had been made by cutting away unwanted parts of high shoes.

The composite picture that emerges from these random observations is one of life on the raw edge, endured in shelters best described as the wrecks of another era. Many of the unused rooms of the compound were in dangerous disrepair. Roofs leaked, ceilings collapsed, earthen walls caved in, floors sagged, and window glass cracked and fell out. Most rooms were adrift with refuse that had accumulated for over fifty years. Were it not for the prevailing aridity of the Sonoran Desert, the odors and bacteria of abandonment and decay and concomitant rodent and insect infestation would have made them even more of a serious health hazard. The several rooms in use at the time of final abandonment (Unit 3, Room 4; Unit 4, Rooms 1–3) were in better condition but had exposed electrical wiring, heat by cook stoves, no plumbing, and only rudimentary makeshift furniture. By

any evaluation, it was substandard housing.

Burdened with old age lethargy and lack of purpose, crushing poverty, loneliness, and perhaps poor health, these last elderly occupants hung on virtually as wards of the association and of the State of Arizona. Whether technically Chinese American or not, they were survivors who had become lost in a vacuum somewhere between two worlds.

In sharp contrast, the Ying On facilities at the southwest corner of the compound, dedicated in 1950 at a ceremony attended by state and federal officials and numerous Chinese American leaders from other cities, was a blend of Occident and Orient. So, too, was its membership, which was composed of aggressive business and professional men drawn from all the diverse ethnicities present in the city who lived elsewhere in comfortable suburbia. Thus, until 1968 on TUR Block 22 old and new reflections of China in America were present, but both were doomed to fall before the bulldozers.

REVERSE DIFFUSION

If some Tucson Chinese were slow to accept the material aspects of the American life to which they had been exposed for eight decades, the question arises as to what kind of reverse influence might have permeated the host community. Were people eager to acquire Chinese goods, or did the prejudicial climate toward the Chinese curb interest in their cultural exoticisms? In consideration of these questions from an archaeological perspective it is noted that, not unexpectedly, Chinese objects were concentrated in six of the explored city blocks where Chinese occupation had been heaviest. They also were found elsewhere, although in negligible amounts.

A number of reasons may explain this distribution of artifacts. One obvious cause is the dispersed housing-work pattern of the downtown Tucson Chinese up to the 1950s, which consisted of two or three men or a traditional familial unit living amidst an alien community isolated, in terms of immediate association, from other Chinese. Not only were there few individuals in each such household to create refuse, but because they, far more than the compound residents, were on the front lines of integration, the identifiable Old World trash would have been limited.

Moreover, the Chinese always represented a very minor percentage of Tucson's total population (at peak, less than two percent). Their residential and occupational circumstances were such that most of the Euro-Americans would not have had much, if any, interaction with them. The volume of native Chinese goods stocked by retailers was comparatively small. Modest stores of the low income barrio restricted such merchandise to personal articles for use by the Chinese themselves. Stores selling Asian art goods for possible purchase by affluent Euro-Americans are thought to have found their potential market in other parts of Tucson.

An example of a retail outlet within a predominately Hispanic district but partially geared to Asian customers was on the east side of Block 22. William Gin, in 1935 owner of the Arizona Chinese Supply Company at 100 south Meyer Street, noted that his usual inventory included such foodstuffs as duck feet, 47-day-old duck eggs in mud shells, dried animal inner organs, perch packed in lard, canned sugar cane, litchi nuts, oyster sauce, salted vegetables, dried mushrooms, fish bladders, bamboo shoots, and nut meal. Chinese medicines offered for sale were various pills, powders, peppermint oils, and sweet teas used for curative purposes. Miscellaneous commodities were Chinese dishes, silks, inks, stationery, incense, ledgers, and chopsticks (*Arizona Daily Star*, Rodeo Edition, February 22, 1935). Some of the Chinese consumers surely were residents of the adjacent Ying On compound. Despite the name of his shop, Gin also probably handled a fuller line of merchandise to meet the needs of the greater number of non-Chinese neighbors. When these residents visited the store, it is presumed that only a rare food item, a ceramic piece, or a few yards of silk were selected from the Chinese stock. Although the Hispanic housewife may have depended on the Chinese grocer, she had little interest in duplicating his cuisine.

With the exception of an ornate brass lock (Fig. 3.47), the only Chinese materials in zones away from the primary areas of Chinese occupancy were ceramics. Features excavated in ten scattered blocks produced a few such pieces. On seven of these blocks from one to five Chinese-run stores are documented as having been open for business at various times during a seventy to eighty year period. It is tempting to suggest, although entirely unsubstantiated by the available field notes of excavations, that the ceramics related to foodstuffs and spirits had been used by resident Chinese and at least some of the tablewares, particularly late Japanese pieces, once had adorned Hispanic households. Even so, whatever Chinese coloration was afforded, downtown Tucson was soon drowned in a sea of indigeneity. The Chinese were recognized as being part of the local scene, but the items of their inherited material culture that they may have introduced were largely ignored by other segments of the society. Old Tucson was, and has remained, a borderland outpost of *Hispanidad*.

Hong Men History, Oaths, and Regulations as Depicted on the Banner in Figure 3.74.

Translated by Hong Yu

Since the separation of heaven and earth, the three kings and five emperors pass the power to Yao and Suan [legendary ancestors], all of whom observed virtue in their policies and controlled the world by benevolence. This shows us that sand can be piled up into a mountain; the finest fragments of fox fur, sewn together, will make a robe. It is not difficult for a good man to be a success in his businesses. By making friends with good people and refusing bad people, one is assured of success. The ancient heroes give us many good examples. Guan and Zhong shared the coat when they were poor; finally they became famous. Liu Bei, Guan Yu, and Chang Fei became sworn Brothers in the Peach Garden [the Peach Garden refers to the place where Kuan Kung and these two heroes allied themselves to defend the Han Dynasty until death; thus, a metaphor for the Triad Society]. They were very brave and very loyal to each other, and by being brave and loyal, they established an empire. The heroes of Wa Gang became blood Brothers, though they were not born at the same time. They died the same day. Their spirits have influenced people for many, many years. The heroes of Liang mountain became blood Brothers. Neither fire nor boiling oil would keep them from helping their Brothers. The spirit of Liang mountain is remembered by people over hundreds of generations. People who have the spirit can control the mountains and the sea. Our China has been occupied by Men Yi [Manchu people, founders of the Qing Dynasty]. The rancor has not been forgotten. Today, July 5, 50th year [Chinese calendar], we became sworn Brothers under Hong Men [Triad Society]. Since today our blood mixes together. We swear we must revenge for Shao Lin Temple [destroyed in 1671 by Qing government because of alleged subversion of monks]; we must revenge for King of Chong Zhen [last king of the Ming Dynasty, who, while fleeing to Burma, was strangled by Manchu agents; Davis 1971: 66]. We will reestablish our country [Han nationality]. All of us are from different families, but we share a common fate. Starting today, we will always help each other. We will always echo one another, and our odors will merge together. Whether we are rich or poor, we will always be Brothers. Today we have pledged to follow the 36 oaths and 21 regulations. We will observe these oaths and regulations until we die.

THE 36 OATHS

1. Everyone should follow the lead of Two Capitals [Nanjing and Beijing] and 13 states [provinces in south, east, west, and central China]. No one should take any reward from outside of Hong Men. Those who break this law will be punished by cannon or die under the blade.

2. No one should work for the Men Yi government to seize Hong Men Brothers. Those who break this law will be punished by death.

3. No one should take liberties with another Brother's wife or sister. Those who break this law will be sentenced to die with pestilence.

4. Those who work in Men Yi government should report Men Yi government secrets to the Hong Men. Those who do not will be sentenced to die with pestilence.

5. No one should be jealous of his Brother's wealth. Those who break this law will be sentenced to die by sword and spear.

6. At home everyone should keep these laws in mind. Those who break this law will be sentenced to die by being struck by lightning.

7. No one shall tell the secrets of the Hong Men to his relatives. Those who break this law will be sentenced to die by natural and man-made calamities.

8. Everyone should share his wealth with his Brother. Those who break this law will be sentenced to die by natural calamities.

9. No one should let personal considerations interfere with his duty. Those who break this law will be sentenced to die by snake and tiger bite.

10. No one should make trouble with his Brother. Those who break this law will become blind and die.

11. No one should pass the flag and code number of the Hong Men to his family members. Those who break this law will be sentenced to die without burial.

12. Anyone who sees his Brother fight with somebody else, should help his Brother fight. Those who break this law will be sentenced to die by drowning.

13. No one should rob his Brothers. Those who break this law will be sentenced to die by drowning in a river.

14. When a Hong Men's Brother has trouble, everyone should help him out of this trouble. Those who break this law will be sentenced to die in a field littered with corpses.

15. No one should steal his Brother's money or property. Those who break this law will be sentenced to death by spider bite or snares.

16. Everyone should be loyal to his Hong Men's Brother. Those who break this law will be sentenced to die by spitting blood.

17. Everyone should celebrate the god's birthday on July 25 [July 25, 1674, is considered by the society as the date of its founding; by extension, the birthday of its patron saint]. Those who break this law will be sentenced to death by the god.

18. Everyone should celebrate the Long Big Brother's [a master or head official] birthday on September 15. Those who break this law will be sentenced to die by spitting blood. [*Arizona Citizen*, October 25, 1895, reports a Tucson Chinese Masonic holiday observance on September 9, which possibly could have been recognition of this Hong Men oath.]

19. Everyone should celebrate the Guan Gong's birthday on May 13. Those who break this law will be sentenced to die by spitting blood.

20. When a Hong Men's Brother visits, everyone should treat him nicely, offering him food and drink. Those who break this law will be sentenced to die in the field without burial.

21. Anyone who works for a Hong Men Brother, even if he is fishing or plowing, should not make trouble. Those who break this law will be sentenced to die an unnatural death.

22. When the Hong Men Brother comes, everyone should make sure he is a member of the Hong Men. No one is allowed to give Hong Men secrets to anyone else. Those who break this law will be sentenced to die without burial.

23. Everyone should wear mourning for his parents or relative for three years. During this period he should not behave improperly. Those who break this law will be sentenced to die at Shao Yang mountain.

24. No one should rape the wife or sister of a Hong Men Brother. Those who break this law will be sentenced to die in jail.

25. When monks visit, no one is allowed to insult them. Those who break this law will be sentenced to die in jail.

26. Everyone should love his parents and be nice to his neighbor. Those who break this law will be sentenced to die by choking on his own tongue.

27. Everyone should be loyal to the Hong Men and loyal to his Hong Men Brothers. Those who break this law will be sentenced to die and become a ghost.

28. When traveling by boat, everyone should help his Hong Men Brother. No one is allowed to rob his Brother. Those who break this law will be sentenced to die and be cut into pieces.

29. When flooding occurs, everyone should help his Hong Men Brother. Those who break this law will be sentenced to die by being eaten by fish.

30. When a Hong Men Brother is lost, everyone should help him find his home. Those who break this law will be sentenced to die by being smashed to pieces.

31. No one should insult a Hong Men Brother. Those who break this law will be sentenced to die under the blade.

32. No one should kidnap women. Those who break this law will be sentenced to die and become a ghost.

33. No one should visit a friend without advance notice.

No one is allowed to make trouble in his friend's family. Those who break this law will be sentenced to die by pig or dog bite.

34. When a Hong Men Brother's family has trouble, everyone should help as much as possible. Those who break this law will be sentenced to die by spitting blood.

35. Everyone should remember that our king died at sea during an enemy invasion. We must revenge his death. Those who break this law will be sentenced to die.

36. When the god appears to lead us to reestablishing our country, everyone should be brave and fight the enemy. No one is allowed to escape. Those who break this law will be sentenced to die by being eaten by pigs and dogs.

LAWS AND STATUTES OF THE BROTHERHOOD
The 21 Regulations

1. Those not loyal to the king and those who do not love their family will be sentenced to die.

2. Introducing bad people into the Hong Men will be punished by 720 blows with a club.

3. Telling Hong Men secrets to outside people will be punished by death.

4. Giving the code name or Hong Men shirt to outside people will be punished by death.

5. Taking outside people into a Hong Men meeting will be punished by 360 blows with a club.

6. Insulting people by using Hong Men power will be punished by death.

7. Using Hong Men power to treat people unfairly will be punished by losing one's job.

8. Kidnapping children will be punished by death.

9. Cheating a Hong Men Brother will be punished by 36 blows with a club.

10. Making trouble without reason will be punished by 36 blows with a club.

11. Insulting the Hong Men will be punished by 21 blows with a club.

12. Knowing of friends who are in trouble but not helping them will be punished by 72 blows with a club.

13. Breaking the regulation not to insult old people will be punished by 72 blows with a club.

14. Provoking fights between Hong Men Brothers will be punished by 108 blows with a club.

15. Stealing Hong Men Brother's money or personal seal will be punished by 360 blows with a club.

16. Refusing worthy people permission to join the Hong Men because of jealousy will be punished by 210 blows with a club.

17. Helping Men Yi government arrest Hong Men Brother will be punished by 210 blows with a club.

18. Hiding important Hong Men documents will be punished by 36 blows with a club.

19. Refusing to follow Hong Men leaders will be punished by death.

20. Not being brave in war will be punished by death.

21. Threatening a Hong Men leader will be punished by 108 blows with a club.

Chinese Inscriptions on Selected Artifacts of Medicinal Use

Translated and Interpreted by John W. Olsen

Glass bottle with liquid medicine. Name: *Huang Xiang Hua Wan Yin Ru Yi You* (U-I-Oil). Sole manufacturer: Wong Cheung Wah, Guangzhou, China. Purpose: cure-all, panacea, especially for fainting. (A–49363; TUR 22:2, Unit 2, Room 24.)

Glass bottle, liquid medicine. Name: *Bao Xin An (Po Sum On)* oil. Manufacturer: unnamed, main office in Hong Kong, branch offices in Guangzhou, Aomen (Macao), China, and Hanoi, Vietnam. Trademark registered in China and abroad. "Beware of imitations." (A–49364a, b; TUR 22:2, Unit 2, Room 9.)

Medicinal gum. Name: *Zheng Hu Gu Jiao* (Real Tiger Bone Gum). Manufacturer: Daning Shenrong Yaohang (Daning Ginseng and Antler Pharmacy, Aomen). Purpose: soaked in wine, then taken internally for rheumatism and related disorders, injuries. Good for health, the older the better. Inside wrapper is advertisement for other medicines made by Daning Pharmacy, such as tiger, monkey, turtle bone gum, and antler gum. (A–49365a, b, c; TUR 22:2, Unit 4, Room 11.)

Glass bottle. Name: *Jing Bu Jing* (Refined Energy Powder). Manufacturer: Lei Ming-chun, Hong Kong. Purpose: cure of male sexual dysfunction and female infertility. Brewed as tea, or pills taken individually. Slogan reads, "Selected by imperial doctor, used in palace." (A–49366; TUR 22:2.*)

Box. Name: *Wan Yin Gan He Cha* (cure-all; mild, sweet tea). Manufacturer: Liu Ze Tang, owned by Yuan Ji-lin, location unknown. Purpose: for cure of influenza, especially in summer, vomiting, indigestion, drunkenness, and similar disorders. Brew one box in one bowl of water, steep for one to two minutes. Take two or three bowls per day. (A–49368a–k; TUR 22:2, Unit 4, Room 8.)

Herbal medicine. Name: *Yan Ying* pills, two per carton, herbal medicine sealed in wax. Packed in Guangzhou, Guangdong, China, manufacturer unknown. Purpose: panacea. Specifically mentions old age, tired blood, diphtheria, typhoid fever, cough, stomachache, rheumatism, gum bleeding, sore throat, difficulty in breathing, menstrual cramps, birth pains, low blood pressure, excessive sweating, sunstroke, miscarriage. Should be broken into small pieces and eaten. (A–49369a–d; TUR 22:2.*)

Glass jar, metal cap. Name: *Wan Jin You* (Tiger Balm). Made in China, specific location unknown. Purpose: relief of symptoms of rheumatoid arthritis, colds, general cure-all. (A–49372; TUR 22:2.*)

Cloth covered cardboard box, plastic vial. Name: *Lu Shen Wan* (Lu Shen pills). Trademark: Qian Xiu (practice piety). Manufacturer: Lei Yunshang Pharmacy, location unknown. Plastic vial also inscribed *Qian Xiu, Lu Shen Wan*. Purpose: for relief of sore throat, especially tonsillitis. (A–49376a, b, c; TUR 22:2.*)

Glass vial with cork, white powder. Name: *Shi Ling Dan* (Ten Effective Powder). Manufacturer: Ling Zhi Pharmacy, location unknown. Owner: Liu Zuo-fan. Purpose: cure-all, panacea. (A–49383; TUR 22:2, Unit 2, Room 17.)

Cardboard box, glass vial, cork, pills, and instructions. Name: *Shen Xiao Shuang Liao Hong Wan* (magical, effective, extra-quality red pills). Manufacturer: He Ming Xing Tang, packed in Guangdong, China. Purpose: for poisoning, constipation, various sexual problems; dosage is one bottle every thirty days. (A–49386a, b, c; TUR 22:2.*)

Plastic vial and cardboard box. Name: *Bao Ji Wan* (pills of relief), from Hong Kong. Purpose: summer cold, vomiting, fever, headache, travel sickness, cholera, drunkenness, cure-all. Dosage: one or two bottles with tea, milk, or water every two hours. Children under three years old, half of adult dosage. (A–49387a, b; TUR 22:2, Unit 4, Room 11.)

Paper envelope for medicine. Name: *Bao Ji Wan* (pills of relief). Manufacturer: Li Chung Shing Tong, Hong Kong. (A–49388; TUR 22, Unit 2, Room 15.)

Cardboard box. Name: *Zhu Po Hong Ling Yao Gao* (Pearl and Amber Red Efficient Medicine Salve). Manufacturer: Ji Chun Tang Pharmacy, Guangzhou and Hong Kong, China; Luo Zhi-ting, owner. Purpose: for skin irritation, "muscular rot," to relieve aches, remove poison, regenerate muscle. (A–49396; TUR 22:2.*)

Glass bottle with cork. Name: *Zhi Ke Wan* (pill to stop cough). Owner: Liang Pei-ji, location and name of pharmacy unknown. (A–49398; TUR 22:2, Unit 2, attic of outhouse, east of Room 16.)

Cardboard box. Name: *Ren Dan* (Kindness Pills). Manufacturer: Aigun Pharmacy, Shanghai, China. Purpose: to cure emergencies, medicine for travel, for adapting to new food, water. Also effective for influenza, indigestion, typhoid fever, stomachache, diphtheria, and angina. (A–49399; TUR 22:2.*)

Glass bottle with cork. Name: *Er Liu Er* (Two Six Two). Manufacturer: Yao Hua Pharmacy, Shanghai, China. Also inscribed, *Zhen Ji Zhong Shui*, meaning unknown. Purpose: "cures 72 dangerous diseases," particularly plague, tuberculosis, and various infants' diseases. (A–49400; TUR 22:2, Unit 3, Room 2.)

Paper envelope for medicine. Name: *Qing Huo San* (powder to relieve hotness). Manufacturer: Liu De-zhi Pharmacy, Toisan, Xining, Guangdong, China. Made in 1946. "An agent in every city." Purpose: for fever, headache, arthritis. (A–49403; TUR 22:2.*)

Glass bottle, bamboo applicator, cardboard box, paper description. Name: *Xuan Lai Pi Fu Xiao Du Shui* (ringworm,

leprosy skin disinfectant). Manufacturer: Ou Jia-chuan ("Au Kah Chuen") Pharmacy, Guangzhou, branch office in Hong Kong. Bottled in 1929. Paper included is advertisement for Ou Jia-Chuan Pharmacy, with display of seals authorizing manufacture. Purpose: ringworm, leprosy, minor skin diseases. (A–49411a–d; TUR 22:2, Unit 2, Room 19.)

Glass bottle, sealed wooden stopper, red pills. Name: *Li Zhi Du Tong Wan* (pills for immediate cure of stomachache). Manufacturer: Yong Shou Tang, Guangzhou and Shanghai, China. Owner: Su Rui-sheng. Dosage: adults, one bottle; children, one-half bottle. (A–49413; TUR 22:2.*)

Glass bottle, wooden stopper, pills. Name: *Wan Ying Bao Ji Wan* (all-effective pills of relief). Manufacturer: Li Zhong-sheng Tang, original enterprise on Zumiao Street, Foshan, Guangzhou, Guangdong, China. Purpose: panacea. (A–49416; TUR 22:2.*)

---

*Items were recovered in TUR 22:2, but specific room location is not available.

Inscriptions on Ceramic Opium Pipe Bowls

Translated and interpreted by John W. Olsen. Chinese characters drawn by Hong Yu.

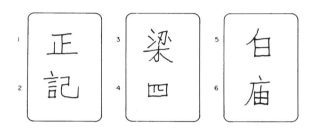

Figure C.1. Style One Inscription. 1, 2, Zhēng Jì (correct or exact mark), trademark? 3, 4, Liáng Sì (Liáng Four), Liáng is a surname, probably that of the manufacturer; factory designation? 5, 6, Bái Miào (White Temple), probably a place name. 7, Shūang (two, a pair), kiln number?

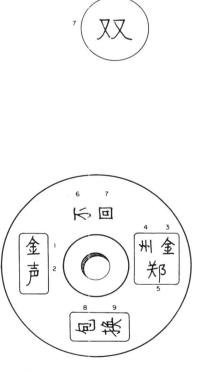

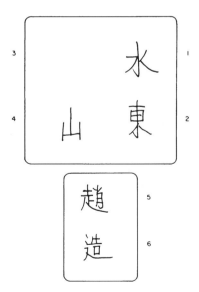

Figure C.2. Style Two Inscription, on pipe bowl base (plan view). 1, 2, Jīn Shēng (Golden Sound), brand name or manufacturer's given name? 3, 4, Jīn Zhōu (Golden District), place name? 5, Zhèng (surname, probably of manufacturer). 6, 7, Bú Húi (no return) and 8, 9, Bāo Huàn (exchange) mean "Exchange, but no refund."

Figure C.3. Style Three Inscription. 1, 2, Shǔi Dōng (East of the Water), probably a county or district name. 3, illegible (could be hǎi "sea" or méi "plum"). 4, Shān (mountain), part of another place name, probably that of a village. 5, 6, Zhào Zào (Made by Zhào).

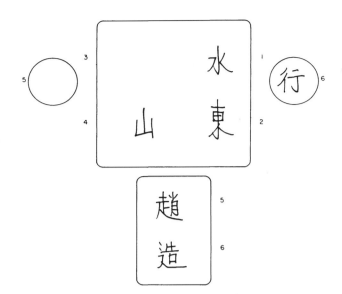

Figure C.4. Style Four Inscription. 1, 2, Shuǐ Dōng (East of the Water), probably a county or district name. 3, illegible (could be hǎi "sea" or méi "plum"). 4, Shān (mountain), part of another place name, probably that of a village. 5, illegible. 6, Háng (business, firm), probably meant to be read with illegible character 5. 7, 8, Zhào Zào (Made by Zhào).

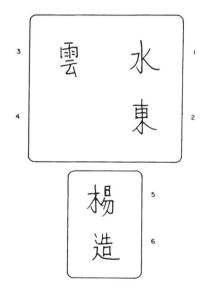

Figure C.5. Style Five Inscription. 1, 2, Shuǐ Dōng (East of the Water), probably a county or district name. 3, Yün (cloud). 4, illegible. 5, 6, Yáng Zào (Made by Yáng). Characters 3 and 4 are probably meant to be read together as part of a place name.

Figure C.6. Style Six Inscription. 1, 2, Bái Miào (White Temple, probably a place name. 3, 4, Tíng Jì (Mark of the Imperial Court), trademark? 5, 6, Liáng Zào (Made by Liáng).

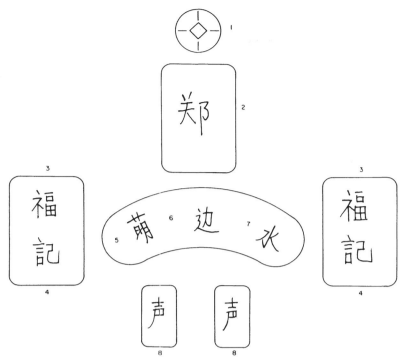

Figure C.7. Style Seven Inscription. 1, coin or flower motif. 2, Zhèng (surname, probably of manufacturer). 3, 4, Fú Jì (The Mark of Luck or Happiness), trademark? 5, 6, 7, Méng Bīan Shǔi (Bud Beside Water), product name? 8, Shēng (sound, reputation), meaning unknown.

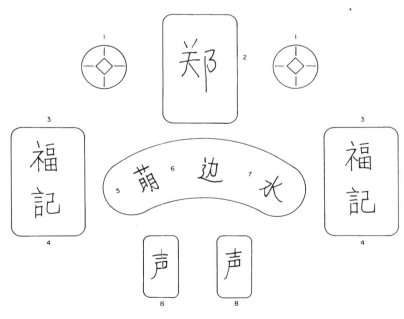

Figure C.8. Style Eight Inscription. 1, coin or flower motif. 2, Zhèng (surname, probably of manufacturer). 3, 4, Fú Jì (The Mark of Luck or Happiness), trademark? 5, 6, 7, Méng Bīan Shǔi (Bud Beside Water), product name? 8, Shēng (sound, reputation), meaning unknown.

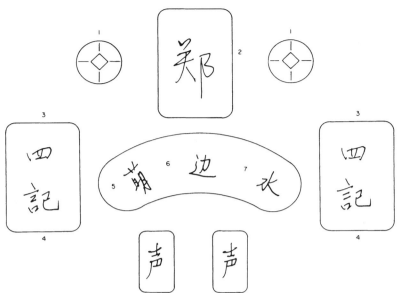

Figure C.9. Style Nine Inscription. 1, coin or flower motif. 2, Zhèng (surname, probably of manufacturer). 3, 4, Sì Jì (Mark Four), trademark? 5, 6, 7, Méng Bīan Shǔi (Bud Beside Water), product name? 8, Shēng (sound, reputation), meaning unknown.

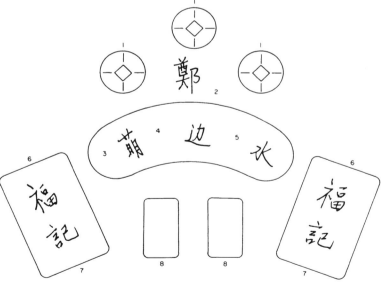

Figure C.10. Style Ten Inscription. 1, coin or flower motif. 2, Zhèng (surname, probably of manufacturer). 3, 4, 5, Méng Bīan Shǔi (Bud Beside Water), product name? 6, 7, Fú Jì (The Mark of Luck or Happiness), trademark? 8, illegible (probably Shēng).

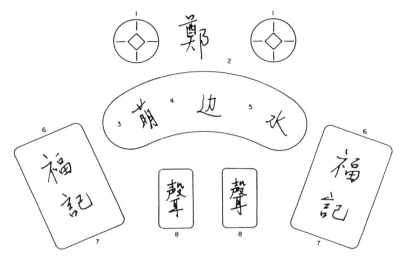

Figure C.11. Style Eleven Inscription. 1, coin or flower motif. 2, Zhèng (surname, probably of manufacturer). 3, 4, 5, Méng Bīan Shǔi (Bud Beside Water), product name? 6, 7, Fú Jì (The Mark of Luck or Happiness), trademark? 8, Shēng (sound, reputation), meaning unknown.

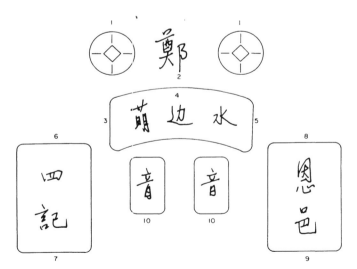

Figure C.12. Style Twelve Inscription. 1, coin or flower motif. 2, Zhèng (surname, probably of manufacturer). 3, 4, 5, Méng Bīan Shǔi (Bud Beside Water), product name? 6, 7, Sì Jì (Mark Four), trademark? 8, 9, Ēn Yì (place name?). 10, Yīn (sound, tone, message), meaning unknown.

Figure C.13. Style Thirteen Inscription, on pipe bowl base (plan view). 1, 2, Qīn Zhōu (Imperial District), probably a place name. 3, 4, Měi Yīn (Beautiful Sound), product name? 5, Huáng (Yellow), probably manufacturer's surname. 6, pictographic potter's mark (rabbit?), not illustrated, trademark?

References

Anderson, E. N., and Marja L. Anderson
  1977 Modern China: South. In *Food in Chinese Culture, Anthropological and Historical Interpretations*, edited by Kwang-chih Chang, pp. 317–382. New Haven: Yale University Press.

Arizona Historical Society
  1898 Tucson Block Book. Maps on file in the Arizona Historical Society, Tucson.

Awald, John
  1968 Bottle Identification: TUR 22:2–2e. Manuscript on file, Arizona State Museum, University of Arizona, Tucson.

Ayres, James E.
  1968a Field Notes, Conditions of Buildings at TUR 22:2. Notes on file, Arizona State Museum, University of Arizona, Tucson.
  1968b Field Notes. TUR 38:4. Notes on file, Arizona State Museum, University of Arizona, Tucson.
  1968c Urban Renewal Salvage Archaeology in Tucson, Arizona. Paper presented at the Annual Meeting of the Society for Historical Archaeology.
  1980 Analysis of Artifacts from Tucson, Arizona's Urban Renewal Area. Final report to the National Endowment for the Humanities, Grant No. RO–21419–75–217. Manuscript on file, Arizona State Museum, University of Arizona, Tucson.
  1988 Chasing the Dragon with an Opium Pistol. Paper presented at the Annual Meeting of the Society for Historical Archaeology.

Ayres, James E., William Liesenbein, and Lee Fratt
  1968 TUR Beer Bottle Report. Manuscript on file, Arizona State Museum, University of Arizona, Tucson.

Ball, John C.
  1966 The Chinese Narcotic Addict in the United States. *Social Forces* 46: 68–72.

Barnes, Mark
  1983 Tucson: Development of a Community. MS, doctoral dissertation, Catholic University, Washington.

Bluden, Caroline, and Mark Elvin
  1983 *Cultural Atlas of China*. New York: Facts on File.

Brandes, Ray
  1962 Guide to the Historic Landmarks of Tucson. *Arizoniana* 3(1): 27–38.

Bret Harte, John
  1980 *Portrait of a Desert Pueblo*. Woodland Hills: Windsor.

Brott, Clark W.
  1982 *Moon Lee One: Life in Old Chinatown Weaverville, California*. San Diego: Great Basin Foundation.

Burkhardt, V. R.
  1953 *Chinese Creeds and Customs*. Hong Kong: South China Morning Post.

Butler, Bill, and Joyce McCormick
  1968 Soda Bottle Industries of Tucson. Manuscript on file, Arizona State Museum, University of Arizona, Tucson.

Chace, Paul G.
  1976 Overseas Chinese Ceramics. In *The Changing Faces of Main Street*, edited by Roberta S. Greenwood, pp. 509–530. San Buenaventura: Redevelopment Agency.

Chavannes, Edourd
  1973 *Five Happiness*. New York: Weatherill.

Ch'en, Jerome
  1979 *China and the West, Society and Culture, 1815–1937*. London: Hutchinson.

Chesneaux, Jean
  1971 *Secret Societies in China, in the Nineteenth and Twentieth Centuries*. Ann Arbor: University of Michigan Press.

Clayre, Alasdair
  1984 *The Heart of the Dragon*. Boston: Houghton Mifflin.

Clonts, John B.
  1969 Field Notes, TUR 14:1. Arizona State Museum files, University of Arizona, Tucson.
  1970 TUR 22:2, a Faunal Analysis. Manuscript on file, Arizona State Museum, University of Arizona, Tucson.
  1971 Butchering Analysis, a Possible Tool. Manuscript on file, Arizona State Museum, University of Arizona, Tucson.
  1983 Some Long Overdue Thoughts on Faunal Analysis. In *Forgotten Places and Things, Archaeological Perspectives on American History*, edited by Albert E. Ward, pp. 349–354. Albuquerque: Center for Anthropological Research.

Clyde, Paul H., and Burton F. Beers
  1966 *A History of the Far East, of the Western Impact and the Eastern Response (1830–1965)*. Englewood Cliffs: Prentice Hall.

Courtwright, David T.
  1982 *Dark Paradise. Opiate Addiction in America Before 1940*. Cambridge: Harvard University Press.

Culin, Stewart
  1890a Chinese Secret Societies in the United States. *Journal of American Folk-Lore* 3(1): 39–43.
  1890b Customs of the Chinese in America. *Journal of American Folk-Lore* 3(1): 191–200.
  1891 The Gambling Games of the Chinese in America. *Publications of the University of Pennsylvania, Series in Philology, Literature, and Archaeology* 1(4). Philadelphia: University of Pennsylvania.
  1896 The Origin of Fan Tan. *Overland Monthly* 28: 153–155.
  1970 *The I'Hing or "Patriotic Rising," a Secret Society Among the Chinese in America*. San Francisco: R & E Research Associates.

Dai, Bingham
  1964 Opium Addiction: A Socio-psychiatric Approach. In *Contributions to Urban Sociology*, edited by Ernest W. Burgess and Donald J. Bogue, pp. 643–654. Chicago: University of Chicago Press.

Davis, Fei-Lung
1971   *Primitive Revolutionaries of China.* Honolulu: University Press of Hawaii.
DeBary, William Theodore, Wing-tsit Chan, and Burton Watson
1960   *Sources of Chinese Tradition.* New York: Columbia University Press.
Dillon, Richard H.
1962   *The Hatchet Men: The Story of the Tong Wars in San Francisco's Chinatown.* New York: Coward-McCann.
Etter, Patricia A.
1980   The West Coast Chinese and Opium Smoking. In *Archaeological Perspectives on Ethnicity in America,* edited by Robert L. Schuyler, pp. 97–101. Farmingdale: Baywood.
Evans, William S., Jr.
1980   Food and Fantasy: Material Culture of the Chinese in California and the West. Circa 1850–1900. In *Archaeological Perspectives on Ethnicity in America,* edited by Robert L. Schuyler, pp. 89–96. Farmingdale: Baywood.
Farrar, Nancy
1972   The Chinese in El Paso. *Southwestern Studies Monograph* 3. El Paso: University of Texas at El Paso.
Farris, Glenn J.
1979   "Cash" as Currency: Coins and Tokens from Yreka Chinatown. *Historical Archaeology* 13: 48–52.
Felton, David L., Frank Lortie, and Peter D. Schulz
1984   The Chinese Laundry on Second Street: Papers on Archeological Investigations at the Woodland Opera House site. *California Archeological Reports* 24: 1–120. Sacramento: California Department of Parks and Recreation.
Fong, Lawrence M.
1978   Chinese Manuscript Collection from the Tucson, Arizona, Urban Renewal Project. Historical and Explanatory Report and Inventory. Manuscript on file, Special Collections, University of Arizona Library, Tucson.
1980   Sojourners and Settlers. The Chinese Experience in Arizona. *Journal of Arizona History* 21(2): 22–56.
Franke, Herbert
1974   Siege and Defense of Towns in Medieval China. In *Chinese Ways in Warfare,* edited by Frank A. Kierman and John K. Fairbank, pp. 150–201. Cambridge: Harvard University Press.
Gates, William C., and Dana E. Ormerod
1982   The East Liverpool Pottery District: Identification of Manufacturers and Marks. *Historical Archaeology* 16(1–2): 1–358.
Gernet, Jacques
1982   *A History of Chinese Civilization.* Cambridge: Cambridge University Press.
Giles, Rikke, and Thomas N. Layton
1986   An Analysis of Imports from China to San Francisco, 1850–1860. A Small Sampling of Items Listed on Ships' Manifests. Paper presented at the Annual Meeting of the Society for Historical Archaeology.
Goree, Patricia
1971   Identification of Button Types Found in the Chinese Areas of Tucson. Manuscript on file, Arizona State Museum, University of Arizona, Tucson.
Greenwood, Roberta S.
1978   The Overseas Chinese at Home. *Archaeology* 31(5): 42–49.
1980   The Chinese on Main Street. In *Archaeological Perspectives on Ethnicity in America,* edited by Robert L. Schuyler, pp. 113–123. Farmingdale: Baywood.
Grosier, J. B.
1981   *The Chinese.* New York: Crescent.
Hahn, Emily
1968   *The Cooking of China.* New York: Life-Time.

Hill, Herbert
1973   Anti-Oriental Agitation and the Rise of Working-Class Racism. *Society* 10(2): 43–54.
Jenyns, Soame
1951   *Later Chinese Porcelain, the Ch'ing Dynasty (1644–1912).* London: Faber and Faber.
Kane, Harry Hubbell
1976   *Opium-Smoking in America and China.* New York: Arno.
Kisch, Bruno
1965   *Scales and Weights.* New Haven: Yale University Press.
Lee, Chiang
1975   *Chinese Calligraphy, an Introduction to its Aesthetic and Technique.* Cambridge: Harvard University Press.
Lee, Lim P.
1938   The Chinese in Tucson, Arizona. *Chinese Digest,* April: 8–9, 19.
Lee, Rose Hum
1948   Social Institutions of a Rocky Mountain Chinatown. *Social Forces* 27(1): 1–11.
1960   *The Chinese in the United States of America.* Hong Kong: Hong Kong University Press.
Light, Ivan H.
1972   *Ethnic Enterprise in America. Business and Welfare Among Chinese, Japanese, and Blacks.* Berkeley: University of California Press.
Lydon, Sandy
1985   *Chinese Gold. The Chinese in the Monterey Bay Region.* Capitola: Capitola.
Lyman, Stanford M.
1970   The Asian in the West. *Social Science and Humanities Publication* 4. Reno: Desert Research Institute.
1974   *Chinese Americans.* New York: Random House.
Matter, Ellie
1969   Opium Smoking in Tucson. Manuscript on file, Arizona State Museum, University of Arizona, Tucson.
McGuire, Randall H.
1982   The Study of Ethnicity in Historical Archaeology. *Journal of Anthropological Archaeology* 1: 159–178.
Melzer, Barbara A.
1969   Pen T'sao. The Identification, and some Background, of a Collection of Chinese Medicines Found in the Tucson Urban Renewal Area. Manuscript on file, Arizona State Museum, University of Arizona, Tucson.
Myrick, David F.
1975   *Railroads of Arizona.* Vol. 1, *The Southern Roads.* Berkeley: Howell-North.
Nakata, Yujiro
1983   *Chinese Calligraphy.* New York: Weatherill.
Noel, Donald L.
1968   A Theory of the Origin of Ethnic Stratification. *Social Problems* 16: 157–173.
Olsen, John W.
1978   A Study of Chinese Ceramics Excavated in Tucson. *The Kiva* 44(1): 1–50.
1983   An Analysis of East Asian Coins Excavated in Tucson, Arizona. *Historical Archaeology* 17(2): 41–55.
Ong, Paul
1983   Chinese Laundries as an Urban Occupation in Nineteenth Century California. *Annals of the Chinese Historical Society of the Pacific Northwest:* 68–85.
Pastron, Allen G., Jack Prichett, and Marilyn Ziebarth
1981   *Behind the Seawall: Historical Archaeology Along the San Francisco Waterfront,* Vol. 3. San Francisco: Wastewater Management Agency.
Pastron, Allen G., Robert Gross, and Donna Garaventa
1981   Ceramics from Chinatown's Tables: An Historical Ar-

chaeological Approach to Ethnicity. In *Behind the Sea-wall: Historical Archaeology Along the San Francisco Waterfront*, Vol. 2, edited by Allen G. Pastron, pp. 365–469. San Francisco: Wastewater Management Agency.

Perkins, Clifford Alan
1984   Recollections of a Chinese-Immigration Inspector. In *Arizona Memories*, edited by Anne Hodges Morgan and Rennard Strickland, pp. 217–232. Tucson: University of Arizona Press.

Peterson, Thomas H.
1966   The Buckley House: Tucson Station for the Butterfield Overland Mail. *Journal of Arizona History* 7(4): 153–167.

Praetzellis, Adrian, and Mary Praetzellis
1978   *Ceramics from Old Sacramento*. Sacramento: California Department of Parks and Recreation.
1979   The Lovelock Ceramics. In *Archaeological and Historical Studies at Ninth and Amherst, Lovelock, Nevada*, edited by E. M. Hattori, pp. 140–198. Carson City: Nevada State Museum.

Prazniak, Roxann
1984   The Chinese in Woodland, California. In "The Chinese Laundry on Second Street: Papers on Archeology at the Woodland Opera House Site." *California Archeological Reports* 24: 121–138. Sacramento: California Department of Parks and Recreation.

Quellmalz, Carl Robert
1972   Chinese Porcelain Excavated from North American Pacific Coast Sites. *Oriental Art*, n.s., 18(2): 148–154.
1976   Late Chinese Provincial Export Wares. *Oriental Art*, n.s., 22(3): 289–298.

Renk, Thomas
1968   Field Notes. TUR 2:1–5a, TUR 3:4–2a, TUR 3:4–3a, TUR 3:4–5a, TUR 3:4–5b, TUR 22:2–2a–g, TUR 22:2–5A–B. Arizona State Museum files, University of Arizona, Tucson.

Robertson, Frank
1977   *Triangle of Death, the Inside Story of the Triads*. London: Routledge and Kegan Paul.

Sarna, Jonathan D.
1978   From Immigrants to Ethnics: Toward a New Theory of "Ethnicization." *Ethnicity* 5: 370–378.

Schlegel, Gustave
1974   *Thian Ti Hwui, The Hung-League or Heaven-Earth League*. Reprinted from 1866 edition. New York: AMS Press.

Schweitzer, John Louis
1952   The Social Unity of Tucson's Chinese Community. MS, master's thesis, University of Arizona, Tucson.

Sheridan, Thomas E.
1986   *Los Tucsonenses, the Mexican Community in Tucson, 1854–1941*. Tucson: University of Arizona Press.

Siu, Paul E. P.
1952   The Sojourner. *American Journal of Sociology* 58(1): 34–44.
1964   The Isolation of the Chinese Laundryman. In *Contributions to Urban Sociology*, edited by Ernest W. Burgess and Donald J. Bogue, pp. 429–442. Chicago: University of Chicago Press.

Smith, Cornelius C.
1967   *William Sanders Oury, History-Maker of the Southwest*. Tucson: University of Arizona Press.

Society for Historical Archaeology
1987   *Newsletter*, No. 3: 17–18.

Sonnichsen, C. L.
1982   *Tucson, the Life and Times of an American City*. Norman: University of Oklahoma Press.

Spence, Jonathan
1977   Ch'ing. In *Food in Chinese Culture, Anthropological Interpretations*, edited by Kwang-chih Chang, pp. 259–294. New Haven: Yale University Press.

Spicer, Edward H.
1971   Persistent Cultural Systems. *Science* 174: 795–800.

Spier, Robert F. G.
1958   Food Habits of Nineteenth-Century California Chinese. *California Historical Society Quarterly* 37(1): 79–84; 37(2): 129–136.

Tang, Esther
1977   A Chinese Success Story. In *This Land, These Voices*, edited by Abe Chanin and Mildred Chanin, pp. 202–207. Flagstaff: Northland Press.

Tucson City Directory
1908–   Tucson Urban Renewal Document Collection. Special
1950   Collections, University of Arizona Library, Tucson.

U.S. Federal Census
1870   Arizona Territory
1880   Arizona Territory
1900   Arizona Territory
1910   Arizona Territory

Wallace, William J., and Edith Wallace
1981   *Digging into Death Valley's History, Three Studies in Historic Archaeology*. Ramona: Acoma.

Wallnofer, Heinrich, and Anna von Rottauscher
1965   *Chinese Folk Medicine*. New York: Crown.

Wang, Cheny
1982   *The Kuomintang, a Sociological Study of Demoralization*. New York: Garland.

Ward, J. S. M., and W. G. Stirling
1925   *The Hung Society, or the Society of Heaven and Earth*. 3 vols. London: Baskerville.

Wells, Mariann Kaye
1971   *Chinese Temples in California*. San Francisco: R & E Research Associates.

Whitlow, Janice I.
1981   Soya Sauce, Bean Cake, and Ginger Ale: Chinese Material Culture. MS, senior honors thesis, San Jose State University, San Jose.

Wiant, Bliss
1965   *The Music of China*. Hong Kong: Chinese University of Hong Kong.

Wilcox, R. Turner
1965   *Folk and Festival Costumes of the World*. New York: Scribners.

Willetts, William, and Lim Suan Poh
1981   *Nonya Ware and Kitchen Ch'ing. Ceremonial and Domestic Pottery of the 19th–20th Centuries Commonly Found in Malaysia*. Kuala Lumpur: Oxford University Press.

Williams, C. A. S.
1960   *Encyclopedia of Chinese Symbolism and Art Motives*. New York: Julian.

Wilson, Rex L.
1981   *Bottles on the Western Frontier*. Tucson: University of Arizona Press.

Wong, Bernard L.
1982   *Economic Adaptation and Ethnic Identity of the Chinese*. New York: Holt, Rinehart, and Winston.

Wylie, Jerry, and Richard Fike
1986   A Survey of Opium Pipes and Related Smoking Paraphernalia. Paper presented at the Annual Meeting of the Society for Historical Archaeology.

Yarwood, Doreen
1978   *The Encyclopedia of World Costume*. New York: Scribners.

Newspapers

Phoenix

Arizona Republican, July 15, 1898
     August 7, 1898

Prescott

Journal Miner, August 25, 1908
     August 8, 1909

Tucson

Arizona Citizen, November 4, 1876
     February 3, 1882
     February 5, 1892
     March 7, 1893
     March 15, 1893
     May 16, 1893
     October 25, 1895
     February 18, 1901
     April 9, 1901
     October 11, 1902

     November 4, 1904
     March 22, 1906
     February 12, 1907
     January 5, 1911
     February 7, 1972
Arizona Daily Citizen, December 17, 1900
     August 8, 1968
Arizona Daily Star, January 10, 1878
     September 3, 1879
     November 9, 1884
     April 24, 1889
     May 11, 1889
     May 21, 1889
     June 19, 1889
     November 1, 1889
     May 2, 1890
     March 28, 29, 1908
     February 22, 1935, Rodeo Edition
     April 18, 1950
Arizonan, June 18, 1870
Tucson Daily and Weekly Citizen, July 26, 1909

Index

ABSTRACT

Chinese men began arriving in territorial Tucson in the 1870s. Their numbers were greatly increased in 1880 when the Southern Pacific Railroad being built from California eastward with Chinese labor reached the town, and many chose to stay. Gradually a small Chinatown complete with tenements, grocery stores, a joss house, and opium dens formed in what previously had been the oldest Hispanic and Euro-American neighborhood. At the same time other Chinese dispersed throughout the town. In 1912 the Chinatown was leveled, but a second concentration of Asian population formed south of the main business district, where it remained until the urban renewal project of 1968–1973.

The first Chinese arrivals found employment as laundrymen, cooks, domestics, truck gardeners, and shopkeepers. They did not meet the violent resistance that other Chinese encountered in Arizona's mining camps, and they were able to survive as a colony because of some symbiotic interaction with the Hispanic societal component. Gradually an incipient class structure appeared, with an elite group headed by native-born Chinese becoming more economically diversified and assimilated and the conservative heirs of the sojourner movement of an earlier generation remaining without resources, families, or interest in integration.

Archaeological excavations in the area of the original Tucson Chinatown and ethnographic collections from a large tenement compound occupied by Chinese males from 1919 to 1968 produced a sizable assortment of material goods imported from China over nearly a century. The varied ethnographic collection is of special interest because it expands the archaeological record into aspects of the overseas Chinese culture heretofore not so completely represented. Among domestic or personal items are tableware, cooking gear, spirits bottles, medicines and their containers, games and game account books, coins, opium paraphernalia, and personal papers. Inasmuch as one room of the compound had been used as headquarters for the local chapter of the Guomindang and another as a lodge for the Chee Kung Tong, two highly traditional organizations of early twentieth century Chinese life, an array of objects left by them greatly enriches the historical reconstruction. Moreover, the physical environment from which these collections derived, which researchers were able to observe prior to its destruction, adds to an understanding of the mode of life followed by the ultimate survivors of a vanished era.

RESUMEN

Los hombres chinos empezaron a llegar a Tucsón territorial en los 1870. Su número fue muy aumentado en 1880 cuando el ferrocarril Southern Pacific, cual se estaba construyendo desde California hacia el este con mano de obra china, llegó al pueblo y muchos eligieron permanecer. Gradualmente se formó un pequeño barrio chino completo con sus viviendas, tiendas de comestibles, un templo, y guaridas de opio en la vecindad que antes había sido la mas vieja de los hispanos y euro-americanos. Al mismo tiempo, otros chinos se dispersaron por todas partes del pueblo. El barrio chino se destruyo en 1912, pero una segunda concentración de asiáticos se formó al sur del mayor centro de negocios, en donde permaneció hasta que se inició el proyecto de renovación urbana de 1968–1973.

Los primeros chinos que llegaron hallaron empleo como lavanderos, cocineros, hortelanos, y tenderos. No encontraron la resistencia violenta que otros chinos encontraron en las poblaciones mineras de Arizona y pudieron sobrevivir como colonia a causa de alguna interacción simbiótica entre ellos y la sociedad hispana. Gradualmente apareció una incipiente estructura de clase, con un grupo selecto, acabezado por chinos indígenos, convertiendose a ser más diversos economicamente y asimilados y los herederos conservadores del movimiento morador de una generación previa quedandose sin recursos, familias, o interés en la integración.

Las excavaciones arqueológicas en el área de la original población china en Tucsón y las colecciones etnográficas de un grande complejo de viviendas ocupadas por hombres chinos desde 1919 a 1968 produjó una considerable variedad de generos materiales importados desde China durante casi un siglo. La colección etnográfica es de interés especial porque extende el registro arqueológico hacia aspectos de la cultura china ultramarina que hasta este punto no había sido tan completamente representada. Entre los objetos domesticos o personales hay vajilla, utensilios de cocina, botellas de alcohol, medicinas y sus envases, juegos y sus libros de cuenta, moneda, parafernalia de opio y papeles personales. Ya como un cuarto del complejo tuvo uso como la sede del capítulo local de la Guomindang y otro como casa de club para la Chee Kung Tong, dos muy tradicionales organizaciones de la vida china al principio del siglo veinte, un surtido de objetos que ellos dejaron ha enriquezado la reconstrucción histórica. Además, el ambiente físico de donde originaron estas colecciones, y que los investigadores pudieron observar antes que se destruyera, añade a nuestro entendimiento del modo de vida seguido por los últimos sobrevivientes de una época desaparecida.